Strategic **MRO** *Powered by* **DSC**

A Roadmap for Transforming Assets
into Strategic Advantage

Richard L. MacInnes and Dr. Stephen L. Pearce

Most Productivity Press books are available at quantity discounts when purchased in bulk. For more information contact our Customer Service Department at (800) 394-6868. Address all other inquires to:

Productivity Press
444 Park Avenue South, Sutie 604
New York, NY 10016
Telephone: 212-686-5900
Fax 212-686-5411
Email: info@productivityinc.com

Printed and bound by Malloy Lithographing, Inc. in the United States of America

Library of Congress Cataloging-in-Publication Data
MacInnes, Richard L.
     Strategic MRO powered by DSC : a roadmap for transforming assets into strategic advantage / Richard L. MacInnes and Dr. Stephen L. Pearce.
          p. cm.
Includes index.
     ISBN 1-56327-293-8
   1. Strategic planning. 2. Business planning. I. Pearce, Stephen L. II. Title.
     HD30.28.M255 2003
     658.4'012—dc21 2003007883

07 06 05 04 03 • 5 4 3 2 1

Special Dedication—to the son of Stephen and Rhonda Pearce
Joshua Davis Gray
August 4, 1979 to June 21, 2000

To our family members—Rhonda Pearce, Julie MacInnes, Melissa McAuliffe, Brendan McAuliffe, and Ann MacInnes—who made continual sacrifices throughout the writing of this book

Author's Message

It is proper that we the authors boldly admit that this book could not and was not created by our efforts alone. We would like to acknowledge the following individuals and companies for their contributions.

Net Results Technical Review Team—Kobus Blomerus, Dirk Labuschagne, Julie MacInnes, and Don Smith.

MRO Software Technical Review Team—Jim Battle, Rob Bloom, Steve Caslick, Anthony Honaker, Pete Karns, Rudie Roy, Terry Saunders, Judith White, and Jack Young.

Corporate Contribution—Fisher-Rosemount Systems, MRO Software Inc., Syclo Corp., Rockwell Automation, a business of Rockwell International Corporation, and Work Technology Corporation.

Publishing Staff—Tom Gale, Modern Distribution Management, Editor, and Julie MacInnes, Desk Top Publishing.

Special Recognition—Clearly a special thank you goes to two individuals who have enabled this process. The first is to Chip Drapeau, President and CEO of MRO Software Inc., for his forward-thinking support of this effort. The second is to Kobus Blomerus for his technical contribution to the Demand Supply Compression™ methodology.

Table of Contents

Chapter 11 – Program Management 281

Chapter 12 – Solution After Next 297

Index 305

About the Authors 313

Preface

Why Strategic MRO
powered by DSC?

Why would we—a couple of somewhat sane, normal people—choose to write a book combining the concepts of enterprise asset management (EAM) and the associated maintenance, repair and operating/overhaul (MRO) materials supply chain under a single banner called Strategic MRO? And why would we suggest that asset management and MRO are strategic rather than purely operational activities for most companies?

These are valid questions. The answer lies partly in the magnitude of the maintenance and MRO dollars spent by those owning and maintaining assets. In 1997, the last U.S. Economic Census estimated the value of manufacturing shipments at $3.8 trillion. The book value of assets to produce these shipments was estimated at $1.6 trillion, equivalent to $2.47 in shipments for every dollar in asset value. In addition, $151 billion was spent on capital expenditures, $6 billion was spent on outside services to repair and maintain facilities, $28 billion was spent on outside services to repair and maintain equipment, and nearly $47 billion in assets were retired. These estimates do not include the internal costs spent by companies to maintain and repair their assets. The pure magnitude of asset management expenditures makes MRO strategic. Perhaps we take assets and their associated costs for granted, but without them we have no earnings. And, poorly managed, these very same assets devour earnings.

Strategic MRO by its nature requires complex labor and materials management practices just to ensure the right person, with the right parts, repairs the right asset, in the right order of priority, at the right time. What's the strategic goal? Achieving the absolute advantage in one's marketplace.

The absolute advantage, in economics, is a concept of trade in which an entity produces products and services more efficiently, using fewer resources of labor, and/or capital, while maintaining market agility superior to its competition.

What is the potential impact of getting Strategic MRO wrong?

- 5% of capacity is lost due to poorly managed maintenance practices.
- 10% of yearly capital budget is spent on the unnecessary replacement of assets due to premature failure.
- 10% extra maintenance staff exists due to poor planning practices, unnecessary planned maintenance tasks, and not involving asset operators in autonomous maintenance.
- 25% of maintenance labor overtime is due to responding to less critical demands during normal work hours and thus displacing work on higher criticality assets.
- 25% extra administrative staff exists due to lack of EAM system integration.
- 30% excess MRO inventory is due to fundamental lack of understanding of asset consumption patterns.
- 10% additional inventory exists because of lack of asset standards and no guidance on planned obsolescence decision making.
- 50% of improvement dollars is spent to find solutions to poor asset designs that create excessive functional failures.
- 10-15% price penalty is due to lack of MRO material strategic sourcing strategies.
- 20% excess MRO is spent because the consumables, spares, and repair strategy are not implemented by asset criticality classification.
- 5% extra labor cost per day or an average 30 minutes per day per maintenance resource is wasted because of the inability to quickly source and locate materials.
- 80% of the purchasing staff's sourcing activities are allocated to acquiring MRO or indirect materials.
- An MRO purchase order transaction with an average cost of $175 to $250.
- One to two inventory turnover range exist for asset owners. This means that on average, six months to a year's worth of MRO expenditures exist in inventory.

Asset Inequalities Require a Strategy

A company's primary product or service is a strategic consideration. So why wouldn't the system that acquires and maintains enterprise assets be strategic as well? It is clear that not all assets are equal in their purpose. Some assets are used to directly produce revenue while others are not. Not all failures are equal. Some failures are catastrophic while others are simple annoyances.

The strategic implication of these inequalities is that all supply responses need not be equal. But too often all supply responses to any asset demand are the same. What if we have no strategy for supply responses? Even worse, what if we had no strategy for assets? What if we did not understand the nature of asset demands? And what if we allowed supply to respond to asset demand without any clear system of priorities? Each "what if" can be answered simply... excess downtime, money, time, and labor.

Strategic MRO Defines the Scope

Strategic MRO as we refer to it in this book encompasses the entirety of EAM and the MRO supply chain. It includes the materials, labor, tools, and outside services employed in the process of keeping facilities, equipment, machines, and people in the condition needed to produce the firm's primary products.

EAM and MRO supply chain management have traditionally been viewed as separate functions within a company. EAM consists of designing, building, specifying, buying, using, and maintaining the production capacity provided by those assets that produce a company's products or services. EAM can be considered to be the demand side of the supply=demand equation.

MRO supply chain management consists of specifying, sourcing, buying, receiving, storing, and eventually issuing items and equipment. It also includes dispatching the human resources needed to maintain and support the running of a company's facilities, mobile assets, and production equipment. MRO supply chain management necessarily includes managing the vendors who supply these items, understanding when and what needs to be purchased, and managing inventories of these items. In addition to managing products, MRO supply chain management practices include the sourcing, procurement, and coordination of such MRO services as outsourced maintenance activities, leased assets, service agreements, and warranty and repair services. This is the supply side of the supply=demand equation.

Strategic MRO looks upon those two functions as being so tightly intertwined that they must be planned for and managed as a single function. In other words, we advocate a very tight, seamless integration between the demand side and the supply side of the equation. We also suggest that design of facilities and mobile assets and the design and specification of production processes are part and parcel to the success of Strategic MRO endeavors.

We differ so greatly in our treatment of MRO that we view the end user's maintenance practices such as condition-based monitoring, maintenance scheduling, and the setting of MRO inventory levels (to name just a few) as a part of the larger strategic MRO process. Therefore we will investigate those practices in this book and suggest changes that can result in benefits to all.

Strategic MRO *powered by DSC* Defines the Strategy

Demand Supply Compression (DSC) is the methodology we will employ to address the challenges of Strategic MRO. Strategic MRO *powered by DSC* provides a practical path to guide an organization's thinking and doing as they seek performance improvement. Focused on achieving a future perfect and guided by meaningful principles, organizations will learn to apply compression strategies to drive out waste, time, and non-value adding activities from their Strategic MRO practices.

We will be led on our Strategic MRO journey by Paul who is the CEO of a fictitious chemical company. His company will be joined by a water utility, an automotive manufacturer, a mobile telecommunications company, a military base operation, and a truck load freight carrier. The message is clear: Strategic MRO *powered by DSC* can be successfully applied to any business concern.

If you are looking to read another maintenance management book, this is not it. If you are looking to read another supply chain book, this is not it. If you are looking to transform your assets into a strategic advantage, you have found the right book.

Asset management and the MRO supply chain are strategic considerations that have been largely ignored. This book provides the roadmap showing how a proper focus on enterprise asset management and the associated MRO supply chain can be a source of huge savings and strategic advantage to companies that choose to alter their views on these subjects.

Let's get to work!

Chapter 1

MRO: The Strategic Imperative

Executive Summary: A key performance indicator for every company to focus on is revenue generated per dollar of asset investment. Developing total cost of ownership guidelines for using assets efficiently and effectively not only preserves capital and expense dollars, but also provides resources for investing in key business development parts of the business—research and development, sales and marketing, operations, and human resources. Similarly, these freed-up funds could drop straight to the bottom line or be used to acquire new assets needed to respond to changing market demands. Organizational agility, absolute advantage, and market domination each require a holistic view of asset management—Strategic MRO.

Another tough day started. As CEO of a major chemical producer in the United States, Paul struggled to understand why operating results were poorer than planned. True, the economy was hurting sales; even so, some other chemical producers were significantly outperforming him. How had all of the money poured into company assets and information technology not resulted in increased revenue or reduced costs as promised by his executive management team? Every one of the business cases looked so promising. Now, after three years, the bottom line looked more like trench warfare—entrenched thinking and doing. And, sad to say, the results were bloody "red" with no promising news from the front lines.

His CFO was advising the divestiture of some assets and the acquisition of others. His COO advised getting sales to do their job—fill the plants with orders. Sales complained of low and mostly "wrong" inventory levels that lost sales

1

because of ever-shrinking customer lead-time requirements. The newly titled supply chain manager recommended developing supplier performance metrics tied to incentives and disincentives.

Intuitively, Paul wrestled with the idea that all these efforts should be coordinated by an underlying set of guiding principles. But trying to visualize the common thread made his head hurt. Paul thumbed through an extract on U.S. manufacturing. It was part of the latest U.S. Economic Census, and he was intrigued and a little overwhelmed by the data he found.

Asset Turnover

Paul's company was not alone in its struggles. As a participant in the 1997 U.S. Economic Census, he knew the U.S. manufacturing sector had required $1.6 trillion in book value of assets to generate $3.8 trillion in shipment value. This equated to $2.47 in revenue for every dollar in physical, tangible, or real asset value.

1997 – U.S. Industry	Value of Shipments	Book Value of Asset	% Asset/Value Shipped	Asset Turnover
Manufacturing – All	$ 3,834,700,920	$ 1,551,319,045	40%	$2.47
Paper	$ 150,295,890	$ 139,378,691	93%	$1.08
Chemical	$ 415,616,508	$ 246,033,140	59%	$1.69
Primary Metals	$ 168,117,728	$ 89,574,167	53%	$1.88
Plastics & Rubber	$ 159,161,346	$ 75,923,401	48%	$2.10
Petro & Coal Products	$ 177,393,098	$ 78,004,070	44%	$2.27
Fabricated Metals	$ 242,813,453	$ 90,925,758	37%	$2.67
Computer & Electronic Products	$ 439,381,300	$ 159,250,346	36%	$2.75
Machinery	$ 270,687,165	$ 83,792,229	31%	$3.23
Transportation Equipment	$ 575,306,996	$ 172,385,913	30%	$3.33
Food	$ 421,737,017	$ 119,140,412	28%	$3.54

Table 1.1 - Asset Turnover by Industry

The chemical sector, where Paul had staked his career, had averaged $1.69 in revenue for every dollar in book value of assets. His rough calculations indicated his company was achieving only $1.27 in revenue for every dollar of book asset value (equipment and structures). He wondered what allowed other companies in his industry to generate more revenue per dollar of asset investment. How could his company's performance be so far below average?

The company clearly needed assets to generate revenue, but why was it that some competitors generated so much more revenue per invested dollar than his company did? What did they know about asset management and utilization that he didn't know? The question haunted him the more he thought about it. The real question, he decided, was what these companies did differently to allow them to use their asset investments more efficiently and effectively?

Paul started to connect the concept of asset turnover with its impact on profitability. As the products in his industry shifted more and more over the past few years to commodities rather than engineered items, margins had decreased steadily.

2

Ever since the days when he completed his MBA, Paul firmly held the view that, although sales were important, shareholders ultimately want a return on their investment. This return on investment can only be sustained, Paul knew, by a steady increase in real profits year after year.

Paul felt he understood the nature of assets and business processes. This understanding caused him to wonder about the sanity of huge cost cutting this year and then large investments next year. Throw in a freeze on maintenance and expansion every now and again and things really get out of kilter. All of these endeavors were undertaken, Paul knew, in an attempt to show profit in a given year. These profits were "engineered," not real, he thought.

Paul recognized that the asset investment required to produce a dollar in revenue varied greatly by industry. He wondered about the forces that resulted in differing amounts of revenue generation per dollar of asset investment for different industries. This was easier for Paul to understand. Surely certain industries require more plants, equipment, and mobile assets because of what they manufacture and sell. For example, the paper industry must require huge, costly machines to make products. In the food industry, machines typically are not subject to extreme operating conditions as in other industrial applications and therefore probably aren't as maintenance and repair intensive, thus extending the assets' lifecycle.

And then Paul quickly recognized two key points:

- Comparisons of revenue produced per dollar of asset investment across industries could be misleading for a number of reasons but made sense within an industry sector.
- He had to understand why his company was less efficient in the use of assets to produce revenue than its competitors.

Paul wondered if other CEOs were aware of how their company measured up in terms of revenue generation per dollar of asset investment.

Future Perfect

Paul's staff had lots of thoughts and good intentions, but no clear vision and no practical path forward. Clearly everyone was trying to do his or her best. Each functional area had rational performance measures and goals. It was as if there was no one to blame for poor performance and yet everyone was at fault all at the same time. How could that be?

Paul kept coming back to the idea of coordinating functions with regard to efficient asset utilization and a set of guiding principles to direct that coordination. He spun out a series of questions:

- Ideally, what are we trying to do?
- How can our company make precisely what the market demands with the absolute minimum investment in assets?

- What does our company need to do to strategically leverage its assets to improve both the top and bottom lines?
- If we could achieve a future perfect, what would it be?

Despite knowing that future perfect represented an ideal state and would be initially rejected for its impracticality, Paul still felt that clarifying a vision of future perfect could help guide his staff in the right directions. Paul's revelation about future perfect boiled down to a simple statement:

For any functional area, know what the future perfect state might be. Then take me there. If you can't take me all the way there, then take me part of the way this year, another part of the way next year, and so on. The key is envisioning future perfect. If we do not have that vision, how will we know what to try to attain?

Paul began by writing his future perfect objectives for assets:

- Produce exactly what is consumed in the market.
- Invest only in assets necessary to produce what is consumed.
- Invest only in assets that never fail over their useful life.
- Achieve zero total cost of ownership (TCO) for all assets.
- Invest only in resources that enable the first four future perfect objectives.

Paul believed that if he could make progress toward a future perfect, then his company had the best chance at achieving the absolute advantage in a cutthroat market.

The absolute advantage in economics is a concept of trade in which an entity produces products and services more efficiently, using fewer resources of labor, and/or capital, while maintaining market agility superior to its competition.

Somehow Paul needed to convince everyone in his company that integrating enterprise asset management and MRO (maintenance, repair, and operations/ overhaul) supply chain management was a strategic issue. Clearly his company was less efficient and effective with the deployment of its assets as compared to the industry. Paul needed a simple way of expressing the behavior he needed from his company. Being an engineer, he sketched his thoughts.

As he looked at the graph, Paul was sure his team would understand that if the company operated at a point to the left of best practice, total cost would be much higher than what would be possible in the future. Paul liked his graph. It held true for the entire operation of the company, not just the way the company managed its fixed assets. Paul felt he could use this simple graph to create common goals and direction for the company's improvement efforts.

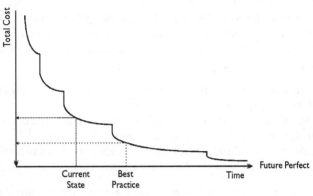

Figure 1.1 - Desired Behavior

Paul decided the process should begin with a consensus understanding of future perfect. He knew his staff had different interpretations of their current state and what constituted best practices. Ultimately, the desired behavior would implement best practices that resulted in the lowest total cost of operations. For asset investments he knew the goal was the lowest total cost of ownership (TCO). TCO consists of costs associated with purchase price, acquisition, possession, and disposal of an asset.

Operational Insight

Paul began with a quick review of his planned budget for the upcoming year. Less than 3.6% of sales were finding their way to the bottom line. From a net earnings perspective, every dollar saved was conservatively equivalent to $28 in sales. Sales predicted a stagnant market with business growth coming from the loss of business by the competition. There was no question competition was coming after their market share, and no question they were vulnerable. Operations had requested nearly $5 million in capital expansions and improvements, in addition to $12.5 million in budgeted maintenance costs. Paul wondered whether the mix between the capital improvement budget and the maintenance budget was correct. Should we spend less on capital improvements and more on maintenance or the other way around? What happens to the maintenance budget if we do a better job of acquiring assets that lower the total cost of ownership? He knew his equipment was aging, but it seemed that the most critical assets weren't getting the kind of attention they needed. Had they really managed the maintenance process or had they reacted as needed?

Paul came back to the idea that enterprise asset management should be governed by an underlying set of guiding principles. For the first time he contemplated the notion that the purchase of new capital assets must consider factors other than who can supply equipment meeting a certain specification at the lowest initial purchase cost. What consideration did existing brands deserve? How fully did they understand the cost of maintaining equipment over time?

Paul wondered whether the operations director or the financial director could give him the financial history of the assets over the last ten years. Paul's head started spinning again:

- What did an asset cost initially and what was the annual operating cost and the maintenance and repair cost?
- Were there any trends in labor, materials, insurance, and other costs that would provide insight to improved asset management practices?
- What about the cost of spares inventory and unplanned downtime?
- Do we understand what the bottom line impact is as a result of these costs?

By now Paul couldn't control his thoughts. Was it possible to reduce the amount of production downtime and improve the production cycle time of the existing assets and perhaps save half of next year's capital asset expenditures? That would surely improve the fixed asset to sales ratio and improve return on assets. And the resulting savings in maintenance, operating, interest, and investment cost, not to mention the impact on the facilities, Paul realized, would have a major impact on profitability.

Paul started to realize that capital expenditure decisions made in the past had resulted in an inflated maintenance budget. They had competing equipment from nearly every major supplier in the plant. Had they been penny-wise and pound-foolish by acquiring capital equipment based on the lowest bid only factor?

Paul decided to spend the rest of the day continuing his review of planned endeavors for the coming year. Purchasing was launching a strategic sourcing initiative to reduce the supply base and aggregate expeditures. This was supposed to reduce purchase prices. Paul wondered if this would in fact result in more bulk purchases, more cash up front, and higher inventory levels.

It occurred to him that purchasing should acquire what was needed, when it was needed, instead of always buying in bulk to get the best piece price – especially for MRO materials. Paul came back to the notion of guiding principles for efficient enterprise asset management:

- Do my purchasing performance metrics work for me or against me?
- Could inventory levels of materials be reduced if sound guiding principles were in place and followed?

Paul's Reflections

When Paul was nearly ready to go home, he spent a few minutes thinking about everything that had challenged him that day. He reflected on the results of the Economic Census and how it had made him think about asset management. Higher efficiency and effectiveness in the use of assets preserves capital and expense monies. These funds can then be redirected to research and development, sales and marketing, operations, and human resources, or go to the bottom line.

Further, these freed-up funds could be used to acquire new assets required to respond to changing market demands. Paul knew his company needed a simple integrated approach to identifying and implementing best practices in asset management that would free up these funds and reduce costs.

Tough times had hit the chemical industry, but it wasn't the only industry tagged by recent downturns in investor confidence. News headlines rang of layoffs in technology, aerospace, automotive, food, and pharmaceutical industries. Paul's company served all these sectors. He wondered how well they were doing with the capital they had tied up on the expectation of higher earnings.

In the not too distant past, Paul's team had looked at significant investment in e-commerce technology. They thought the technology would increase the number of sales channels, reduce the cost of doing business, and be a must-have for global market penetration. The concept was simple: be able to do business with anyone, anytime. Yet the adoption rates had been slow and the vendor list for the technology providers was getting smaller each day. Paul even had read that the leading e-commerce exchange companies would be a good buy for firms looking for already-trained IT staffs. "I guess," Paul mused, "the investors have figured out that it takes real people, using real materials and real assets, to produce real products that can be sold profitably."

Paul's anxiety grew as the potential for his assets and people to sit idle grew. Getting his company back on track and staying there was his first priority. He owed it to his shareholders, the people of his company, and his family to find a path forward.

If Paul's tough day seems uncomfortably familiar, then this book is a must-read for you. Better asset management leads to organizational agility, achieving an absolute advantage, and ultimately market domination. One caveat: Your product or service must bring recognized value to the market. However, our discussion will not focus on this caveat.

Chapter 2

Channel Dynamics

Executive Summary: This chapter classifies the somewhat complicated channels through which industrial products flow and introduces the Strategic MRO principles used to optimize the supply chain. It defines the key channel relationships in a variety of asset management environments. An asset's user (asset owner) can pick from a range of channel options to manage the supply stream and maximize return from the other channel participants (asset maker and asset service provider). The ideal Strategic MRO solution should be focused totally on the asset lifecycle experienced by the asset owner. Lessons learned from the direct materials space—accelerated time to market, lean enterprise, just-in-time manufacturing, contract manufacturing and others—can be directly applied to the asset management and indirect materials market space.

Being at the top of a corporation can be a lonely proposition. Paul found some support as a member of an executive forum of industrial organizations that meets monthly to share common business challenges. The meetings serve two purposes. First, the participants share business experiences and insight without fear of competitive eavesdropping. Second, the peer group analyzes case studies presented periodically by each member. Paul found the executive forum to be a great place for him to raise critical thoughts without sounding early warnings or spurring miscommunications within his own company.

Paul approached the forum's topic committee with his thoughts about Strategic MRO. Specific figures from the U.S. Census led him to think about the efficient use of assets. He needed to get more out of his real assets; as did other companies attending the forum sessions. The forum had executive participation from a broad spectrum of industries such as utilities, oil and gas, facilities, public sector, discrete manufacturing, process industries, pharmaceutical, transportation, aviation, and telecommunications. Each of the companies within these industries had to deploy assets effectively to achieve its mission. Paul said he thought a Strategic MRO focus could be a major opportunity for each member of the group to improve his or her organization's bottom line.

Sounding more like a board chairman than a friendly peer, the forum's topic committee chair asked Paul for written details with specific discussion areas related to Strategic MRO.

Asset Owners, Asset Service Providers, Asset Makers

Paul prepared a brief summary: "I want to simplify the complexities of asset management and MRO materials supply. The goal is a reasonable path forward for executives seeking a future-perfect vision of meeting market demands using the absolute minimum investment in assets. I believe there are three types of organizations that can benefit from our discussions. Each is singularly important and together they capture the entirety of the asset lifecycle. These are asset owners, asset makers, and asset service providers.

Today, every industrial organization is an asset owner. The nature of these assets consists primarily of structures (buildings), equipment, and mobile assets. Some companies may choose to lease or rent assets owned by other organizations to fulfill their needs. In this case the asset owner is the lessor. The emphasis of our forum should be on achieving future perfect for the asset owner. If we understand that well, we will be able to integrate the other channel members according to every individual organization's strategy. Integrating channel members who support the asset owner will require a clear understanding of how asset makers and asset service providers impact the asset lifecycles experienced by the asset owner.

Paul realized his forum needed to embrace some new terminology to help them understand the Strategic MRO world. For example, organizations that produce or build assets should be classified as asset makers. Asset makers consist of raw material, component, subassembly, and final assembly manufacturers of materials or equipment. They also include the raw materials, components, substructures, and finished structures builders. The premise Paul hoped his forum would come to understand is simple, but he had never heard it stated directly:

Asset makers must work to continually understand the desires and needs of asset owners. They must then transform these desires and needs into the tangible structures and equipment necessary to produce exactly what is consumed in the market, thus generating revenue for the asset owner.

Asset service providers consist of all other entities that service the operational and logistical needs of both the asset owners and asset makers. Asset service providers consist of industrial distributors, logistics providers (air, rail, road, and water), technology providers, operations and maintenance service providers, and other outsourced services such as integrated supply, storeroom management, procurement, automated payment, monitoring and testing, and others.

Paul felt comfortable reading what he had written so far: asset owner, asset maker, and asset service provider. This classification, he realized, made it much easier to discuss the somewhat complicated channels through which industrial products flowed.

Paul understood that each specific industry had distinct challenges in how it generated funding or revenue. Yet all had to effectively leverage assets over their useful life. Paul saw the need to reinforce to his forum the idea that each company within a vertical should focus on its roles and challenges in the context of asset lifecycles. Its solutions, then, should be focused totally on the asset lifecycle experienced by the asset owner.

Asset Lifecycle

Paul briefed the topics committee and ended the discussion with the pertinent elements of the asset lifecycle. Briefly he stated the asset lifecycle as consisting of the elements shown in Figure 2.1.

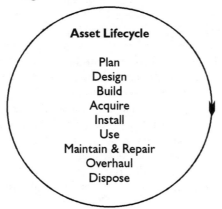

Figure 2.1 - Asset Lifecycle

This was perhaps the most unglamorous subject that the topic committee had considered for presentation to its membership. Past topics had focused on reducing insurance premiums, leveraging customer relationship management software, and mergers and acquisition. This topic seemed more like work to the committee.

However, the members decided, given the state of the economy, why not go back to the basics and rethink the assumptions of asset management. With a few nods the topic committee approved Paul's proposal.

Much to Paul's surprise, his presentation elicited responses such as "you have hit the nail right on the head" and "slowly this asset management thing is starting to make some sense." Clearly it was a new topic and a new way of looking at what seemed to all an important issue for every industrial organization. The meeting ended with a general consensus that the topic deserved more attention.

The committee requested that Paul provide a brief overview of the Strategic MRO players as well as some basics on the channels in which the players coexisted for the next meeting. Paul gladly agreed. He was very happy that they accepted the terminology for the main groups as he had defined it. The asset makers/asset owners/asset service providers classification scheme made sense not only to him but to others as well. Paul felt that an initial discussion focused on players and channels would allow the forum members to locate themselves both within their own channels and within the framework of asset makers, asset owners, and asset service providers.

Strategic MRO Channels

The notion of Strategic MRO is simple, Paul thought, but the channels through which these products and services flow are not, as he soon realized when he started to apply the future perfect objectives to the channel members and their interactions. In generic terms Paul knew that materials that are part of the product are called direct materials and materials that support production activities are considered indirect materials. Traditionally MRO materials are considered indirect materials. It got confusing when Paul noted that what was MRO (indirect) to one entity was the primary product (direct) of original equipment manufacturers (OEMs). He saw that the same product could be used for maintaining an asset owner's asset and as a component part of an asset maker's primary product.

Paul phoned the committee and requested more time to prepare as he realized this was more challenging than he had anticipated. At the next meeting he was immediately greeted with inquiries on his progress and findings. Paul realized that there was a real interest in what he was doing. This motivated him to work even harder at unraveling this Strategic MRO thing.

While preparing, Paul realized that the confusion can go a bit further when he observed that an automotive manufacturer buys bearings through a particular supply chain to repair production equipment. They may also buy the same bearings— through a different supply chain—to use as a component in the original equipment, the vehicle. So the same item could easily be an indirect and a direct material depending on the use it was put to and/or the supply chain through which it was acquired.

Paul started to look closely into this and identified a large number of players. Some are relatively new and are struggling to understand what their roles and ultimate value to their customers will be in the future. Other players in these channels have been around for decades. These older players also struggle to understand what their roles and ultimate value to their customers will be in the future.

Eventually Paul was ready for the next executive forum meeting, and he found he was looking forward to it. Paul's presentation started with a confession: "As I thought and read about this, I quickly realized that I was totally out of my depth. I then remembered a remarkable man I met during my MBA studies. This gentleman has spent more than 25 years in this field and almost everything that I will share here I got from five interviews with him. I want to start the discussion of the Strategic MRO world," Paul told the forum members, "by reviewing the three primary supply channels:

- OEM direct materials channel.
- Industrial repair channel.
- Commercial repair channel.

Our objective is to take a closer look at the channel players, their value propositions, and their challenges." Paul switched on the projector and started his presentation.

Original Equipment Manufacturer (OEM) Direct Materials

The OEM direct materials channel provides goods that otherwise might be thought of as traditional MRO materials to OEMs. For example, automobile manufacturers who build cars use bearings, belts, lubricants, and other items. The same manufacturers who supply these items to industrial end users, as indirect materials, supply them to OEMs through the direct material component channel. Distributors, master distributors, wholesalers, and engineering and construction firms may be intermediaries in this channel. MRO manufacturer-to-OEM direct relationships exist in this channel.

Paul asked the forum members to focus their attention on the inherent design and use of OEM equipment as a key shaper of the MRO supply chain. Because the equipment design dictates (or at least should dictate) the components used and ultimately repaired, the role of engineering and construction (E&C) resources is critical when interpreting end-user requirements back to the OEM manufacturer. Seeing the question marks on everybody's faces, he used a model to explain the channel (see Figure 2.2).

Looking at the model made the channel members and the flow of materials very clear to everybody, and Paul continued with a smile, "It's time to introduce you to the principles that make this channel efficient: consumption transparency, velocity, and liquidity."

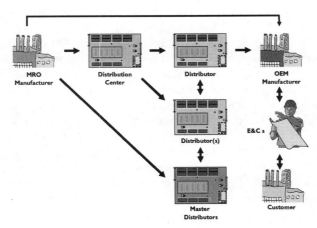

Figure 2.2 - OEM Direct Material Components Channel

Consumption transparency—the manufacturer's ability to know that an item has been consumed at the end-user level—is high within the OEM direct materials channel. Disconnects exist, but where there are direct relationships between the MRO manufacturer and OEM consumer, production schedules and actual production can be monitored to determine the timing of actual consumption. Conversely, information regarding how specific MRO components—once in service—were maintained, repaired, or replaced is not uniformly communicated through any MRO channel back to the producer. Thus, downstream consumption transparency for these MRO products is low.

Velocity in the OEM direct materials channel is good. Velocity refers to the relative rapidity of flow of dollars and products from point of manufacture to point of end use and return. In this channel, velocity is good, in part, because the OEM's focus on low component price requires the channel to be as efficient as possible. The challenge to the OEM is to standardize MRO components to meet broad industry requirements while meeting specific MRO component standards for major end users. If product specifications generally align with industry design requirements, the OEM manufacturer can systematically lower inventory investments to meet actual production orders. If there is misalignment, lead times increase, inventory levels subsequently increase to offset these lead times, and pricing escalates to handle customer-specific requirements.

Liquidity in the OEM direct materials channel is good. Liquidity refers to the ability to exchange inventory for cash. Velocity and liquidity are highly correlated. Higher velocity in a channel generally equates to higher liquidity. This is because high velocity usually means that the items consumers buy are consistently produced as replacements. Noncollaborative design and inefficient production processes that leave intermediaries and component manufacturers holding larger than necessary inventories impede liquidity. So do extended payment cycles. As companies attempt to manage cash flows they tend to extend payment terms by acquiring products and services well in advance of paying for them. Extended payment terms mean that asset makers (component manufacturers) and asset service providers (distributors) finance a portion of the asset user's debt, thereby "slowing" liquidity in the channel.

The Industrial Repair Channel

The industrial repair channel supplies products and materials used to maintain, repair, and operate facilities, plants, production equipment, and mobile assets. Distributors, master distributors, and integrated service and supply firms may be intermediaries in this channel. Few MRO manufacturer-to-end user direct relationships exist in this channel.

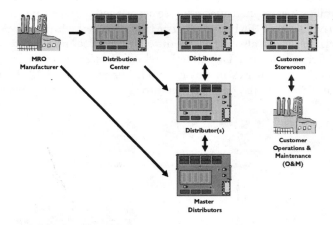

Figure 2.3 - Industrial Repair Channel

Consumption transparency of actual MRO material usage in the industrial repair channel is poor to nonexistent. Moreover, channel intermediaries almost universally fail to distinguish between demand and consumption. For example, the MRO manufacturer will record as demand the sale of a pallet-size quantity of an item to a distributor. This demand is recorded with absolutely no knowledge about whether or not end users are actually consuming the item. To make matters worse, this demand may well cause the manufacturer to plan replacement production for the item.

Self-imposed market mechanisms also generate demands that exceed consumption recorded by industrial repair channel players. For example, an MRO manufacturer may offer quantity discounts to distributors. This causes the distributor to buy larger quantities on a comparatively infrequent basis thus disguising the actual timing of consumption. The distributor, then, may offer quantity discounts to the industrial end user. End-user purchasing agents—often motivated by lower piece prices—fill the plant's storerooms with product that may become obsolete due to production process changes. Thus, the industrial repair channel tends to produce and replenish to an artificial demand that is often far in excess of consumption.

Velocity in the industrial repair channel is poor as a result of production and replenishment to demand rather than to consumption. *Liquidity* is even worse. When the end user is motivated by piece price reductions, storerooms fill with product that becomes obsolete. Examples abound in this channel of situations where 35% to 50% of a plant's MRO inventory investment is virtually worthless.

The Commercial Repair Channel

The commercial repair channel provides materials—that otherwise might be thought of as traditional MRO materials—to an aftermarket that may or may not be industrial. For example, nonindustrial consumers use bearings, belts, lubricants, and other items to repair automobiles. Industrial repair centers, for example, military jet repair, may acquire repair parts and other components through traditional MRO and OEM channels. The manufacturers who supply these items to industrial end users also supply them to aftermarket end users through the commercial repair channel. Distributors, wholesalers, retailers, and service centers may be intermediaries in this channel. For example, 50% of a bearing manufacturer's output may go to market through the commercial repair channel.

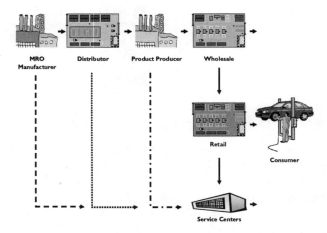

Figure 2.4 - Commercial Repair Channel

Consumption transparency in the commercial repair channel is marginal but disconnected. Forthcoming discussions explore the concept of consumption transparency and its importance to channel efficiency. For now suffice it to say that efficient channels require real-time information about what is consumed so that they can plan replacements based on expected consumption rates.

Consumption transparency in commercial repair is marginal rather than poor or nonexistent because point of sale information is available in parts of the channel.

Information relative to an auto parts store's selling a bearing is quickly communicated to regional and national offices. Disconnects exist because that information does not flow all the way back to the bearing manufacturer. The reasons for the lack of consumption transparency in this channel and others will be explored in detail in later chapters.

Velocity in the commercial repair channel is good, in part, because point of sale data is used in portions of the channel. Velocity would be better without the noted disconnect in consumption transparency.

Liquidity in the commercial repair channel is good but somewhat hampered by the sheer diversity of products needing periodic repair. Likewise, liquidity is impacted by the fact that consumers are unwilling to wait for needed parts. This requires inventories to be held near expected points of use. Point of sale data and efficient logistics have improved the channel's liquidity. Traditionally payment terms in the nonindustrial commercial repair channels are pay upon completion of service. This payment process is not fully ascribed to in the industrial channels. Welcome to the world of industrial purchase orders, invoices, invoice reconciliation, dispute resolution, and credit holds.

MRO Channel Players

Traditionally, MRO channel players have included:

- OEM equipment manufacturers.
- MRO manufacturers.
- MRO industrial distributors.
- MRO industrial end users.
- Engineering and construction firms.
- MRO commercial service centers.
- Consumers.

Increasingly, new and hybrid players are emerging, and these include:

- Distributor integrators.
- Manufacturer directed integrators.
- Third-party procurement integrators.
- Technology provider integrators.
- Engineering, procurement, and construction integrator.
- Operations and maintenance integrators.

At the heart of the Strategic MRO demand-supply chain is a piece of equipment, an asset, whether for industrial or consumer use. This piece of equipment consists of components that may require maintenance, repair, or replacement.

Players in the MRO channel exist to keep this piece of equipment reliable and available for its intended use. The OEM manufacturer (maker) produces the equipment; the MRO manufacturer (maker) produces the equipment components; the MRO distributor (service provider) stocks and resells MRO equipment and components. The industrial end user (owner) uses the equipment to produce its product or services. The engineering and construction firms (service providers) assist the industrial end user or the commercial user (owner) in selection and installation of the equipment. The consumer (owner) purchases equipment for personal use and finally the commercial service center (service provider) operates as both a commercial distributor and repairer of equipment in the aftermarket to the industrial end user or the consumer.

Original Equipment Manufacturers

Original equipment manufacturers are asset makers. They produce equipment, facilities, and infrastructures. They produce everything from planes, cars, trucks, and boats, to cranes, robots, mixers, furnaces, label machines, ultrasound machines, air conditioning units, and computers, as well as buildings, bridges, roads, sewers, water and gas lines, and electricity distribution systems. It is this design and installation of equipment or infrastructure that creates consumption and ultimately requires MRO supply chain support.

The OEM manufacturer must balance the needs of the customer with the target margins it sets for its products. For example, the end-user customer may have standardized on a particular motor manufacturer, Brand Y, and desires this type of motor to be part of the original equipment. The OEM manufacturer has standardized on Brand Z, because of cost and delivery requirements. The difference between customer desires and OEM standards creates a dilemma for all involved. The answer isn't as simple as giving the customer what he wants or politely refusing to play. It is the balancing of these factors that distinguishes a good OEM from a great OEM.

The OEM may or may not realize that the design and use of the equipment or infrastructure ultimately dictates the total cost of ownership for the customer. Highly engineered content without increased reliability generally results in higher maintenance and repair costs. Highly engineered products usually have more convoluted supply chains for repair parts. However a highly engineered item designed with enhanced reliability improves equipment availability and reduces maintenance and repair costs.

The OEM and its customers must make trade-offs between increased reliability and product costs. The shame of these trade-offs is that maintenance and MRO inventory cost are not often analyzed during the capital equipment procurement process. After all—this is the capital project's budget, not the maintenance budget. The goal is to operate within the capital budget—others are left to worry about maintenance later.

The OEM manufacturer fulfills the following needs in the marketplace:

- Designs, produces, and delivers products and infrastructure that enable an industrial end user to produce products or services.

- Designs, produces, and delivers consumer products and infrastructure that are by design consumable or durable in nature.
- Provides product technical support before, during, and after the sale.
- Through design of the product and/or infrastructure establishes nearly 80% of the future operating cost of the user.
- The OEM may maintain and repair its own and other equipment on an outsource and co-source basis.

MRO Manufacturers

As asset makers, MRO manufacturers produce the component products that flow to market through the OEM direct materials, industrial repair, and commercial repair channels. For the most part, these three channels operate independently of one another. Most channel members are concerned only with their own needs.

The MRO manufacturer must balance the use of its own resources against the needs of all three channels and the resulting opportunities. Of course, some MRO manufacturers serve only one or two channels while others serve all three. Product pricing can differ dramatically depending upon which channel material flows through. Likewise profit margins can vary by channel.

The MRO manufacturer is challenged by its customers to produce products that last longer and cost less. Additionally customers want products to easily replace or substitute for other MRO product manufacturers. Not too long ago many of us changed a spark plug in our vehicle's engine every 3,000 miles or every oil change. Today spark plugs last 100,000 miles and may never be replaced. This causes loss of brand identity, unclear definition of the product, service value propositions, and fuzzy product portfolio management of old product designs with new product introductions.

The MRO manufacturer receives varying levels of information flow regarding consumption in the marketplace. In theory, those channels that can provide more timely consumption information should be more desirable to the manufacturer. This is because that information could be used for better production planning. Better consumption information could also reduce the investment in buffer inventories held by the manufacturer. Surprisingly, many manufacturers are not internally positioned to effectively use this information even when it is available. Most still live and die by old-line batch systems focused on producing to inventory-based demand rather than real-time consumption information.

The MRO manufacturer fulfills the following needs in the marketplace:

- Designs and manufactures MRO component products.
- Balances quality, functionality, and price.
- Extends asset lifecycles by improving product reliability.
- Shortens product acquisition cycle times by producing in anticipation of demand.

- Holds buffer inventories.
- Provides paper and/or electronic catalogs.
- Provides technical support.
- Provides technical product specifications.
- Provides service parts for current and, where practical, past designs.

MRO Industrial Distributors

The MRO industrial distributor is an asset service provider that acts as an intermediary between the MRO manufacturer and the industrial end user, the commercial repair center and, often, the consumer. The term *industrial distributors* refers to the fact that this channel sells predominately to industrial end users. Thousands of industrial distributorships have relatively small yearly sales volumes. Their outlets are often in close proximity to industrial plants. They tend to have superior expertise in the application of the products they stock and sell to industrial applications. This application expertise often exceeds that of the MRO manufacturer of the product.

The MRO industrial distributor is frequently challenged to provide the lowest cost product in the shortest possible time. Given the nature of end–user demand, the customer lead time (the time from when an MRO need is known to the time the need is communicated to the supply chain) is invariably less than the time it takes to manufacture the product and deliver it to the customer site. Thus inventory sits in the channel, waiting for the order to come from the customer.

The MRO industrial distributor is the manager of the inventory risk in the channel for both the MRO manufacturer and the MRO customer. The MRO industrial distributor can significantly impact an MRO manufacturer's profitability by how it conducts sales and inventory management activities. Likewise the MRO industrial distributor can significantly impact the cost of operations of an end user by the advice its gives and the products it sells.

Rumors of bypassing MRO industrial distribution increases as channel players review how MRO products can be manufactured and delivered similar to just-in-time direct materials. Given the current state of MRO manufacturing practices and end–user asset management practices we find these rumors quite humorous. Predicting failure for everything that could possibly be maintained, repaired, or replaced for most operations is impossible. This prediction of failure, where practical, will lower inventory in the channel. Because all failures are not predictable, MRO industrial distributors will continue to serve their channels for the foreseeable future.

The challenge for MRO industrial distributors is to grow their understanding of the customer's maintenance and production practices. To the extent that they can provide guidance on improving consumption patterns for the products they sell, they are of greater value to their customers. Distributors must begin to sell products that last longer, enable the customer to achieve lean (just-in-time) manufacturing requirements, and ultimately reduce the customer's total cost of ownership of assets. Further, distributors need to manage the quantity being purchased by the customer so that it matches consumption patterns.

In the United States the expressions "fat chance" and "slim chance" have the same meaning. One current assessment of the MRO channel is that there is a "fat chance" that the distributor knows enough about manufacturing to aid the customer in the reduction of MRO consumption. This assessment goes on to note that there is a "slim chance" that the customer knows enough about distribution practices to correctly align inventory quantities and stocking practices to meet consumption requirements.

Accordingly, MRO channel players need to get deeply involved with the lean thinking concepts detailed in this book if real progress is to be made. This implies a closer relationship and understanding of roles among all channel members.

The industrial distributor fulfills the following needs in the marketplace:

- Manages inventory risk in the MRO channels.
- Provides availability of MRO product at the right time and place.
- Provides appropriate cross section of complementary products from many different MRO manufacturers.
- Provides product application information.
- Provides information regarding newly introduced products.
- Holds buffer inventories.
- Provides technical support.
- Provides technical product specifications.
- Provides paper and/or electronic catalogs.
- Provides feedback to the MRO manufacturer on product performance.

Nonindustrial Consumer

The nonindustrial consumer is an asset owner who consumes a significant percentage of the product delivered through the commercial repair channel. This channel has been designed to support both do-it-yourselfers and those who use outside assistance for their repair needs. The industrial supply channel offers the nonindustrial consumer retail sales of MRO components, product warranties, insurance, and product guarantees.

There are a number of lessons that the industrial sector can learn from the consumer sector. For instance, before a customer leaves a retail store, the MRO component is paid for. When a customer returns a product that is not working properly it is accepted immediately by the selling organization. If the customer desires a refund it is provided immediately. If the customer selected the wrong product it can be quickly exchanged for the correct one. Service personnel respond patiently and quickly to customer inquiries. Help desk and service counters greet the customer immediately upon entrance to the store.

Nonindustrial consumers expect and are willing to pay for support and service. Premiums are routinely paid for in-house service. They are willing to pay for the travel time of the service technician.

These same consumers enter the business world and completely change standards. When was the last time a major industrial account actually paid for the product when they took possession? A special case, to be fair, is when the customer uses a procurement card to pay for a purchase. Of course, the finance charges associated with the p-card purchases are usually borne by the seller. When did a product return happen without questioning and delayed reimbursement to the buyer? The differences are striking and work counter to future perfect. The nonindustrial consumer expects, gets, and pays for a relatively efficient system.

MRO Commercial Service Centers

MRO commercial service centers are asset service providers. They provide skills the asset owner may not have and perform repair activities that the asset owner does not want to perform internally.

Commercial service centers tend to service a geographically dispersed customer base. One of their major goals is achieving the highest customer service and response levels while simultaneously maximizing labor utilization. Most commercial service centers require that the asset owner bring or ship the asset to a centralized location. Centralized locations are designed to maximize labor utilization. This is accomplished by eliminating the transit time to customers' locations, centralizing both the stocking of repair parts and access to the expertise required to diagnose and repair the asset.

Commercial service centers that provide on-site services face the challenges of sending the right resource, with the right materials and equipment, to the right location, while minimizing non-value added activities, such as transit time behind the steering wheel of a repair truck. Commercial repair centers must constantly evaluate the effectiveness of their diagnostic and repair processes. Industry statistics reveal that commercial repair centers that obtain greater than 25% of actual repair time ("wrench time") for on-site services are performing well.

MRO commercial service centers fulfill the following needs in the marketplace:

- Sell maintenance, repair, and overhaul services to both the industrial and consumer sectors.
- Increase consumer confidence as an asset owner that if something does go wrong it can be remedied. This increased consumer confidence increases future sales.
- Provide timely and convenient service minimizing the asset owner's downtime.

- Make spare parts available for repair of assets that would be difficult for the consumer to obtain through industrial MRO channels.

Industrial End User

The industrial end user is an asset owner who buys MRO products to maintain plant and equipment. The industrial end user has two distinct processes ongoing that ensure its plants continue to have production capability. The first is enterprise asset management and the second is MRO supply chain management.

Enterprise asset management (EAM) consists of designing, building, specifying and buying, and using and maintaining the production capacity provided by those assets that produce a company's products.

MRO supply chain management consists of specifying, sourcing, buying, receiving, storing, and eventually issuing those items needed to maintain and support the running of a company's facilities and production equipment. This process necessarily includes managing the vendors who supply these items, understanding what needs to be purchased and when, and inventory management activities.

Various entities at the industrial end user company perform the following functions:

- Design, specify, and purchase production assets.
- Maintain production assets.
- Extend production asset lifecycles by performing reactive and predictive maintenance.
- Specify, source, buy, receive, store, and issue repair parts for maintenance.
- Hold buffer inventories.
- Provide technical support.

End-user companies impact the MRO supply channels in the following ways:

- Asset design, asset use, and asset maintenance significantly impact the MRO demand that the supply chain must respond to.
- Through use of the asset and supporting technology, the industrial end user can develop extensive asset profiles that can be used to increase both asset availability and reliability. This insight is often more meaningful than that provided by the asset maker or asset service providers.
- Industrial end user MRO policies and practices drive behaviors within their organizations that have dramatic impact on MRO supply channels. Subsequent chapters elaborate on these policies and behaviors. The industrial end user will have to make a paradigm shift and leverage knowledge of Strategic MRO concepts to get the rest of the channel players moving toward future perfect.

Integrated Services and Supply Management

Integrated services and supply management is a term used to describe a wide variety of functions that can be provided to an industrial plant by a single third-party company or group of companies as asset service providers. These functions may be as simple as MRO procurement provided by a local distributor or as complex as an operations and maintenance integrator providing all MRO procurement and plant maintenance.

The most common integrated services and supply management offerings include:

- Integrated supply in various configurations.
- Distributor integrator.
- Manufacturer directed integrator.
- Third-party procurement.
- Technology provider integrators.
- Operations and maintenance integrators.
- Engineering, procurement, and construction integrators.

Some may feel that almost all of these offerings of integrated services and supply management take advantage of the end user's lack of knowledge or focus on a specific element of Strategic MRO. A full understanding of the underlying principles of Strategic MRO is a critical prerequisite to using these kinds of services.

The danger in contracting with integrated services and supply players for the wrong reasons is that doing so runs the risk of perpetuating current practices and relinquishing control to partners who have no incentive to move a company toward lower total cost of asset ownership.

Integrated supply is a concept that evolved in the early 1990s and sought to allow a plant to achieve cost reductions through shrinking the MRO supplier base. The ideas that fewer suppliers are less costly to manage and that increased purchase volume through fewer suppliers may result in lower piece prices may have merit. Integrated supply is generally available through distributor integrators, manufacturer directed integrators, and third-party procurement or pure integrators.

Distributor Integrators

Distributor integrator groups form at the direction of a particular end-user customer or plant or by combining disparate product lines in an attempt to gain competitive market advantage. The customer may choose a number of distributors representing important product lines and request that they work in concert so as to appear as a single source of supply. This allows the customer to issue a single purchase order for many types of products to this integrated source of supply. The order is internally divided among the participating distributors. The integrated source bills the customer on a single invoice. Order fulfillment and delivery may or may not be integrated.

Initial industry drivers for integrated supply were to aggregate MRO spending to increase purchase leverage and to outsource non-core competencies to reduce internal labor costs. The distributor integrator would not only provide their products but also serve as the purchasing agent for other products on behalf of the industrial end user. Integrated supply contracts also drove integrators to support vendor stocking programs, inventory consignment, issue bins, and inventory buybacks for slow-moving and obsolete items.

Distributor integrators fulfill the following needs in the marketplace:

- Provide a single source for sourcing, delivering, and accounting for MRO supplies.
- Provide storeroom stocking and inventory management services.
- Aggregate MRO spend through a single source thus improving price leverage through the channel.
- Provide integrated systems for order fulfillment and accounting activities.

Manufacturer Directed Integrators

The order fulfillment technology investment to participate in integrated supply activities often represents a high cost of entry for mid-sized to small distributors. These costs are often borne by the manufacturer who desires to keep these specialty distributors from losing business otherwise won by larger integrated supply sources. Thus the manufacturer directed integrators enable an MRO manufacturer to protect its product positioning within industrial end users by providing its specialty distributors with integrated supply capabilities.

Added benefits to the industrial end user are a continued relationship with a specialty distributor that emphasizes product knowledge, technical support, and configuration management. Surveys have indicated that industrial end users expect this type of support for power transmission and bearings, pipe, valves, and fittings, safety, cutting tools and abrasives, electrical, and electronics products.

The benefit to the manufacturer who directs such integrated supply activities is visibility of actual customer consumption patterns for their products. This knowledge enables the manufacturer to improve production planning and scheduling activities. Production control improvements result in lower inventory levels needed to meet end-user service requirements. Lower inventory investments mean lower inventory carrying costs for all MRO channel participants.

Manufacturers are now forming e-commerce exchanges under one brand name to provide integrated cataloging and ordering capabilities for multiple product types. E-commerce enabled catalogs are then provided to the industrial end user through their traditional distributors, enabled by MRO manufacturer efforts.

Manufacturer-directed integrators fulfill the following needs in the marketplace:

- Protect product positioning within an industrial end user.
- Provide high-level product technical support and information.

- Provide access to product configurator models for order placement.
- Provide improved production planning for inventory replenishment activities within the MRO supply channels.
- Provide manufacturer catalog data visibility for improved product identification and cross-referencing in the order fulfillment activities.

Third-Party Procurement Integrators

Third-party procurement, or pure, integrators are asset service providers for procurement functions. They neither make nor own MRO inventories. They act as aggregated buying agencies on behalf of their customers. In essence they represent an outsourced purchasing function for the industrial end user. Distributor and manufacturer-directed integrated supply companies may also use pure integrators to source services, specialty and engineered items, and low volume, low demand items.

Pure integrators fulfill the following needs in the marketplace:

- Integrated sourcing of multiple product types.
- Lower cost supplement or replacement of existing purchasing resources.
- Aggregated buying requirements to achieve lower per-piece price in the market.
- Enable customer to receive equivalent bulk quantity discounts for smaller order sizes.
- Manage adherence to local, regional, and national contracts.

Technology Provider Integrators

Technology provider integrators are a recent development through which e-commerce exchanges provide not only the technology for integrated purchasing but also services such as strategic sourcing, contract management, auction and reverse auction services, e-collaboration, catalog management, price book management, workflow, payment, and electronic mail and paging services.

Technology provider integrators fulfill the following needs in the marketplace:

- Provide technology to enable electronic order fulfillment and payment activities.
- R&D efforts that provide step changes in order fulfillment technology and its deployment, enabling lower total cost of ownership for the industrial end user.
- Provide connectivity services for bringing trade entities into e-commerce exchanges.
- Provide technology backbone and redundancy for secure and reliable trade transactions.

Engineering, Procurement, and Construction Integrators

Engineering, procurement, and construction (EPC) firms are asset service providers who design and build structures. They also design, build, and install production processes, install OEM equipment, and establish initial maintenance and MRO supply requirements. EPC firms conduct trade with the industrial distribution channel and MRO manufacturers to complete construction projects on behalf of their customers.

EPC integrators evolved as an additional service provided after construction project activities were finished. The EPC integrator's value proposition provides maintenance support during operations at a cost lower than a company's internal cost of performing these activities. As significant buyers of MRO materials required for construction, the EPC integrator offers to combine its purchasing power with that of the customer to further leverage prices.

To be successful, EPC integrators have to make the difficult transition from project work to repetitive maintenance work. Early efforts focused on the maintenance of facilities. Production assets are considered sacred to the industrial end user and have historically been maintained by an internal maintenance staff. EPCs have found that they need to form separate business units that focus strictly on operations and maintenance to extend their service offerings into this realm. This organizational structure parallels that of most large industrial firms, which separate construction from maintenance and ongoing operations activities.

Engineering, procurement, and construction integrators fulfill the following needs in the marketplace:

- Design and build structures.
- Design, build, and install production processes.
- Install OEM equipment.
- Establish initial maintenance and MRO supply requirements.
- Conduct maintenance functions postconstruction activities.

Operations and Maintenance Integrators

Operations and maintenance (O&M) firms, are asset service providers that serve asset owners by performing both maintenance and MRO supply chain activities. They are often referred to as asset managers. Typically operating under service level agreements, O&M integrators are challenged to improve asset availability and, most recently, asset reliability.

O&M firms have a distinct advantage over most integrated supply solutions in that they address both the demand and supply characteristics of the asset lifecycle. Conversely, distributors, manufacturing directed, and pure integrators tend to focus on inventory replenishment strategies based on stated on-time delivery goals. The goal of the O&M integrator is to improve asset availability and reliability. This requires a thorough knowledge of the asset in use as well as the optimization of the MRO supply chain.

Operations and maintenance integrators fulfill the following needs in the marketplace:

- Monitoring asset availability and reliability to reduce the total cost of ownership for the asset owner.
- Performing on-site maintenance and MRO supply chain activities.
- Acting on behalf of the asset owners to ensure that satisfactory service levels are achieved.

The Ideal Combination

The asset owner has many alternatives from which to sculpt an enterprise asset and MRO supply chain management solution. In truth, there may be many ideal combinations. One of these ideal integrator combinations might include elements from EPC, O&M, distributor, and logistics asset service providers. Logistics service providers include 3PL (3rd party logistics) and 4PL (4th party logistics) service providers that aid the customer in optimizing the flow of goods between trade entities. Such a combination covers the entirety of asset lifecycle activities. However, such a combination has not been formally presented to the asset management market. To date, more focus has been placed on this combination of talent in the direct materials space. Lessons learned from accelerated time to market, lean enterprise, just-in-time manufacturing, contract manufacturing, and others can be directly applied to the asset management and indirect materials market space.

Chapter 3

Islands of Pain

Executive Summary: To change behavior, first understand the problem. Historically, suboptimal supply chain practices within organizations have created "islands of pain." These islands evolve as individual departments implement isolated EAM and supply chain management programs. Like a balloon squeezed at several different points, an organization feels the effects as these localized and isolated management tactics ripple through the organization, most often in terms of added cost and inefficiencies. This chapter classifies the most common islands of pain and outlines alternative practices—the building blocks for a cohesive Strategic MRO solution.

P aul's presentation to his executive forum had gone well. Forum members had been intrigued with his classification of Strategic MRO channel players as asset owners, asset makers, and asset service providers.

While most of the forum members were asset owners, there were a few asset makers. These asset makers quickly realized they too were asset owners —they owned plants, equipment, and other assets used to make the assets that were their primary products. All of the forum members readily identified asset service providers as those firms that supplied them products and services that kept their assets, plants, and equipment running.

The forum members also were quite interested in the revenue created per dollar of asset investment statistics Paul talked about. Over the past week, Paul had received several telephone calls from forum members who had calculated their own company's revenue per dollar of asset investment. The calls seemed to have a common theme: What are the problems within companies that lead directly to below-average revenue generation per dollar of asset investment? This was the same question Paul was contemplating.

Future Perfect Revisited

The phone calls from his fellow forum members directed Paul's thinking toward the next forum topic. He knew the goal was future perfect. In his mind this meant:

- Only produce exactly what is consumed in the market.
- Only invest in the assets necessary to produce exactly what is consumed in the market.
- Only invest in assets that never fail over their useful life.
- Achieve zero total cost of ownership (TCO) for all assets.
- Only invest in resources that enable the first four future perfect objectives.

What Paul didn't know was what was in the minds of his company's top executives. He called a staff meeting to discuss future perfect. He began by redrawing his future perfect continuum and explained its meaning (see Figure 3.1).

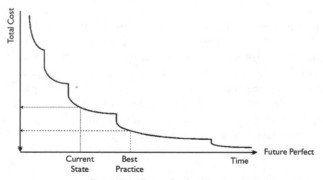

Figure 3.1 - Future Perfect Continuum

The vertical axis represents total costs for the organization, he explained. The future perfect target is zero total costs. The horizontal axis represents the passage of time. Careful analysis and changes in organizational practices involving people, processes, and technology over time should result in lower costs. Thus the graph moves downward (lower cost) as it moves to the right (time passes). Another way to say this is that costs are lower this year compared to last year because we improved our processes. Costs do not go down just because time passes. The graph generally goes down with the passage of time because people take actions that result in improved business processes.

Paul asked the group to look at the left side of the graph. This represents a point in time many years ago when our industry was relatively unsophisticated. Notice that costs are high compared to where we are today, which is labeled Current State on the graph. In the early days of our industry, there were large cost reduction opportunities because practices were unsophisticated. Thus, at the extreme left of the graph, costs declined dramatically with little passage of time as the industry improved its practices. But, when the early, easy improvements have been made, further reductions in cost are more difficult to attain. That is why the cost curve's rate of decline tends to flatten out over time.

The vertical drops in total costs (step changes) are a direct result of deployment of new technology. For example, the change from manual machining operations to computer controlled machining operations represents a change in technology that reduces costs dramatically. The declining curves between the step changes brought on by new technology represent incremental cost reductions due to fine-tuning day-to-day use of the technology, processes, and people currently in place.

Finally, the point labeled Best Practices represents the cost position we will enjoy when we have implemented all of the best practices known today both within and outside of our industry. Points to the right of Best Practices depict cost reductions that may be attainable in the future due to not-yet-envisioned new technology and business practices.

The extreme right portion of the graph represents the use of future perfect business practices and technology that result in costs much lower than today's costs.

Leadership's Vision of Future Perfect

Now that his staff members understood his future perfect vision, Paul asked each person to describe future perfect in their world.

His CFO wanted to be able to produce products without owning any assets or paying for materials until the company was paid for the products they sold. In fact, the CFO really wanted to delay payments to their suppliers until 45 days after they were paid for the products the materials went into.

Paul realized that owning no assets was probably not possible. He was gratified, however, that his CFO understood that future-perfect visions should not be constrained by what you think is possible but, rather, directed toward what would be the perfect case. The example Paul had used to illustrate the folly of thinking something is impossible was a simple one. In 1869 how many Americans would have thought it possible for a man to walk on the moon? Yet a mere 100 years later the moon walk was reality.

Paul's COO wanted to have the lowest cost operation possible that only produced what the customer needed, right the first time, at the time the customer needed it. Though these were great aspirations, Paul wondered if true future perfect for operations might include more than this.

Future perfect for the maintenance manager was more people and materials to deal with the unpredictable nature of the machines. Paul wondered if future perfect in the area of maintenance should be that every failure is predictable. If that was the case, then he could minimize the number of resources needed to react to failures and simply take steps to prevent the failures to begin with.

The supply chain manager wanted suppliers that delivered just what was needed, when it was needed, at the lowest total cost of ownership. What a perfect situation.

Paul thought it remarkable that, so far, no one contemplated a future perfect model that consisted of a totally vertically integrated company. He sat back in his chair, stared at the ceiling, and said: "What if we had a design where all supply resources were under one roof, under one command, and under one system, sort of the Henry Ford idea at the River Rouge facility?"

After a long silence, a free-for-all conversation began. Ideas about dedicated or shared capacity, owned capacity versus bought or leased capacity, and owned or supplied designs had always created much debate. The notion of outsourcing non-core competencies that support core competencies of the organization was another fundamental point of disagreement. The discussion, although thought provoking, quickly diverged. Paul steered the team back to their visions of future perfect.

The engineering staff believed future perfect consisted of product and service designs that required no assets at all to produce. The breakthrough! Now we are getting it, Paul thought. His engineering staff wanted to design products and processes that enabled the company to create revenue at the desired profit levels with no production costs. They knew assets were cost drivers. Their goal was to eliminate them.

Paul knew his assets represented a potentially huge liability in employee safety, health, and welfare. Environmental contamination such as emissions and spills represented threats to his employees and to the community. His legal chief agreed that future perfect for them meant zero legal liabilities for contract performance, health, safety, and environmental practices.

His CIO wanted the lowest cost technology that met the information requirements necessary to support sales, engineering, operational, financial, and legal objectives. The CIO defined the role of information technology as a process-enabling, compliance-assuring, data-driven system that facilitated management direction, communications, and continuous improvement efforts. Not to be outdone by engineering, the CIO indicated his goal was zero DRIP (data rich information poor) processing. In essence, all data collected was to be converted into useful information, at zero cost and zero maintenance, enabling the organization to achieve its future perfect objectives.

At the end of the meeting, Paul compared his future perfect objectives to ones generated by his staff. Certainly his staff was more focused in their application of future perfect. He had to find a way to align his vision with the vision of his executive staff. Misalignments seemed to create joy for some and pains for others. Procurement got the lowest price but operations paid for it in increased failures and maintenance costs. Engineering designed the most reliable equipment in the world, except some of these highly engineered items had 16-week lead times. It seemed as if his staff had local rather than global visions. Visions focused on their own areas sometimes created islands of pain for other areas within the company. Paul wondered how he could get people to think in a companywide or more global way.

Paul reviewed his future perfect continuum and doodled on it. How do I make sure our decisions move us collectively toward future perfect at the lowest total cost?

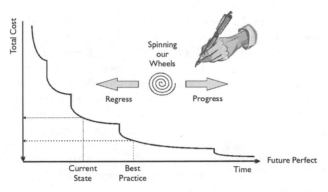

Figure 3.2 - Future Perfect Progress

Paul wondered how he could focus the Strategic MRO initiative while motivating his staff, which seemed—with the possible exception of his CFO—focused on their own individual islands of pain instead of future perfect. The more he thought about it, the more he realized these islands of pain would make a great topic for his executive forum. As he began jotting down his thoughts, Paul realized that behavior could not change if people didn't see or understand the impact of their misdirected behavior. The misdirected behaviors were, in part, what kept companies from moving toward future perfect.

Paul decided to focus on understanding the essence of each island of pain. He also vowed to never forget the bigger picture, the overriding future perfect. His intuition told him the notion of future perfect would help his staff see their short-term pain in the context of the perfect but (for now) unattainable future they had to move toward.

Classifying the Islands of Pain

Behaviors in the industrial market are driven by the desire to satisfy local needs and create local profits. Local decisions are often made for local expediency in a particular business environment and/or geography, lacking a broader viewpoint that considers more far-reaching issues. For example, a distributor may make inventory investments in excess of what is actually needed by local customers. That distributor may lack knowledge of what local customers actually consume, may want to receive price breaks from suppliers for buying in quantity, or fear that if they cannot immediately meet the needs of a customer they will lose a sale.

Expanding the local view of industrial market behavior to a more global view reveals that various inefficiencies are introduced into the components of enterprise asset management and the MRO supply chain by these apparently optimal local behaviors. For example, quantity discounts often drive inventory reorder quantities. To get a piece price reduction, distributors buy in excess of what is needed to support the actual consumption of their customers; subsequent overproduction by manufacturers results.

Overproduction results because the manufacturer of the product that the distributor has stocked in excess mistakenly views product movement to the distributor as consumption by the end user. The manufacturer then schedules to produce more of the material. Thus, excess inventory is introduced into the supply chain. This excess inventory carries with it costs related to storage, obsolescence, taxes, loss of opportunity, and many others. This is but one example of a business practice at the local level that creates waste in the supply chain.

We call actions that are seemingly optimal at the local level but suboptimal in the total supply chain view "pathological behaviors." These behaviors introduce huge inefficiencies resulting in unnecessary costs and seriously hamper overall value stream performance. Those that persist in engaging in such behaviors will not be rewarded with competitive advantage. Those that identify these pathological behaviors and set out to change them will set themselves apart in their respective industries.

Our goal in this chapter is to identify suboptimal practices or islands of pain. Of course, our view is a more global one. Individual businesses, with their understandably local view, will have to define their own place and practices within this global view. We have loosely classified the islands of pain within each of the five future perfect objectives described at the beginning of this chapter.

Islands of pain associated with the future perfect objective:
Only produce exactly what is consumed in the market.

A company today must participate in a complex supply chain to deliver its "unit of value" in the form of products and services to the market. Too much or too little production results in waste or lost opportunities. Finding perfection in volume, timing, and delivery is a constant challenge. The various islands of pain make it evident that both strategic and tactical Strategic MRO initiatives are required to be successful in today's market.

Pain #1: Strategic MRO is not considered an executive imperative.

Rarely do mundane topics such as enterprise asset management, maintenance management, storeroom management, MRO supply chain management, equipment standardization, condition based monitoring, reliability-centered maintenance, total productive maintenance, and other operational issues make it to executive staff meetings.

Operational costs are summarized, reported, and compared to the budget. But what is really important to the executive?

- Our stock value today?
- How sales figures are looking?
- How our margins are?
- What our backlog is?
- Whether there are any potential accounts on the sales horizon?

To slight Strategic MRO issues in favor of these concerns represents a lack of focus in our opinion. Strategic MRO initiatives can and do result in operational cost reductions. For a company earning 5% profit on sales, $50,000 in operational savings equals the same increase in profit as $1 million in additional sales revenue. Understandably the top line is important. Increased sales revenue is a tried and true path to a larger bottom line. Another path to the bottom line is through successful deployment and management of assets. However, this path is often ignored at the executive management level.

Pain #2: Outsourcing your way to the lowest total cost.

As companies pursue various supply chain strategies such as contract manufacturing, outsourcing core competencies, and supply partnerships, the assumption is that the organizations performing the outsourced activities are more cost-effective than funding the activities in-house.

Too often we have observed outsourcing viewed as a bid-and-buy activity. A short-term perspective leads to choice of the low bidder to perform the outsourced activities. The low bidder might have bid at very slim margins to get the job. When this is the case, there may be no way for the bidder to afford to implement the appropriate enterprise asset management and Strategic MRO initiatives needed to assure cost improvement over time. Outsourced cost improvement should be expected in the same sense that internal functions are expected to become more efficient over time.

In the worst case, the low bidder may be counting on a price increase next year to offset the slim margins in the year the bid was originally won. The bidder's thinking may be that in year two it is harder for a company to internalize a set of activities that were outsourced the year before. That bidder may be right.

A contract manufacturer may have no vision for the life of the product being made for a third party. The primary vision may be to maximize profit. Reality suggests that most products must be made in an ever more efficient manner to remain competitively priced in the market.

Contract manufacturers may receive tools and machines from contracting companies. This can create lack of standardization in the contractor's plant. It can hamper efforts toward efficient enterprise asset management and development of low-cost MRO supply chains.

These issues can diminish the ability of the supply chain to produce a combined unit of value that meets the four economic utilities of form, time, place, and possession. One weak link puts the entire chain at risk. Shifting of asset responsibilities does not shift the risk of the value stream.

Pain #3: Ignoring the impact of geographical location on Strategic MRO initiatives.

Imagine your operation attached to both its customer and supply base with a series of rubber bands. What happens when you move operations to a low-cost labor country? Is the infrastructure adequate to handle your operations? What new or different government regulations apply to the operations and maintenance of your assets? What about the MRO supply chain? As companies go global, so must the assets. The value stream is only as productive as its assets.

Islands of pain associated with the future perfect objective:
Only invest in the assets necessary to produce exactly
what is consumed in the market.

Companies must invest in two types of assets to fulfill its market obligations: revenue producing and non-revenue producing assets. We will discuss this distinction in more detail later. However, for now, we will say that over and under investment in both types of assets has associated costs and penalties. Ideally asset investment equals the market requirements for value creation, no more, no less. The following islands of pain focus on the importance of aligning asset requirements to market demands.

Pain #4: The asset lifecycle is the least of our worries.

Companies focus on meeting sales objectives until it is time to expand, sell, or shut down operations. Then what becomes of the assets?

In practice every company that produces a unit of value must manage a product lifecycle. In general, it begins at product concept and ends at obsolescence. The asset lifecycle must be perfectly matched to the product lifecycle to achieve the lowest total cost. Rarely does industry synchronize product and asset planning. The asset planning should encompass design, development, and production as well as obsolescence to achieve the lowest total cost. Which assets will be upgradeable, expandable, repairable, disposable, resalable, or recyclable?

Lifecycle decisions relating to revenue-producing assets impact the profit contribution of the products they produce. Non-revenue producing assets must be managed to improve workplace performance without ballooning operational costs. The asset lifecycle is as important as the product lifecycle if the organization intends to create value as a going concern.

Pain #5: Disconnect between EPCs, product lifecycles, and O&M.

As asset-owning companies outsource their asset design, build, and installation activities to professional asset service providers, managers need to maintain a keen awareness to ensure that Strategic MRO remains an internal core competency. Engineering, procurement, and construction (EPC) companies build plants to a specification put out to bid. These specifications may not align the product lifecycle with the asset lifecycle.

The EPCs do not run the plant, so their limited knowledge of product and market requirements must come from the customer. When these requirements are not effectively contained in the plant specifications, the outcome is inevitable—a mismatch between asset design, build, and startup and product performance objectives. This is the first disconnect between the EPC and the product lifecycle.

EPC bid awards are typically based on the lowest acquisition cost, not necessarily the lowest total cost of ownership (TCO). Too often, parts of the plant and equipment are specified using the words "...or equivalent." This equivalency phrase in the specification creates latitude designed to allow the EPC to shop for the best price. This is well and good, except that it leads to an outcome that creates lack of standardization in components and equipment. This in turn creates a high-cost operating environment for the operations and maintenance (O&M) function that eventually has to maintain the plant; it drives the "operational" cost of assets up. Thus plants are built in a manner designed to reduce the initial construction cost without thought to the years of high MRO spend and high investment in MRO inventories that will result. This is what we describe as a disconnect between EPCs and O&Ms.

As a result of these disconnects, the early maintenance activities often include equipment resizing and changing out of serviceable components to achieve standardization objectives. Changeout may also occur as maintenance installs components for which there is a ready and dependable source of supply. This higher than normal MRO spend in the early years of a plant should be accounted for as a capital project overrun in the plant construction budget, but this rarely happens. Collaboration between the firms constructing the plant and those that will eventually operate and maintain the plant will result in lower MRO spend throughout the planned years of equipment operation.

Pain #6: Operating as if all assets are exactly the same.

This behavior manifests itself in a number of future perfect objectives. However, this island of pain originates when companies make their initial investments in assets. There must be a clear distinction between revenue-producing assets and non-revenue-producing assets. If a choice has to be made between a marble entryway to the corporate office or a more reliable production asset, what do you think the priority should be? If the marble entryway wins because we need to show customers that we are a professional organization then the price we will eventually pay is greater equipment downtime.

Clearly, assets that create the unit of value must be given first priority. First priority must also be given to the best engineering talent, the best maintenance resources, the best supply chain specialists, and the best operators. Simply put, all non-revenue-producing assets may represent unrecoverable costs if revenue-producing assets are not doing their jobs as efficiently as possible.

Islands of pain associated with the future perfect objective:
Only invest in assets that never fail over their useful life.

If the asset never fails, it never needs servicing or replacement. This is future perfect. However, the second law of thermodynamics stands in the way of achieving our future perfect. The second law of thermodynamics states that all unattended, irreversible systems requiring mechanical energy will eventually stop, due to wasted energy, friction, wear, and failures. This is the nature of the assets we use to create value. Our future perfect driver is to mitigate the asset's performance deterioration over its intended useful life. What are the more frequently occurring islands of pain that stand boldly in the way of future perfect?

Pain #7: Lowest acquisition cost wins out over the lowest TCO.

Acquisition cost is often narrowly defined as the purchase price of an asset. The goal of some is to get the lowest price, period. We affectionately call these people price buyers. All sales people loathe them because they hate having to justify the higher price to them. Their single-mindedness is often rewarded with bonuses and the world is their negotiation stage. Our contention is that any untrained person can select the lowest price. Caveman tactics have been around since the beginning of humankind. What's new?

A better approach is where an asset-owning company says, "Time out on outdated practices! What do we need from the asset and what is that worth to us?" This is the essence of total cost of ownership decision-making. What are the "all-in" costs of owning an asset? Price is only one component of TCO calculations. Acquisition includes all costs of design, sourcing, freight, and installation of an asset.

TCO goes considerably farther than this. TCO also considers cost of ownership components such as insurance, maintenance costs, operating costs, MRO supply costs, the cost of downtime, and cost of first-time-through quality and other factors. The final component of TCO is the cost of disposal. Alignment of the asset lifecycle with the product lifecycle is key to minimizing the impact of assets outliving or failing prior to the end of product life in the market.

In practical applications, engineering goals to ensure performance requirements and to minimize liability often result in asset over-design situations. Requiring engineered components or high-end products where commodity components would suffice may unnecessarily drive acquisition costs up. Likewise, purchasing's need to drive down initial acquisition costs by choosing the cheaper alternative without consideration of component failure rates and plant standards may drive operational costs up.

The battle lines are now drawn between engineering and purchasing—lowest operational costs versus lowest purchase price. These battles then move into operations. Construction is pressured by the organization's need to speed up the build, install, and startup process to accelerate revenue creation. This may leave little time or money to consider the longer-term asset maintenance and performance requirements.

In some cases, it could be argued that engineering is looking out for the maintenance impact by designing assets that have the highest reliability and availability. Reality often suggests otherwise. Listen in on most maintenance planning and problem-solving sessions; the first question is invariably, "Who designed this piece of junk to begin with?" Does pain know no boundaries?

Pain #8: All asset failures are the same.

In an ideal world, do all assets and components fail in a similar way? Our contention is that the company loses if engineering designs assets expecting all component failures to be predictable and thus preventable. Why? All failures are not predictable. Reliability and failure studies consistently identify several distinct and common failure patterns. Each failure pattern, like infant mortality where parts fail shortly after being put into operation, requires a different maintenance plan. This infant mortality maintenance plan would be very different than the plan for a component that has long life under planned load.

Earlier we said that all assets should not be treated the same and that first priority should be given to revenue-producing assets. We now suggest that all failures are not the same. Therefore total cost of ownership decisions must be based on some reasonable knowledge of failure patterns of the owned asset.

A failure impacts a function. All functions of revenue-producing assets do not necessarily impact the production of the unit of value. Using this logic, key functions, often described as key control characteristics (linked to key product characteristics), take first precedence for understanding potential failure patterns. Within this priority scheme the organization begins to develop the lowest total cost plan to respond to failures before, during, and after failures occur. Subsequently, this plan becomes the essence of demand planning for labor, materials, and equipment to maintain assets.

Pain #9: Thinking that OEMs know their equipment failure rates and thus your spare parts need.

We notice spares inventories that have never been used in plants . Upon investigation we often find spares for equipment that no longer exists. We have observed this often enough during our routine analysis of MRO inventories that we felt compelled to understand why investment is routinely made in items that are never used.

The answer is surprising but believable. A package of spare parts is available for newly purchased equipment. Many buyers of equipment purchase this spares package reasoning that, "who could better know better what fails and needs replacement than the original equipment manufacturer?" The lesson here is that those who design assets do not always use them. Likewise, those who design and build plants (EPCs) may not have experience operating and maintaining them.

This is not to suggest that all original equipment manufacturers are clueless as to what should be in spares packages, only that some know better than others. The key is to understand how the manufacturers of equipment used in your plants determine failure rates. Buying spares from the OEMs is one of the warranty conditions. However, OEMs seldom agree to buy back unused parts.

Do OEMs perform failure mode and effects analysis? Do they track component failure rates as reported from the field? Do they request failure rate estimates from their component manufacturers? Know the answers to these questions before investing in OEM recommended spares.

Pain #10: Two assets are better than one.

"Don't worry if it fails, we've got a back-up." Why do we need 110 buses when 100 will do? You never know when one will go down? Extra assets are sometimes used to compensate for poor operational and maintenance practices. Engineers should design assets with a reasonable assumption of proper use and maintenance. Planning for and supporting redundant systems is costly.

Continuing the logic of our previous islands of pain, the first priority is given to revenue-producing assets. Focus first on functional failures that impact the unit of value itself. Redundant systems play a significant role in mitigating critical failures that are unacceptable and have a reasonable chance of occurrence. What is a critical failure? Is it related to the cost of the lost asset? What is reasonable? Should it be a 50 % chance that failure will occur during hours of planned operations where the cost of unpreventable downtime is equal or greater than the TCO of the redundant asset?

Pain #11: Who needs standards? All commodity MRO products perform the same.

Some argue that process engineering should actually be called configuration management. They argue that most asset designs are merely a combination of commodity components fashioned in such a way as to perform desired functions. Because we are dealing with commodity components, market channels exist for the parts to repair the asset.

With the exception of highly engineered assets, this is not a farfetched description of the world we operate in. Just because three bearing manufacturers exist and each has an equivalent bearing, does it make sense to have all three bearings in use in a plant? Our price buyer says yes, because it provides the ability to pit competitors against each other to obtain the lowest price. The maintenance person may say it's no big deal. The products look alike and do the same thing. The storeroom clerk smiles as, once again, poor thinking increases his job security. The operations manager wonders why MRO inventory costs are so high. And engineering wonders why maintenance keeps installing Brand X that seems to fail twice as much as Brand Y.

For simple asset components, standardization has little effect on skill required to install and maintain. For more complex components this is not the case, especially if the device requires both hardware and software knowledge. Lack of standardization leads to the proliferation of MRO inventories and increased need for skilled resources to service differing brands of equipment. Design standards— based on failure rates, ease of installation, source of supply, and other cost factors— lower TCO.

Pain #12: Condition-based monitoring is too expensive.

Rather than using condition-based monitoring (CBM) systems, some companies rely on maintaining extra maintenance staff and stocking all possible repair parts. This often is the unintended consequence of running all equipment to failure or replacing items before they even hint at failure. These policies dramatically increase MRO inventory investments and contribute to excessive levels of unplanned plant downtime.

Failure patterns can vary significantly. Each failure pattern drives different maintenance strategies. A primary goal should be to prevent failures that impact the critical functions of a revenue-producing asset. To accomplish this, companies try to determine if an asset or its components can alert us to an impending failure. Early warning systems and CBM systems have been designed for this purpose.

Condition-based monitoring is an automated way to trigger the work order for repair activities. These systems can trigger the demand for purchase of what otherwise would be expensive repair parts that might sit idle in an MRO inventory. Condition-based monitoring systems have become reliable and affordable in the past few years. Still, CBM systems are viewed as too expensive by many companies because of a short-term view that focuses on the initial cost of the system. When used properly CBM can alleviate the need for unnecessary preventive maintenance activities, lower MRO stock inventory, and provide a signal to schedule needed maintenance thus avoiding unplanned plant downtime.

Condition-based monitoring systems are no less prone to failure than any other well-designed system in a plant. They can be sabotaged or circumvented by unhooking or wiring around sensors. Circumvention is often an indicator of a lack of understanding of what the system is supposed to do or the desire to put off needed maintenance. Used properly, CBM systems operate in real time and sense conditions to trigger the scheduling of component replacement, adjustment, or additional testing and inspection.

Islands of Pain associated with the future perfect objective:
Achieve zero total cost of ownership (TCO) for all assets.

For those still unconvinced that Strategic MRO is a strategic imperative, consider the following islands of pain. Achieving zero TCO is a future objective that drives organizations to eliminate all wasteful asset management activities and thus reduce cost of operations. These wasteful activities number in the thousands. We will simply point out the ones we see most often. These wastes begin with design, then are accentuated by how an organization manages the supply response to asset demands. Supply consists of labor, materials, and equipment necessary to satisfy asset demand created through use.

Pain #13: Lack of basic understanding of costs and realization of cost savings.

Costs come in two flavors: hard costs and soft costs. Hard costs savings are savings that result from money not being spent. Soft costs savings are savings in time and in a few cases, space. Savings in time are interesting, but not as interesting as not spending hard currency: "Show me the money!"

Hard currency not spent reveals itself as increased cash in bank accounts and larger net profit. Soft cost savings may not result in any change in hard costs and thus may never have a measurable impact on expense budgets and the bottom line.

As an example of a hard cost savings, consider cutting tools used in a plant. Suppose the tooling vendor sells the plant on using a kind of cutter that costs twice as much as the currently used cutter but lasts four times as long. So, for example, the expenditures for these cutters might be reduced from $40,000 per year to $20,000 per year. The $20,000 not spent is a hard cost savings. That $20,000 remains in the cash account and does not appear as an expense; net profit is $20,000 higher.

Now consider, as an example of soft cost savings, a technology that can reduce the time needed to process purchase orders (POs) by 30%. Those trying to sell such technology will calculate cost savings by multiplying 30% of the time required to process a purchase order by the number of purchase orders processed and then multiply that by the wage rate of the person processing POs. This calculation will result in an estimated dollar cost savings based on reduction in processing time.

But suppose there is only one person processing purchase orders. Due to adoption of our example technology, the person processing purchase orders will now have 30% fewer of their daily hours occupied. Since the time savings is less than one person equivalent of total time, it is likely that no real cost savings will ever occur because it is difficult to reduce the work force by 30% of a person. Time savings are a soft cost savings that can only be considered a hard cost savings when they accumulate to the point where a person can and is removed from that department's payroll.

Sometimes actual savings in processing time never result in decreases in payroll expenditures. The time required to perform the work required can be expanded to exactly fit the time available. People may do this to avoid having to learn new skills or because they fear loss of their job.

Let's review another example. Companies often are frustrated in their efforts to understand the true nature of cost savings from reducing maverick purchases. To reduce maverick purchases a company may consider new technology designed to link purchasing and the maintenance function directly to suppliers in real time. Organizational goals include improving purchasing procedures, increasing responsiveness and eliminating off-contract purchases. Of course, the technology has a cost, so a cost justification that looks at future cost savings must take place.

The new technology will prevent purchases from unauthorized suppliers and will easily and automatically direct purchase of specific items to the supplier who has the contract for that item. These are all positive outcomes. The cost savings mistake comes when a figure of 40% of the yearly dollar value in past maverick purchases is recorded as the cost savings attributable to the new purchasing procedures and technology.

Sure, the new system will help people procure materials from the right source at the negotiated price in the future. Our point: the material will still be needed and bought in the future. The cost savings is not the value of the maverick purchases prevented. It is the difference in price between what was paid in the past and what will be paid in the future when bought on contract from the correct suppliers. You can also estimate the savings in time; just keep in mind that this is a soft cost unless the savings total up to a person equivalent and that person is removed from the payroll.

One more example. Procurement cards (p-cards) are another area where we see mistakes made relative to cost savings. Someone calculates that every purchase order processed costs the company $250. (Where that number comes from is often suspect but, for our example, let's assume it is at least close to correct.) The solution appears to be to issue fewer POs and the procurement card is the mechanism that will allow needed materials to continue flowing into the plant. But to actually reduce costs through processing fewer POs, head count usually must be reduced. This may or may not happen.

With the new p-card strategy comes loss of control in several areas. First, it is difficult to tie demand back to the asset creating the demand when the purchased items are bought using p-cards. Preferred suppliers may not be used. Much time may be wasted driving to suppliers that have the perceived lowest purchase price on selected items. Finally, reconciliation of p-card statements may be the responsibility of the maintenance department. This effectively shifts a relatively unskilled clerical job responsibility to a relatively skilled person in the maintenance department. Did we save money with the p-card strategy?

Finally, in the area of mistakes relative to cost comes the area of inventory investment. MRO inventories create much higher internal costs than many companies realize. Most companies think that inventory investment carries a cost equal to the cost of short-term borrowing. In reality, the cost of MRO inventory investment is much higher than this. At best, the cost should be considered equal to the return on assets expected by the company's equity holders. Even this is probably on the low side. If we take into consideration the cost of insurance, storage, pilferage, obsolescence, asset recovery, and disposal as well as the cost of money, the cost of inventory ownership is 20% of the value of owned inventory per year at a minimum. Most companies would be better off buying MRO inventories as needed even at a slightly higher unit price compared to maintaining large investments in inventory.

To clarify, we endorse endeavors to lower soft costs whether based in technology, process improvement, or both. Even if time savings never impact the bottom line directly, they are important for at least two reasons. First, reductions in cycle time usually result in better customer service. Second, freeing up time allows a company to process additional transactions in the future—brought on by growth, for example—without having to expand head count.

So continue to look at technology and process improvements that will save time. At the same time, understand what will affect the bottom line directly so your assessments of cost savings made to justify technology and other activities today will be close to the reality observed in the future.

Pain #14: 80% of MRO costs are designed and redesigned in.

Most MRO improvement efforts are focused on improving processes and equipment currently in use. This is a natural focus; the equipment and processes in place are what people have to work with when called on to reduce costs. However, 80% of the cost of operating equipment and processes is locked in by the initial design of the equipment and processes. This means the most effective after-design improvement endeavors can only hope to reduce costs by 20% unless redesign occurs.

Because we know assets wear or fail through use, it is reasonable to assume these assets will have to be maintained. Some key questions:

- Does the design lend itself to ease in serviceability? This implies the asset design has been optimized to reduce the time, effort, and expense of changing components and performing routine servicing. Design considerations may include modular design, allowing quick change of component subassemblies.
- Does the design require component standardization across a number of sizes of machines to reduce the number of spare parts required in an MRO inventory? Component standardization further reduces the number of maintenance specialists required.
- Is the asset designed with the MRO supply chain in mind? Or does a special, engineered item drive up replacement lead times, machine downtime, and the cost of critical spares and specialized labor?

- Do we repeat these same oversights during redesign activities? Do we under-stand the impact of uncontrolled modifications to equipment on TCO?

Pain #15: Our problems would be solved if we only had more maintenance resources.

A recent assessment of a manufacturing facility revealed the need for more electricians. The reason given: "If you only knew how many controllers we have, how much programming we must do, how many power substations we must support.... A more detailed study revealed legacy (old) control systems dating back to the early 1980s, six different brands of PLCs (programmable logic controllers), and nearly 600 PLC configurations. When asked about the impact of having one brand, the same PLC model year and sizing standardization on the number of electricians, the response was simple. We would need less, not more resources. Why then would a company continue to pay the labor, material, and downtime premium to operate this way? Our experience is they haven't calculated the total-cost impact of their decisions.

Here is a simple test of the above logic. What if your company operated using DOS, Win 3.1, Win NT, Win 2000, Unix, 12 different database engines, four accounting systems, and 12 different PC brands? What do you think your IT (information technology) staff would look like and how much would it cost to support this wide variety of systems? Are you doing the same thing to your main-tenance staff?

Our next question is even more straightforward. Have you established a hier-archy of asset criticality, with an associated demand criticality classification so that maintenance resources can be scheduled to respond accordingly? The answer for most companies: All assets are treated the same. We have already addressed this island of pain. Studies indicate that the presence of a formal demand response strategies can reduce wasteful labor efforts a full 25%.

Our assessment of the plant used in our example above revealed that less than 25% of a maintenance person's time was actually spent performing tasks to restore an asset to its desired performance level. Because maintenance personnel were spending more than 80% of their time responding to non-critical functions and non-revenue-generating assets, they were not readily available to perform the critical tasks that impacted the company's revenue creation. It's no wonder many plants see maintenance costs going up and think they need more people.

Pain #16: No time for planned maintenance or downtime when we are building to stock anyway.

Two quite different production philosophies exist. One is make-to-order and the other is make-to-stock. Companies that pursue a make-to-stock production strategy should always build planned downtime for planned and preventive

45

maintenance into their schedule. Unfortunately, too often we see companies building stock to a forecast and putting off maintenance. Why? Because the forecast demands it.

In fact, the forecast is nothing more than an educated guess as to what future consumption will be. Why put off planned and preventive maintenance when we are building inventories? No customers suffer as a result of selling off inventories during maintenance. Base production on consumption in the market. This reduces finished goods inventories and leaves time for planned maintenance.

Pain #17: Internally supplied functions have no cost to us.

Incremental cost analysis is a pathological behavior in many companies. We define incremental cost analysis as the general practice of observing that performing one additional activity adds no cost because we own the function that performs the activity. Examples of this behavior abound. It is often said that the cost of taking one more order is nil because we already have the order entry person working an eight-hour day.

Maintenance is another example. Rather than investing in condition-monitoring equipment and utilizing real-time predictive maintenance, companies rely on a run-to-failure strategy because "we already have a maintenance workforce and the labor cost of one more repair is near zero." The same holds true with material handling. Rather than redesign production facilities and warehouses to drastically reduce material movement, companies use existing forklifts and operators to move materials in circuitous paths.

Inventory cost analysis is another area where incremental cost analysis leads to suboptimal decisions. Warehouse people and space occupied are not deemed to be a part of the cost of ownership of MRO inventory "because we already have the space and the people." Acknowledging these costs means a much higher (and more accurate) inventory carrying cost. This in turn would increase efforts to reduce inventory investments.

Incremental cost analysis is not inherently wrong. It is simply not well understood and often misapplied. In many areas, costs change as a step function rather than in a linear way as activities increase. That is to say, adding activities may not change costs until the point is reached where another person must be added to the workforce. Then total costs go up by the amount of that person's salary plus benefits. At that time activity costs increase dramatically because the additional person initially is underutilized.

Internally supplied functions have a cost that, averaged over time, should remain fairly constant on an activity-performed basis. The notion that total cost does not change as activities are increased is purely a short-term view that leads to poor long-term decision-making.

46

Pain #18: Managing labor utilization instead of TCO.

Some think that human resources must be fully utilized to justify their existence on the payroll. That mindset can lead to hard dollars spent on non-value-adding activities, such as rushing to repair or replace non-revenue-generating assets.

A maintenance person creates real value by brainstorming how to improve the efficiency of production assets, not by performing activities to fill the day and show high labor utilization. The prime objective must be to improve the availability and reliability of revenue-generating assets. Labor content should be measured relative to total cost reduction and revenue enhancement.

For organizations whose assets are geographically dispersed, travel time can be significant. Work-order reporting may indicate high labor utilization if travel time is counted as a part of the total time to perform maintenance. This is misleading. We would really like to see the effect of all non-value added time so that it can be prevented in the future. Management by TCO aggregates work orders by geographic proximity, thus reducing the cost of non-value-adding activities, such as travel.

Pain #19: Not integrating production and maintenance planning.

Idle resources and inventory increase when production and maintenance planning are not integrated. For example, suppose that a manager of a mechanized deep-level mining operation is given what he perceives as a relatively easy production goal. Imagine his surprise when actual production is only 80% of that planned for a particular month. Two of eight continuous mining rigs had to be withdrawn from production for a 3,000-hour and a 5,000-hour time-based maintenance service. Serious under-performance occurred simply because production and maintenance planning was not integrated.

Revenue-generating assets are the first priority and ensuring their availability to planned production schedules is critical to business success. TCO statistics indicate there is no less than 5% unplanned downtime in virtually every organization. Further, there is no less than 10% maintenance overtime, no better than an average of 35% maintenance labor utilization, and no less than 30% excess MRO inventories (just in case we need them)...need we say more?

Pain #20: Buying office products is the same as buying maintenance products is the same as buying direct materials.

Not all MRO products are equal. This is true from the perspectives of criticality, sourcing complexity, specifications, and many other attributes. It is sheer folly to purchase all MRO items using the same procurement policies and procedures. This is analogous to applying the same maintenance practices to all failure types. This practice can only result in over-specification of some items and under-specification of others. Thus, cost of procurement and use are driven higher.

To adequately address this island of pain, it is necessary to examine the underlying system of financial control used by many companies. All properly managed companies have implemented systems that allow for checks and balances for purchases and cash disbursements. These checks and balances seek to provide for efficient use of purchasing expenditures and prevent outright fraud and theft. These systems include the purchase order (PO) system, receiving verification, accounts payable, matching of invoices with receipts and POs, as well as invoice auditing procedures.

In general, financial control systems evolved over time and started their lives as manual systems backed by paper. Almost without exception, these systems were put in place to provide proper accountability and control over relatively large expenditures made to purchase raw or direct materials. Because any one of these expenditures was large, a complex set of checks and balances was needed for accountability and to prevent misuse of funds.

Now consider the typical MRO purchase. It is usually quite small in value compared to the typical raw material purchase. However, that small MRO purchase may well be subject to the same purchasing controls and procedures used to assure proper management of larger direct materials purchases. No wonder we find that the average PO for MRO materials has a transaction cost of $175 to $250. Purchasing procedures should be geared to the type of product being bought and to the engine generating the demand.

The demand engine for direct or raw materials is the material requirements planning (MRP) or enterprise requirements planning (ERP) system. The demand engine for maintenance items is the asset or equipment the items are used to support. The demand engine for office products is the person using the products.

Use the ERP or MRP system with complex financial controls to manage large expenditures for direct materials. Do not subject purchases for MRO materials to the same level of control. The engine responding to demand for MRO materials should be the enterprise asset management (EAM) system. EAM can associate demand with the asset producing the need for MRO material. Likewise the EAM system can record and make available differences in MRO component parts and consumable needs that vary when a particular asset is used in different locations within a plant. For example, a pump used in a wastewater application in a plant might have the need for a different impeller than the same pump used in a caustic chemical application. The ERP or MRO system generally cannot capture these differences in maintenance need, based on location.

Procurement of most office supplies, then, should be left to the people using those supplies. Of course, logical enforcement of pricing and purchasing agreements as well as aggregation of demand should be provided for but, in general, the buying of office supplies should be a desktop requisitioning procedure. There is little need for the complexity of even EAM for office supplies because lack of such supplies will rarely shut down a plant and the level of specification for them is low.

Pain #21: MRO supply consumption/demand confusion.

This island of pain is significant and represents immediate cost savings. The differences between product demand and product consumption are not well understood by participants in industrial supply chains. We define demand as the anticipated need for product at a particular point in the supply channel. Most channel planning is called demand planning. This planning seeks to have the appropriate products and quantities at the points of need at the right time. Perhaps this approach to planning would more appropriately be termed "demand anticipation," because in practice we find that little attention is placed on understanding end-user product consumption except when demand planning has created excess inventories. Then the attention is an after-the-fact focus on why demand planning failed.

Consumption, on the other hand, is the actual use of a product by an end user. The key difference between demand and consumption is that demand is anticipated usage and consumption is actual usage. Ultimately the efficient supply chain must be driven by replenishment of actual consumption—not anticipated demand. This is revolutionary thinking. Past practices have been predicated on lack of actual consumption data availability to participants in the supply chain. Consumption data must be available to all channel participants in the future.

To illustrate why demand planning rather than communicating actual consumption to channel participants creates inefficiency, consider the following scenario and its ripple effect back up through the supply chain. First, a maintenance technician in a plant is dispatched to repair a failed bearing in a pump. The technician requisitions the bearing and two seals. Only one seal is actually required, but the technician fears the second one will be needed if the first is damaged in the installation process. As it turns out, the second seal is not needed but— rather than return it to the storeroom—the technician keeps it in his toolbox as it is a common item.

The requisition of two seals throws the storeroom inventory below its order point. A replenishment economic order quantity (EOQ) is calculated based on average past usage. Suppose this order quantity is eight seals. This seems like a reasonable number because two were used in the current month. Eight seals represents a four-month supply. The storeroom orders eight replacement seals from the local seal distributor.

When the distributor fills the order for eight seals, their seal inventory is depleted; an order for replacement seals is triggered to the seal manufacturer. The distributor's EOQ recognizes demand of eight in the past month and orders a three-month supply, or 24 seals. The manufacturer receives the order and schedules production for a two-month supply, or 48 seals. The production planner rounds the quantity up to 50 because a particular raw material for the seal is packaged in packs of ten.

Conventional demand planning has triggered the production of 50 seals when only one seal was consumed. The demand planning process has actually hidden the timing of future demand from all participants in the supply chain. The next time a seal is needed in the plant, the maintenance tech uses the one in his toolbox. The distributor wonders why the plant has not ordered any seals recently; they simply delay their next seal order to the manufacturer. The manufacturer has no clue when the distributor will order more seals and, in fact, wonders why their inventory of seals is so high.

Some will say our example above is contrived and misleading. They may say the law of averages applied across many players in the supply chain evens things out. And to a limited degree that's right. Nevertheless, the above scenario plays out every day across many items and channel participants. The result is that inventory turnover in industrial channels is dismally low and inventory obsolescence is surprisingly high.

Planning for production, product positioning, and movement in the supply chain based on actual consumption rather than demand—is revolutionary thinking for industrial products supply chains! It is common practice in other supply chains. Consider the consumer products channels. Fifteen years ago, Wal-Mart and others invested in systems that could report point-of-sale (consumption) information on a daily basis to their suppliers to avoid inefficient inventory deployment in their supply chains.

Whether a channel player sees demand or consumption depends on its position in the channel. Some see a confusing mixture of both. For example, the end user can track actual issues of material from the storeroom. This material may or may not be consumed as shown in our above example. The end users of industrial products project demand for the future based on past consumption. The demand projections are what trigger replenishment orders for storeroom stock in many systems.

For the most part, distributors see only demand because they are filling orders for replenishment that are demand based. The demands they see are almost always larger than actual consumption during the period in which they see the demand. Likewise, periods of time pass when consumption takes place at the end-user facility that the distributor knows nothing about.

As we move further away from the end-user consumer, upstream channel participants see demand at various levels of aggregation. An individual distributor projects demand based on the aggregated past purchases of all of its customers. The manufacturer projects demand based on the aggregated past purchases of all of its distributors. The aggregation of demand at the manufacturer, in theory at least, should approximate consumption by the end user. This is rarely the case due to incentives that induce sporadic large purchases by all participants downstream of the manufacturer. This disguises the timing of actual consumption to the point that the best a manufacturer can do is project future demand based on past purchases by its distributors. As noted earlier, the timing and quantity of these demand projections may be grossly different than actual consumption of material by end users. These differences lead to shortages or excess inventory in the channel.

So consumption is *actual* usage of material by the end user. Demand, on the other hand, is the projection made by suppliers as to what they *think* consumption should be in the current and future periods based on past purchases by the channel players. The supply chain would be better served if the timing of consumption was known to all players. This allows all involved the opportunity to produce and/or stock replacements for what is actually consumed. This is generally not the case for industrial supply chains.

Demand in excess of actual consumption is created in the industrial supply chain by a variety of mechanisms. This excess demand not only creates excess inventory in the channel, but also creates shortages of other materials. When manufacturing capacity is used to create these excesses, it is not available to make other items that are in short supply. Bottom line: the right parts aren't built simply because of the timing mismatch caused by not knowing what is actually being consumed.

There are several contributing factors to the excess demand dilemma. The first mechanism is when various channel players try to reduce procurement transaction costs. Companies buy larger quantities less frequently to reduce the volume of purchase orders, which reduces the frequency of accounts payable activities. Electronic procurement and funds transfer can drastically reduce these costs by making it easier for companies to buy the right quantity based on true need; it essentially removes the administrative overhead factor. To date, companies have been slow to adopt e-commerce technology and business practices to fully leverage procurement transaction cost reductions.

Another mechanism that inflates demand compared to actual consumption is a company's desire to transfer ownership of inventory to one of their channel partners. For example, a manufacturer might want to minimize their finished goods inventory levels and maximize cash flow. They might offer discounts to distributors to encourage larger quantity purchases. The distributor now has an incentive to buy ahead of actual consumption. However, the manufacturer also creates a demand in their product movement history that may be far in excess of actual consumption—the inflated demand cycle is in full swing! Contrast that scenario with a planning system geared toward manufacturing replacements for what is actually consumed at the end-user level.

A simple desire to increase sales in the current period also creates demand in excess of actual consumption. The same incentives to transfer inventory ownership also are used by channel members to influence the timing of sales recorded on their income statements. A company's motivations for increasing sales in the current period are varied: financial performance targets, higher factory utilization rates, as well as bonuses at the individual or department level.

We view most industrial supply chains as push systems. Driven by artificial demand, manufacturers use production planning systems to produce quantities in excess of actual consumption. These products and quantities are pushed down through the channel using various incentives. Viewed from a total supply chain level, excess inventories and shortages created by these mechanisms translate into higher costs and lower overall service levels.

A pull system must be based on knowledge of consumption as we have defined it in the market. When consumption takes place, a replacement is scheduled for production or "pulled" through the supply chain. Recognition of usage by the end user must be near instantaneous and propagated back up the channel so channel members can restock or schedule a replacement for manufacture. In a pull system driven by recognition of consumption, the only idle inventory will be that in transit and stocks necessary to satisfy customer lead times shorter than manufacturing and transit time.

Pain #22: Lack of transparency of consumption data.

Real-time consumption information is absolutely critical to increase inventory efficiency throughout industrial supply chains. Several business practices hinder information flow through the channel. One is the wide variety of computer systems in use by channel members today. Often, these systems have trouble "talking" to each other automatically. The technology to connect disparate computer systems exists today. But business philosophies tend to hinder consumption information flow. These philosophies relate to ways of doing business that have evolved over time, lack of business process discipline, and perceived advantage by channel players.

End users may fear that timely communication of consumption data may harm their ability to negotiate better piece prices based on volume. Often, these price negotiations are predicated on an end user's estimates of volume that are in excess of actual need. They can become self-fulfilling prophecies as purchasing organizations buy ahead of need to stay within negotiated volume requirements.

End users may want to split purchase volume among several suppliers for a variety of reasons. When this is the case, they may not want suppliers to know their total consumption. A perceived point of leverage, then, results in the choice not to convey exactly the information needed to make the channel more efficient.

Poor business practice discipline contributes to lack of consumption information in the industrial products supply chain. Unlike consumer markets where almost all products have a universal product number, the players in industrial markets commonly use their own product numbers. This leads to a nightmarish cross-referencing endeavor for those who want to communicate product use information electronically. To add to the problem, it is not uncommon for end users to have the same item represented in their business systems multiple times. Thus, consumption information is distributed among multiple part numbers that represent exactly the same item.

Likewise, distributors in industrial markets may see reasons not to communicate actual consumption information back to manufacturers, even if they could get it from end users. They might fear volume pricing negotiations could be hampered by this information. And distributors may want to split volume among several manufacturers.

Distributors have evolved their business practices to gain advantage by participating in favorable "spot" markets that exist periodically due to overproduction by manufacturers. Lack of product consumption data creates these opportunities. These distributors perceive that knowledge of actual consumption by manufacturers would lessen the magnitude and frequency of overproduction. This, in turn, would reduce the need for the manufacturer to offer price discounts to move excess product. Of course, excess products of one kind often means shortages of others because manufacturing capacity was used to make the wrong products. To a degree, however, the distributor sees these shortages as another kind of opportunity and has learned to live with and even profit from them.

Manufacturers, in general, like to see transparency of product consumption data in their supply chains. This allows them to continuously fine-tune production scheduling to make the replacements for the products actually being consumed. But many manufacturers will have to adjust their business processes to make appropriate use of timely product consumption data. Flexible manufacturing systems that can accommodate smaller batch sizes and quick changeover of machines will have to evolve in many manufacturing organizations.

Many manufacturers currently offer incentives to their customers for buying in bulk. These bulk purchases increase manufacturing lot sizes and decrease the manufacturer's transaction costs associated with order processing, storing, and shipping of finished goods. These incentives disguise the timing of consumption. The manufacturer needs this information to drive a production system that makes the right products at the right time. This seems to imply that incentives for bulk purchases create inefficiency in the supply chain. If this is so, in addition to developing flexible manufacturing systems, many manufacturers will have to implement more efficient small-order processing systems.

The notion of which players in a supply chain might desire transparency of consumption information is not as simple as noting that manufacturers want it while distributors and end users do not. It may be more accurate to say that the sell side of the organization in the supply chain sees great value in consumption data transparency while the buy side of those same organizations can see reasons to hide that information from their suppliers.

For example, an end user of industrial products may maintain a storeroom that "sells" product to maintenance people. They certainly want to know what is consumed and when. They do not want that product use data adulterated by maintenance people requisitioning quantities larger than they actually use. But the purchasing or "buy" side of the end user's organization may not want product consumption data passed on to the their suppliers for the reasons noted previously. As we direct our view of the supply chain upstream we find that the same is true of distributors.

Pain #23: Demand engine is not connected to supply engine.

Assets, not people, create their own demand for repair parts and consumable items. This rate of demand varies depending on such factors as production rate, asset design, and level of preventive maintenance. For companies that use enterprise asset management systems, the EAM system is the engine that fulfills demands from the asset. When the asset needs maintenance, a human creates a work order in the EAM system.

Too often, the repair parts (MRO) inventory is maintained on the central enterprise resource planning (ERP) computer system. The EAM work order system may not be able to access these inventory records without a manual lookup by a human. Thus, time is lost and labor is employed trying to determine whether or not parts needed for a repair are available. If parts must be ordered, notification that the parts have been received by the ERP system may be a manual process. Further time is lost.

Most ERP systems cannot associate MRO material usage with particular assets. This means material usage can only be tracked at the aggregate level. Tracking consumption at the aggregate level means future demand predictions may include quantities for machines that a plant no longer uses simply because past usage for these parts exists in the historical usage database.

A better solution is to use the equipment assembly structures available in EAM systems to associate material demand to the asset that caused the demand and consumed the material. Then, procurement for MRO materials can be based on an analysis of equipment used today and the rate at which those assets have consumed repair parts and consumables in the past. This represents a tight coupling of MRO supply with MRO demand.

We predicate our reasoning that supply and demand for repair and consumable items should be tightly coupled on an examination of how direct materials procurement systems are designed. These systems tightly couple procurement of the raw materials used in the manufacturing process to the near-term production schedule by exploding the bills of material for what is scheduled to be built.

Procurement of MRO materials should consider the demand created in the past for the actual machines in use today adjusted for the rates these machines are scheduled to run in the future. MRO material needs derived in this manner will be quite different from needs determined from an analysis of total past usage if there are differences between assets used in the past and assets to be used in the future.

Pain #24: Thinking that the maintenance function is the demand engine rather than the asset.

Assets create demand for repair parts and consumables. That is, the use of the machine causes it to need lubricants, belts, bearings, and other parts. Assets used sporadically create less demand for these parts while assets used continuously create correspondingly higher demand.

Different assets create wear part and consumable demand at different rates. For example, consider two different brands of a machine designed to do the same manufacturing operation. Because of inherent design differences, these two machines doing the same operation can produce different demands for wear parts and consumables even when run at the same production rates! The same notion applies to vehicles, conveyors, and any other kind of equipment and facilities used in organizations of all types.

Organizations think that the maintenance department should predict the demand for specific materials to be purchased. This is a fundamental mistake that has little to do with the individual in the maintenance department.

People intuitively think of historic consumption as a way of estimating future needs. However, people generally do not take failure rates into consideration. For example, it is easy to note that we used a particular item this month. Therefore we need another one. But if the failure rate of the specific equipment is once every two years, items will be bought to sit on the shelf. People also tend to protect themselves by estimating a higher future demand "just in case."

Significant inventory reductions can be achieved without increasing availability risks if organizations realize that the assets are the demand engine. Knowing what materials a specific asset consumed in the past—given a specific production rate—will produce much more accurate demand predictions. Thus, the maintenance person is simply an interpreter of equipment needs (demand). Condition-based monitoring combined with skilled maintenance personnel and operators act as the best interpreters of asset demand, but they do not create the demand. The asset itself creates the demand.

When procuring parts and services to maintain an asset, clearly link these parts or services with the particular asset to create a profile of the asset demand. Rather than focus on MRO spend per maintenance person, we should concentrate on MRO spend per asset. Then we can identify assets that are expensive to run versus those that are less expensive, even given the same production rates. The goal should be to reduce absolute MRO parts and labor spend per unit of production by gravitating to assets that are inherently less expensive to run. This is difficult to do without having first connected demand to each asset.

Pain #25: Thinking that cost should be controlled via better inventory management while ignoring the underlying generation function.

In many enterprises today, more emphasis is placed on cost control via better MRO inventory management than on managing the underlying demand for MRO materials. While better inventory management is a noble quest, larger cost savings come from understanding how and why enterprise assets are creating demand for MRO components and consumables. Remember: the assets themselves create the demand for MRO materials.

Inventory management generally strives to use an investment efficiently and effectively. If the investment is caused to turn over beyond a certain target annually, inventory management is said to be efficient. If low stock-out rates or high fill rates are achieved, the inventory management is deemed to be effective. From an inventory management perspective, both high fill rates and high turnover are desirable and probably reduce the cost of maintaining inventories. Greater cost savings, however, are achieved by altering the demand generation functions of enterprise assets.

Enterprise assets are designed to eat components and consumables through natural and forced deterioration. Natural deterioration occurs when equipment, machinery, or vehicles are deployed, used, and maintained exactly as they should be. They wear and use consumables at a natural rate. Forced deterioration occurs when assets are deployed in harsh environments or are not maintained at optimum intervals. Forced deterioration causes expenditures for wear parts and consumables to be much higher than they otherwise would be. Most enterprises would be better served by understanding and reducing the need for MRO materials caused by forced deterioration rather than just focusing on moving these expenditures efficiently and effectively through an inventory system.

Enterprise assets are what they eat. That is, equipment, machines, and vehicles may experience lower overall maintenance costs when fed a diet of better quality consumable materials. A higher quality bearing costing twice that of a standard bearing may last five times as long. In other cases, overall cost savings can be achieved through feeding an asset more of a consumable. Certainly many vehicles and other types of equipment perform longer at lower cost with more frequent oil changes. These are total cost of ownership issues. Unfortunately, efforts focused on cost savings through better inventory management rarely consider total cost of ownership issues.

Please do not interpret our comments in this area to mean that we are not in favor of better MRO inventory management. We applaud all efforts that result in more efficient and effective use of an inventory investment. That said, we would like to reinforce the idea that the best inventory management efforts may do little to manage the creation of demand by enterprise assets. Reducing the demand for wear parts and consumables typically realizes cost savings far in excess of those realized through better inventory management.

Pain #26: The notion that purchasing controls can reduce the maintenance spend.

MRO purchasing policies and procedures exist for various reasons. Primary among these is the desire to establish financial accountability standards within that part of the organization. Unfortunately, in many cases these standards evolve over time into controls seeking to regulate the amount spent for procurement of MRO materials. This type of control is inappropriate and destined to failure because it is misdirected.

Assets create the demand for MRO materials. The supply side of the organization (purchasing) simply buys the material to satisfy the demand. Controls on the supply side that slow the procurement of material needed to satisfy demand simply delay needed repairs to assets supporting the value stream.

In extreme cases, maintenance people circumvent purchasing and buy the parts they need. When this happens not only does maintenance take longer than it should, the maverick purchases may be made from suppliers outside of existing price contracts. In general maverick purchases are an indicator of malfunctioning supply processes. Maintenance people do not purchase in a maverick manner on a whim. They do so because they need parts to fix malfunctioning assets and they believe they cannot get those parts in a timely way through use of normal procurement procedures.

The designation of preferred suppliers by purchasing is another supply side control that can cause inefficiency and delays in procurement of MRO materials. Purchasing policies and procedures usually establish how suppliers are awarded a preferred status. The preferred designation may or may not take into consideration the ability of those suppliers to directly supply all key materials needed to maintain organizational assets.

When preferred suppliers cannot directly supply the materials needed to properly maintain equipment, one of two things happens. Either the maintenance people buy the needed materials outside the system or purchasing orders the material from a preferred supplier who must then source it from an unpreferred supplier. Both of these cases result in wasted effort and are likely to cause a delay in obtaining needed MRO materials.

We contend that supply side or purchasing controls designed to reduce MRO expenditures are misdirected. Control of MRO expenditures should be directed at the demand side of the system. Assets used to support the company's value stream create demand for replacement parts and consumables. If these expenditures are higher than desired, look to replacement of the assets, preventive maintenance programs, condition based monitoring, and any other endeavor designed to reduce the underlying demand for MRO materials.

Pain #27: Inventory expensed directly to a job or department as it is acquired does not show on my books.

Some companies expense any MRO material directly to jobs upon acquisition, whether or not it is consumed or goes into a stockroom. This is a highly misleading practice—an island of pain. It is true that no inventory investment shows on the balance sheet. Yet inventory exists, but since there is no accounting entry for it, no one is concerned about managing it.

The practice of expensing MRO inventory upon acquisition often leads to a distorted view of which assets are consumed for what and when. The distortion occurs because this association of MRO materials with an asset is not done or not done correctly. Material is purchased and expensed to a particular asset but often ends up being used on another piece of equipment.

Likewise, the timing of material use is skewed. Material is charged against a piece of equipment when bought but not used until much later, if at all. A subsequent analysis of MRO material consumption patterns can be quite misleading. Maintenance may be tempted to requisition more MRO material because it appears that material has been used in the past when, in fact it still exists, unused, in the plant.

In the worst case, MRO material is acquired and expensed to a department. Now we lose track of all association of material with assets. We also lose track of what MRO materials should be available for use. The MRO inventory escapes into the black hole of that department and becomes untraceable. True, there is no inventory shown on the balance sheet and people mistakenly believe that return on assets will be higher in the absence of the balance sheet inventory amount. This, however, is untrue. Expenses are higher due to expensing of inventory at time of purchase. Thus, return on assets is affected whether or not the inventory is treated as a balance sheet item as it should be.

Expensing inventory as it is purchased leads to a lack of accountability. Purchasing controls degenerate into a system of approval limits seeking to indirectly regulate the MRO spend. A much better approach is to buy as needed, associate expenditures with the asset requiring repair or consumable materials, and inventory what is not used so that all can know what materials are available for use. Then, focus on reducing MRO spend by focusing on assets that are overconsuming materials and seek to reduce inventories by focusing on the level and timing of purchases that are inventoried.

Finally, expensing MRO material upon acquisition leads to a lack of focus on material recovery and disposal. Since there is no inventory investment to call attention to dead stock, there is no effort to identify items that are in the plant but unneeded. Thus the opportunity to recover a portion of the value of these items is missed.

Pain #28: Thinking MRO inventory is an asset.

Companies that properly account for MRO inventories are not immune to pain. It is just a different sort of pain than experienced by those who expense all MRO materials upon acquisition. We believe that inventorying MRO items and expensing them on use is the proper way to account for MRO spend. This facilitates the association of demand with the asset creating the demand and creates visibility of the items held in inventory.

Over time, MRO inventories tend to get bloated with investments in excess of what they should be. The actual items associated with the investment cannot be located, are obsolete, or otherwise unusable. These inventories should be purged of these items, salvage attempted to the extent possible, and the remaining investment written off. As a part of this process, assess why the excess investment occurred in the first place. Then put procedures in place to stop investing in items that are either unneeded or become unusable over time.

The pain arrives with the realization that the inventory write-off will create an expense and lower net profit. For a variety of reasons, companies do not want to endure the pain of lowered profits. We have observed that the fortunes of the company do not particularly matter with regard to this aversion to taking a write-off that will harm the bottom line. For example, if the company is having a great year profitwise, there will be those who say, "we can't take the write-off this year. It will spoil a record profit year." Conversely, if the company is having a poor year they will say, "we can't take the write-off this year because our profits are already way too low."

So, for whatever reason, nobody cleans up the MRO inventories. The cash flow opportunity from salvaging those items with residual value is missed. The inventory continues to occupy space. It has to be maintained, counted, and sometimes taxed.

MRO inventories should be evaluated on a continuous basis. Dispose of obsolete and excess inventory as quickly as possible to maximize salvage value. Constantly evaluate procedures to keep the value of MRO inventories held to an absolute minimum. Most companies are better off crafting a supply chain that can supply MRO materials as needed and buying only what is needed in the near term. This is true even if it means paying a slightly higher piece price for the material.

Pain #29: The notion of "buy bulk and save money."

Many procurement organizations measure success by comparing piece prices on key items to prices a year ago. In times of general price inflation, this is modified to measure whether piece prices rose more slowly than the price inflation rate. This focus on piece price as a procurement performance measure is a pathological behavior; it ignores significant cost factors. A procurement organization wants to know they have bought at a fair price. But this focus on price must be balanced with knowledge of how total costs related to acquisition, receipt, storage, use, and disposal of material are affected by the desire to get the best piece price.

In general, purchasing agents are motivated by pricing and availability. Given availability and the same product specifications, better piece price wins the order. This makes sense under most circumstances. However, a blind focus on better piece price can sometimes dramatically increase total cost.

For high-usage items, buying a larger quantity than actually needed to qualify for the next price break seems to make sense. However, increasing the quantity bought to get a better price can quickly increase the procurement spend while inflating inventories. Purchasing staff members often look at the next price break quantity and routinely increase the quantity ordered. Inventories of slow-moving stock build up. A better strategy is to buy what is consumed and nothing more for all but a tiny fraction of MRO items.

Even for items consumed regularly and repetitively, buying more than needed to replace actual consumption for the sake of lower piece prices increases cost. In many cases these cost increases exceed the piece price reduction savings.

Inventories create hidden costs that are not easily measurable. These include storage, taxes, pilferage, obsolescence, and the cost of the people necessary to manage, store, and keep the inventories orderly. It is common to find 25% to 40% of the value of an industrial plant's MRO inventory either missing, unusable, or obsolete. This represents millions in MRO spend that is virtually worthless. Much of this accumulated over time due to the mentality of "buy bulk and save." These companies would have been better off to have paid a slightly higher piece price for what they actually needed and not bought the excess materials.

Pain #30: Thinking that reverse auctions drive down total cost.

The popularity of the Internet has enabled the use of reverse auctions for MRO materials. Typically a company will place a list of items and quantities needed on their website and ask suppliers to respond with pricing. The current low price may be shown for each item with the idea that competitors will bid the price to the lowest possible. Then, presumably, the lowest price supplier by item or item category is awarded the contract to supply those items in the future at that price.

Of course, it is important for a company to pay a fair price for all of the products it needs. However, the concept of a reverse auction fails to consider total cost of ownership in choosing future suppliers. Terms and conditions can and do vary greatly among suppliers. Ostensibly, all suppliers participating in the reverse auction implicitly agree with the terms and conditions set forth by the company for the supply of the MRO materials in question. In reality, the total cost of acquiring, receiving, storing, and using the products supplied by the low bidder can be higher than the total cost of supply from a higher bidder.

The reverse auction extends the three-bid purchasing model into that of many bids. Part of the strategy can be to aggregate the demand of many plants into a corporate demand to try to achieve quantity price breaks. Suppliers are understandably leery of this aggregated demand strategy because they suspect that many companies exaggerate the potential demand. Further, suppliers know they will likely have to ship small orders to many different plants, thus negating much of the savings they might have realized from selling larger quantities.

Reverse auctions tend to neglect the value of long-term relationships with key suppliers. They disregard the services and emergency support these suppliers have provided in the past and will provide in the future. The reverse auction process shifts focus away from the key suppler relationship, which evolved because a plant could count on the supplier for timely help when the plant was down. Instead the focus becomes that of lowest product cost.

Too many plants have found that the supplier of a product at the lowest price is not the supplier that can bring the latest product innovation and problem solving information into the plant on a continuous basis. Technical support often suffers when the absolute lowest prices for products are attained. The result can be additional plant downtime expenses that far exceed the reduction in product price savings.

Corporate sourcing of MRO products may not consider inventory practices and preferences maintenance may have for particular brands of products. These practices and brand preferences exist, for the most part, because they support plant and asset uptime. Thus a corporate procurement endeavor may not be supported at the plant level with the plant citing special needs as the justification for not participating in the corporate program. When this occurs, total cost of MRO materials supply will likely be driven up because plants may have to take measures to hide their lack of participation in the corporate endeavor.

In other cases plants may be required to take possession of larger than desired quantities of MRO materials bought as a result of a reverse auction. See our previous comments on the notion of buying in bulk to save (Pain #29).

Islands of pain associated with the future perfect objective: Only invest in resources that enable the first four future perfect objectives.

If 80% of the cost of operations is designed in, then 80% of improvement dollars should be spent on redesign efforts. How can our improvement efforts be guided? Are our efforts driven to obtain future perfect? Let's take a closer look at people, processes, and technology islands of pain that keep companies from advancing as rapidly as they should.

Pain #31: No Strategic MRO strategy is the best strategy.

Our experience is that enterprise asset management and MRO supply chain management initiatives that comprise Strategic MRO have not been guided by an understandable set of principles. Typically, there is no definable strategy or practical path forward to guide people's actions.

Questions that help to develop a Strategic MRO strategy include:

- What is the result of not having a set of guiding principles? Does the existence of more than 30 islands of pain provide a hint?
- Do future perfect objectives exist to guide organizational decision making?
- Are you buying the best assets for the task at hand?
- Will future assets be managed to achieve availability and reliability expectations?
- Do maintenance strategies such as run-to-failure, preventive, condition-based, and risk-based maintenance exist?
- Is TCO a common metric for driving cost-based decisions?
- Are there metrics that ensure progress is being made toward a future perfect?

Great thinking precedes great doing and ends with great results. Organizational focus on Strategic MRO improves both the top and the bottom line.

Pain #32: Assets perform functions; maintenance repairs things.

Any review of work orders at a typical plant will undoubtedly indicate that many assets were maintained or repaired. Likewise, at plants with efficient maintenance organizations, all maintenance resources will show to be fully employed and MRO inventory investments will probably achieve good turnover. Nowhere in the work orders, however, will there be an indication of what functions were restored to operational status.

Throughout our islands of pain discussions we have indicated that assets can be placed into two basic groups. The asset either contributes directly to revenue creation or it does not. Assets perform functions. Maintenance tasks maintain or restore these functions. Not all functions are critical thus not all maintenance and repair activities are critical. Simply constructing a maintenance strategy to repair things misses the target by more than a mile and more than a few dollars. Maintenance strategy should be organized and managed in a manner that takes asset criticality into consideration.

Pain #33: Thinking that maintenance is a "do and don't think" function.

A huge waste is incurred any time an organization loses any portion of insightful human thought and creativity. This may occur when an organization implicitly or explicitly conveys the message that maintenance is to "do as they are told, not think." Failures happen regardless of the strength and depth of Strategic MRO activities. Because of this, maintenance resources must swiftly diagnose symptoms, analyze the impact of the failure, and treat the root cause. These are the actions of an asset doctor, not a mechanic who merely replaces motors per instructions.

Any improvement initiative relies on the analytical and practical thinking of its resources. Understanding failure patterns, applying appropriate maintenance prevention and response modes, crafting the lowest total cost of ownership solutions, streamlining and improving the effectiveness of work order management, coordination of labor, materials, and equipment to respond to asset demands, and orchestrating a complex MRO supply chain requires more than doers.

Thinking by an asset custodian is paramount to the success of the Strategic MRO initiative. This requires the maintenance and improvement of perhaps the most important asset, the asset custodian.

Pain #34: The goal of OEE is 100%.

Overall equipment effectiveness (OEE) is quickly becoming recognized as the metric of choice for tracking the productivity of equipment. OEE components consist of availability (AV), performance efficiency (PE), and first time through quality (FTT). The mathematical equation is OEE = AV x PE x FTT.

As an example suppose the following:
Availability (AV)	*= 95%*
Performance Efficiency (PE)	*= 90%*
First Time Through Quality (FFT)	*= 99%*

$$OEE = AV \times PE \times FFT = .95 \times .9 \times .99$$
$$OEE = .8465 = 84.65\%$$

Most other metrics have a goal of 100% if the measure is of something good like "shipments on time," or 0% if the measure is errors, for example. The goal of OEE is "it depends." Rarely is the goal for OEE 100%.

Availability is defined as equipment availability to the schedule. Availability of 100% may imply that no scheduled downtime or maintenance is considered. No planned maintenance is a short-sighted planning strategy for most equipment.

Performance efficiency is defined as the ability of the equipment to run at its design speed. Equipment can sometimes be sped up to meet production needs. Certainly, most equipment can be slowed down to meet production schedules or balance its speed with other physical assets or bottlenecks in the production process.

First time through quality is a measure of what percentage of products were produced right the first time. FTT should also take into consideration first piece inspection, quality samples, and rework.

The industry benchmark for OEE is 85%. OEEs of 45% aren't necessarily bad. That level of OEE might mean that equipment has been slowed down, extra quality samples were taken, or maintenance performed whether routine or overhaul.

Striving to reach high OEE goals just for the sake of showing "great equipment utilization numbers" might make no sense at all. It depends on the circumstances. For example, if a plant is working hard to reduce a backlog of actual customer orders and is not scrimping on maintenance, a quite high OEE is very good. On the other hand, if high OEE is achieved by building to stock resulting in inflated finished goods inventories, this may not be good at all.

Pain #35: Lack of visibility of asset demand behavior.

What did each asset cost your company last year? Did the cost exceed the benefit? What assets should be repaired versus replaced? What decision support processes exist to answer these questions?

The only way to consistently answer these questions is to improve the demand visibility of an asset. When issuing parts and/or performing services to maintain an asset, clearly link these parts or services with that particular asset in order to create a profile of the asset demand. Rather than focus on MRO spend per maintenance person we should concentrate on MRO spend per asset. Then we can identify assets that are expensive to run versus those that are less expensive even given the same production rates.

The goal should be to reduce absolute MRO parts and labor spend per unit of production by gravitating to assets that are inherently less expensive to run. Lack of visibility of asset demand patterns is a quite serious pain that industrial organizations face when challenged with improving performance (availability and reliability) and the total cost of ownership.

Pain #36: Confusing management decisions with technology impact.

Recently, much emphasis has been placed upon the use of technology as a key to decreasing costs. Our notion is that technology in and of itself does nothing to reduce costs. We base this observation on our experiences with too many companies who have spent millions on technology and then additional millions making the new technology work exactly like their previous computerized or manual system worked. They end up with business processes that are marginally improved at best and realize little if any cost reductions from their investment in technology.

Interestingly, we occasionally visit companies that have achieved dramatic cost savings through careful business process analysis and refinement. Some of these companies have spent virtually nothing on additional technology. Technology does not reduce costs—the proper application of technology, and sound business practices, based on rational management decisions can reduce costs.

The truth of the matter is that, most often, a careful redesign of business processes along with technology to automate, reduce search time, provide mobile handheld connectivity, and replace paper documents yields the largest cost savings. The technology is secondary to the decision to improve the underlying business process.

It is not uncommon for us to hear about technology providers that claim to be able to help companies achieve price reductions from their supplier of up to 20%. Companies that are successful in realizing such price reductions do so through implementing effective strategic sourcing practices. No technology is necessarily required, though technology can streamline the process by acting as a gatherer of information and as an instrument to facilitate compliance with strategic sourcing decisions.

The key, then, to more efficient, effective business processes is management vision, the decision to undertake the activities to improve and the tenacity and drive to stick to the improvement initiative. Technology has nothing to do with these. Technology is an enabler, a compliance mechanism and a way to automate and streamline processes. Make sure you apply technology to business processes that have been improved to the highest levels of effectiveness and efficiency. After all, technology that automates poor business processes allows you to make mistakes more rapidly than ever!

The Path Forward

Paul's executive forum responded quite favorably to his presentation on islands of pain. In fact, the participants suggested islands of pain he had not thought of or uncovered in his research. What a mess, Paul thought. How does a company get started when faced with a list of problems of this magnitude?

What Paul needed was a path forward that would force his resources to focus on future perfect. He hoped to define his current behavior using this process, best practices, and the technology necessary to achieve the absolute advantage he sought in the market. He felt that his executive forum couldn't offer him a succinct roadmap for his issues. Paul had to seek specialized assistance.

One of his executive forum colleagues suggested that he investigate the Demand Supply Compression (DSC) methodology applied to Strategic MRO. His colleague related that he had become familiar with the DSC approach at an international enterprise asset management conference in Paris. Why not check it out? So Paul did.

Chapter 4

Demand Supply Compression: Guiding Principles

Executive Summary: The change management process must be guided by principles that can be easily understood and followed. Demand Supply Compression consists of the thinking and decision-support methodologies to guide organizational Strategic MRO efforts. The principles challenge organizational intelligence and provide an organizational framework for implementing Strategic MRO practices. Its language is designed to simplify the complexities of enterprise asset management and MRO supply chain management. The five principles—defining the value stream, connecting the asset to the value stream, connecting demand to the asset, connecting supply to demand, and compressing demand supply connections—guide the use of tools and methodologies.

Paul had just finished a round of morning meetings that would have shaken the confidence of most senior executives. Shareholders were dismayed that share prices were slowly but steadily falling. They looked to him to reverse this trend. Wall Street analysts at the institutions that owned big blocks of his company's stock had identified poor cash flow management as the primary reason for the stock price decline.

Paul's next steps were clear. He had to identify the direction and focus his company needed, and do it fast. Paul knew his product offerings were solid, but his operational costs were sky high. Perhaps this was the time to begin implementing the MRO issues that he had been discussing with the executive forum. He knew from his research that focus on the MRO space could yield considerable savings in short order. Paul's pressure to improve cash flow was mounting, and he dreaded the possibility of more layoffs and early retirements to achieve this. He knew these layoffs didn't change his operational practices, only added more work to those who remained. The deer in the headlight looks he received during the last announcements of layoffs were unforgettable; he didn't want to repeat that experience.

Sitting at his desk, still somewhat motivated from his first round of executive forum discussions on islands of pain, Paul saw his own island of pain growing. He realized that addressing the issue of Strategic MRO was not an "in the mood" thing—it required constant attention. As he looked through his forum notes he spotted the recommendation to investigate the Demand Supply Compression (DSC) methodology applied to Strategic MRO. Was DSC just another gimmick, another popular tool re-branded, that implemented the same MRO practices that were not working well in his company today?

Lately Paul's business had been inundated with tools that were supposed to help them achieve success in one area or another. From his perspective, *analysis tools* existed to study people, products, and market performance, monitor current performance, and predict future performance. *Process improvement tools* existed to help analyze past practices, understand current practices, and develop new processes for future practices. In simple terms, tools existed to help compare desired outcomes to actual outcomes. Further, these tools sometimes provided help in understanding why desired outcomes were or were not achieved or, in some cases, exceeded. Paul's organization had all the tools. They just needed something to guide their application. Could DSC light the path they needed to take, he wondered?

Paul went to the World Wide Web to see if he could better understand what DSC was all about. He immediately discovered that Demand Supply Compression was based on five guiding principles, impacted five critical business cycles, and ultimately sought to increase the value content of business assets and activities. He soon discovered that the DSC principles have been applied to both Strategic MRO for indirect materials and market driven system for direct materials. He clicked on the Strategic MRO link. Here is what Paul found.

Physical Assets Versus Intellectual Assets

It is our experience that organizations have a difficult time applying analysis and process improvement tools in a succinct and thoughtful manner. The question is why. Our thoughts are simple. Organizations have spent considerable time and much money to institutionalize their physical infrastructure and the information systems required for operating the physical infrastructure. Clearly, when you enter an automobile assembly plant, a layman can instantaneously discern the process and the desired result. A refinery looks and acts like a refinery, a jet repair center looks and acts like a jet repair center, and a bottling plant looks and acts like a bottling plant. The physical assets of your organization tell a compelling story.

But what about the intellectual assets of a company? What does organizational intelligence look like? What does it act like? What is the process of managing and extending organizational intelligence? What are the results of organizational intelligence? The physical assets of a company are relatively constant. However, the intellectual assets of an organization change daily given such events as new hires, promotions, retirements, acquisitions, and layoffs. Thus, the process of what and how we think changes constantly. It is quite normal that companies struggle with a consistent vision and understanding of how to best use their assets to serve their markets. It is normal for companies to struggle with priorities for investments: do we improve this, do we acquire that, and do we shut down this or restructure this other?

Leveraging Intellectual Assets

Strategic MRO *powered by* DSC is a procedure for introducing a systematic process for leveraging intellectual assets to turn your physical assets into a strategic advantage.

Strategic MRO *powered by* DSC considers all of the complexities of Enterprise Asset Management and MRO Supply Chain Management and simplifies the process to give you, the organizational leader, a well-trodden roadmap to achieving Strategic MRO goals.

The process for change, no matter how described, requires the organization to examine the performance gaps between the current state and a desired future perfect as Paul had previously diagramed in Chapter 1 and later reintroduced in Chapter 3.

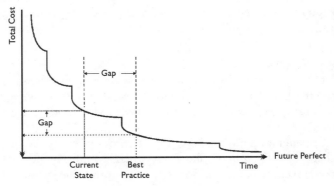

Figure 4.1 - Future Perfect Performance Gaps

In Chapter 1, Paul introduced his notion of future perfect objectives or general rules of action. As a brief reminder let's review them:

1. Only produce exactly what is consumed in the market.
2. Only invest in assets that produce that which is consumed in the market.
3. Only invest in assets that never fail over their useful life.
4. Achieve zero total cost of ownership (TCO) for all assets.
5. Only invest in resources that enable the first four future perfect precepts.

The Demand Supply Compression methodology uses five guiding principles to achieve these future perfect precepts. The principles are sequential in nature. The first must be considered before the second and so on. The principles both challenge organizational intelligence and provide an organizational framework for implementing Strategic MRO practices.

The Demand Supply Compression guiding principles are:

1. Define the value stream. This principle guides our thinking as we make progress towards only producing what is consumed in the market.
2. Connect the asset to the value stream. This principle guides our thinking as we make progress towards the future perfect objective to only invest in assets that produce that which is consumed in the market.
3. Connect demand to the asset. This principle guides our thinking as we make progress towards the future perfect objective to only invest in assets that never fail over their useful life.
4. Connect supply to the demand. This principle guides our thinking as we make progress towards the future perfect objective to achieve zero TCO for all assets.
5. Compress demand supply connections. This principle guides our thinking as we make progress towards the future perfect objective to only invest in resources that enable the first four future perfect objectives.

The purpose of this chapter is to briefly introduce you to these guiding principles. Chapters 5 through 9 spend considerable time clarifying and providing specific business examples of each.

Define the Value Stream

The first DSC principle focuses the company on defining the unit of value it offers to the market. The unit of value refers to the products and services for which the company receives remuneration. These products and services are sometimes referred to as trade assets.

For profit generating entities, the value stream represents the sequence of activities that creates the unit of value from which revenue is generated.

If your organization is a not-for-profit entity, your value stream is that set of activities that assure future sources of funding for some delivered unit of value. Requirements may vary for not-for-profit organizations. For example, levels of readiness and mission capability may be required for military or disaster response organizations. Still, the value stream is a set of activities that produce or can produce the output desired by the entities funding the organization.

Connect the Asset to the Value Stream

The second DSC principle focuses the organization's enterprise asset management priorities. Priorities are based on the future perfect objective of only investing in assets that produce that which is consumed in the market. Future perfect represents ideal, not what is currently attainable in the market.

Ideally asset owners build, procure, and maintain assets that have a definable purpose relative to the value stream. In the strictest sense organizational assets are either working for or against the value stream. In a broader view some assets are not supporting the value stream directly but are inherently necessary to allow for future responsiveness, which may or may not be needed. It is essential that these assets be at least neutral in their impact on the value stream.

We divide organizational assets into two categories, revenue and non-revenue generating. Revenue or funding generating (mission critical) assets, must work for the goals of the value stream. Non-revenue or non-funds generating (non-mission critical) assets, at best, must remain neutral in their impact. They can never be permitted to become a distraction, or other resource-eating pit.

Connect Demand to the Asset

This principle guides our thinking as we make progress toward the future perfect objective to invest only in assets that never fail over their useful life. In connecting assets to the value stream, the goal is to improve asset *availability*. In connecting demand to the asset, the goal is to improve asset *reliability*. As asset reliability improves, supply costs go down. As asset reliability improves, availability improves. For revenue producing assets, this means more trade potential.

Ideally, if an asset never fails, never needs servicing, and never needs overhaul, we have mitigated the need for the MRO supply chain. However, this is not the real world. Assets wear, assets fail, and often assets need to be upgraded. The goal is to understand asset demand patterns to either prevent or respond to them at the lowest total costs.

Connect Supply to Demand

For every demand there is supply. Supply is defined as the labor, materials, and special equipment/tools needed to respond to asset demand. Unmanaged supply is extremely costly. Idle labor, excess inventory, and specialty tools increase costs rapidly. The connect supply to demand principle guides our thinking as we make progress toward the future perfect objective to achieve zero TCO for all assets. TCO is comprised of the acquisition, possession, and disposal of assets. Supply impacts all three elements.

Understandably, the superior asset availability and reliability required to achieve business performance objectives cannot be achieved without supply costs. The question is: If not all assets are equal, and not all demands are equal, should all supply response be equal? This question raises another question: What level of supply response is necessary to mitigate business risks of unavailable and unreliable assets?

Compress the Demand Supply Connections

The principle of compressing the demand supply connections guides our thinking as we make progress toward the future perfect objective to invest only in resources that enable the first three future perfect objectives.

As a quick reminder, the first four future perfect objectives are:

1. Only produce exactly what is consumed in the market.
2. Only invest in assets that produce that which is consumed in the market.
3. Only invest in assets that never fail over their useful life.
4. Achieve zero total cost of ownership (TCO) for all assets.

The goal of compression is to increase the value adding content of all assets and supporting activities. An activity is classified as adding value if it directly contributes to the production of services and products for trade. Conversely, non-value adding activities are non-contributing. This classification is consistent with the distinction between revenue and non-revenue producing assets. Revenue producing assets are value adding assets. Non-revenue producing assets are non-value adding assets.

In Chapter 3 we introduced a number of islands of pain associated with enterprise asset management and MRO supply chain management. Chapters 5 through 9 introduce specific compression strategies to eliminate waste (non-value adding activities) and to compress time, distance, and space.

The universal metric used to quantify compression strategies is value density. Value density is defined as the percentage of value add to the entirety of the asset or activities being performed. Value density metrics aid us in determining where we need to focus specific compression efforts. Examples include:

- A robot is scheduled to be in production for 37 hours during a one-week period. Due to unplanned downtime, the robot is available only 32 hours. The resultant availability metric of 32/37 or 86% is a value density metric. Suppose the robot produced 95% good parts at 97% of the design performance speed. The combination of availability, first time through quality, and performance efficiency is commonly referred to as overall equipment effectiveness (OEE). OEE is a value density metric.
- An electrician is hired to perform eight hours of overhaul work to update and expand the capacity of the circuit breaker box located in a hotel. Throughout the day the electrician must search for various parts and special tools. Total wrench time where physical work is being performed is 4.5 hours. The value density of the labor effort is 4.5/8 or 56%.

Demand Supply Compression consists of the thinking and decision-support methodologies to guide organizational Strategic MRO efforts. Its language is designed to simplify the complexities of enterprise asset management and MRO supply chain management. The five principles of defining the value stream, connecting the asset to the value stream, connecting demand to the asset, connecting supply to demand, and compressing demand supply connections guide the use of tools and methodologies.

Next Steps

Paul pondered what he had researched on Demand Supply Compression. He thought that the five guiding principles represented a simple, common language that could be easily communicated throughout his organization. Demand for Strategic MRO was the demand created by the asset in use. Supply was the necessary response to restore the asset to acceptable performance levels. Compression represented the elimination of non-value adding activities and islands of pain (wrong thinking). Value density metrics allowed him to monitor progress toward a future perfect where all assets, activities, and systems were value adding.

He thought the island of pain discussions in his executive forum had gone extremely well. Using the Demand Supply Compression guiding principles Paul felt he had a focused and manageable process for making progress.

Chapter 5

Define the Value Stream

Executive Summary: Every organization has a purpose, to deliver its products and services "unit of value" to the marketplace. The value stream is defined as the activities, supporting labor, materials, assets, and information required to produce the desired unit of value. In seeking to produce only what is consumed, the value stream allocates precious resources to ensure that value is delivered and value is achieved by the producing organization. The end result is an absolute advantage in the marketplace.

T he recent islands of pain discussions invigorated the executive forum. With the permission of the topics committee, Paul outlined the agendas for the next several meetings. Paul felt that these meetings should discuss the DSC guiding principles. He reasoned that the principles should be addressed one per meeting and in the order suggested by the DSC methodology. He also thought that the forum members should be broken into groups based upon the industries member companies represented.

Each group elected the most qualified facilitator to help focus their discussions. Each DSC principle was to be discussed in both theory and practice. A case study was to be prepared to illustrate application of the DSC principle to a specific company within the group's assigned industry vertical. The facilitators from each group agreed in advance on a format to guide discussions for DSC principles one through four. Principle five, compress demand supply connections, would be applied to each guiding principle as it was discussed.

The format structure was an eight-step process:

1. Review DSC guiding principle.
2. Review future perfect precept.
3. Determine organizational impact.
4. Reflect on the islands of pain.
5. Define value density metrics.
6. Identify compression strategies.
7. Develop case study examples.
8. Define the management strategy.

At the next forum meeting Paul outlined the process for the forum members. They then broke into their assigned groups and started their discussions relating to the first DSC principle.

Review DSC Guiding Principle #1: Define the Value Stream

The value stream discussion begins with a clear definition of the unit of value that a company's value stream offers the market. The unit of value refers to the products and services offered for trade. The value stream, then, is defined as the activities, supporting labor, materials, assets, and information required to produce the desired unit of value.

Review Future Perfect Precept

The first guiding principle guides our thinking as we make progress toward only producing those units of value that will ultimately be consumed in the market. Some have successfully argued that this future perfect objective does not go far enough. The waste of overproduction should be eliminated as well as any waste in the production process of the unit of value. Further, the units of value should be designed, deployed, and used in a manner that will eliminate any waste associated with acquisition, use, and disposal of those units of value.

Finally, future perfect suggests that both society and industry share the responsibility to produce units of value that are, where practical, recoverable assets. By recoverable, we mean assets that when depleted or used up, have recoverable value. This value is recovered, for example, by recycling the materials from which the asset is made.

To summarize, waste occurs if producers produce more than what is actually consumed by consumers. The same is true when wasteful production processes are used. Therefore, special efforts should be employed to define value streams that, as efficiently as possible, produce only those value units that are consumed. Excess production represents needless and costly deployment of people, materials, and physical assets. The same is true for inefficient production.

Determine Organizational Impact

To achieve the future perfect of producing only what is consumed, the organization must become keenly aware of how it uses all of its resources. An important goal for most industrial CEOs is to increase shareholder value by focusing on five strategic initiatives that consume resources. These are:

1. Sales growth.
2. Sales cost leadership.
3. Direct material costs leadership.
4. Transformation costs leadership.
5. Strategic MRO costs leadership.

Strategic MRO is comprised of enterprise asset management and MRO supply chain management and is not a "hand off to an employee" initiative. Asset strategies, directions, initiatives, processes, and procedures have a profound impact on an organization's ability to thrive or survive in its market. The executive team must lead the process of leveraging its assets to achieve market objectives.

Executives are challenged daily to focus on share value, revenue objectives, new markets, and new products. These alone are significant challenges even if it were not necessary to maintain a unique focus on assets. However, the top line numbers must somehow make their way to the bottom line. This path to the bottom line flows through assets. The company that plans for, uses, and optimizes its assets has the best shot at achieving satisfactory profit levels and absolute advantage in the market.

The absolute advantage, in economics, is a concept of trade in which an entity produces products and services more efficiently, using fewer resources of labor, and/or capital, while maintaining market agility superior to its competition.

Reflect on the Islands of Pain

The executive forum teams quickly agreed from their previous discussions that achieving an absolute advantage in the market requires that *Strategic MRO be an executive imperative.*

Today companies must participate in complex global supply chains in order to deliver their units of value in the form of products and services to the market. Too much or too little production in the wrong parts of the world results in waste or lost opportunities. Finding perfection in location, volume, timing, and delivery is a constant challenge, even if the assets are finely constructed and tuned to the same mission. Ignoring the impact of geographical location on Strategic MRO strategies will only drive operational costs up and counter any labor and delivery cost advantages.

Define Value Density Metrics

The universal metric used to quantify compression strategies is value density. Value density is defined as the percentage of value-add to the entirety of the product produced or activities being performed. Value density metrics aid us in determining where we need to focus specific compression efforts.

The value stream has several value density metrics that impact the value stream. Two prominent ones are:

Percentage of value adding functions versus desired consumer functions. The goal of this metric is to align the features, functions, and other properties of the unit of value with what the consumer (customer) wants and needs. For example a VCR has 128 features and functions available to the consumer, but only 9 are consistently used. To most customers the value density of the VCR features and functions is 9/128 or 7%. How does this impact Strategic MRO? Why should a company pour money into assets to produce units of value that have little or no value in the market?

Percentage of the number of units of value produced versus consumed in the market. This is an important but hard to determine metric. Organizations tend to focus on the number of products sold versus the number consumed. Logic suggests that not all products that are sold are actually consumed. Knowledge of the actual consumption rates in the market aids us in driving our asset investment, maintenance, and disposal strategies. If, for example, there are six months of excess inventory in the channel, what should our assets be doing now? How should we have deployed our assets to begin with, to prevent the six months of excess inventories?

Identify Compression Strategies

The value stream attempts through market forces to optimize two basic elements. The first is the unit of value itself. The second is the set of activities that make up the value stream. When both of these elements are optimal or nearly so, the units of value are recognized as having high value.

An economist would describe this high value by saying that the unit of value has high economic utility. Overall economic utility is the combination of four basic utility elements:

1. Form utility is the ability of the product or service to meet customer wants and needs.
2. Time utility is the ability of the product or service to be delivered to the customer at the time desired.
3. Place utility is the ability of the product or service to be delivered to the customer at the desired location.
4. Possession utility is based on the ability of the customer to take possession of the product or service. This is a function of the product's value relative to the ability of a customer to expend funds.

As we will further explore in connecting assets to the value stream, assets must assist the producing organization in producing the right products/services, at the right time, delivered to the right location, at a price that represents value to the market. Let's briefly review analysis tools that impact our ability to achieve Strategic MRO future perfect objectives.

Value engineering (VE) is a technique used to define form utility functions of the unit of value. These functions are first and foremost evaluated for their perceived or known value to the customer. Alternative designs are explored to deliver these value-creating functions over the intended useful life of the product or service. For example a function of the automobile is to transport a person from point A to point B. Certainly the combination of ignition system, engine, power train, and cab of the vehicle has significant impact on ability to transport someone. As we delve deeper into how these value-based functions are achieved we answer questions like: Do we use gasoline, natural gas, methane, hydrogen, diesel, or electric as the source of power? A natural consequence of these choices is the design of the assets and activities to deliver the form utility requirements. Certainly assets required to produce a combustion engine versus an electric engine are quite different. Value engineering activities typically lead to costing activities that subsequently support or drive changes in unit of value design.

Target pricing is a compression technique to define the price at which a unit of value must be sold to ensure that it is indeed consumed in the marketplace. Target costing models are then applied to ensure that the producer can provide the unit of value profitably. The combination of target pricing and costing determines the ability of a company to meet possession utility objectives.

Quality function deployment (QFD) is a tool that maps customer wants and needs to product or service specifications. QFD is a natural progression of activities from value engineering. Through a series of matrices, QFD maps product requirements to process requirements. Finally, process requirements are mapped to asset specifications.

Ultimately an organization's QFD efforts enable it to link customer wants and needs to the correct temperature, pressure, and cycle time or other operational aspects of a production asset. Then, for example, the impact of poor asset maintenance can be directly linked to a product's perceived value in the market.

Time-based strategies attempt to meet the market's expectation of quickly evolving solutions. Time compression strategies have many names such as lead time reduction, first to market, time-based competition, and cycle time management. These all attempt to focus the company's attention on the time utility as a primary market driver.

Lead time reduction activities impact asset design, selection, installation, and maintenance practices. The notion is that assets should be sized to support needed production volumes and deployed in continuous flow production designs. Assets should be flexible enough to respond to unexpected changes in the market demand, and they should be quickly deployable to other locations as required. Finally, assets should be available to produce on demand.

Supply chain optimization includes tools such as a network analysis. These tools attempt to define the best location of assets to deliver products to target markets while achieving the lowest cost place utility.

Distance is time and time is money. Since the early 1980s companies have adopted low-cost country strategies for selection of plant and facility sites. In short, companies move assets where the overall operational costs (primarily the labor component) are the lowest. Then they ship products to the customer locations worldwide. Thus, the location of production assets impacts the ability of the producer to deliver products in a timely, cost-effective manner.

As assets are relocated, so must be the skills, supply chains, and information systems needed to maintain the assets. A low-cost producer is only as good as the availability and reliability of its assets. Production losses quickly offset any advantages gained through lower wages.

In summary, compression strategies are driven by the knowledge that assets and asset deployment have a profound impact on all four elements of economic utility. Assets must produce the unit of value right the first time (form), at the right time (time), deliver it to the right location (place), at the right cost (possession) for an organization to be successful.

Develop Case Study Examples

With this introduction and subsequent discussions, the executive forum selected five different companies to model DSC guiding principles. These companies reflected the wide range of executives in attendance.

Superior Water

Superior Water is a regulated public utility that delivers water to both residential and commercial accounts. Superior Water generates revenue through the sale of water. Two methods of determining revenue are employed. The first is a fee established as a percentage of the value of the property served and the second is a metered rate applied to actual water consumption.

Outages, poor quality, and leaks diminish value stream performance and revenue generation. Regulators place considerable constraints on how revenue can be generated and how much profits can be made. Superior Water is under constant price pressure to perform equal to or better than other water companies. Upon comparison with other water producers, Superior Water finds that they are a high-cost producer. Due to recent price cuts Superior is now faced with having to reduce operational costs. As an asset-intensive industry, Superior has no choice but to improve asset availability and reliability in order to reduce overall water supply costs.

Superior Water wants to be recognized as a community-oriented firm that promotes conservation of water, while at the same time meeting customer service needs. It recognizes that leaks are a daily occurrence. In addition to more leaks, water quality diminishes as its infrastructure ages. Most of Superior's service activity is driven by response to complaints. These activities invariably are to repair older pipeline networks and equipment. Superior Water feels that it must reduce the occurrence of complaints and outages if it is to improve its customer value density.

EuroCar

EuroCar is an assembler of passenger cars for the global market headquartered in Europe. The EuroCar assembly plant creates revenue through the sale of its vehicles in the consumer market. However, EuroCar receives payment at a fixed rate from the parent company when a vehicle is shipped. Automobile production impacts nearly one in four industrial sector jobs. These jobs include those in industry sectors that supply paint, steel, carpeting, and many other products and services.

EuroCar is under intense market pressure to attain superior product quality and functionality, at the lowest cost, for several different models aimed at various buyer segments. EuroCar focuses primarily on the family-oriented, luxury car- buying segment.

Yearly marketing studies have caused EuroCar to constantly reevaluate the feature packages consumers place a value on and how to price those packages. They feel their value density is quite high based on consumer response to these feature packages. Their competitors have done the same. Now the price war is back on! The goal is to reduce operational cost by no less than 5% per year.

EuroCar Corporation is undergoing consolidation efforts at its assembly plants. This places an additional burden on a few selected plants where new vehicle production is being added to existing production activities.

Consolidation is meant to reduce costs. However, some plants are seeing costs increase. In those EuroCar plants, additional models mean additional assets, new production methods, and increased line availability pressure. What some see as growth and job security, others see as trouble. How do we maintain plant assets to ensure we meet production and cost objectives? This is a question on the minds of more than a few EuroCar plant managers.

MobileTel

MobileTel is an international provider of mobile telecommunications services. MobileTel generates revenue based on actual minutes of usage. Local and long distance fares for land-based telecommunication systems have been under siege for several years. Because of this, MobileTel's parent organization has placed high earnings expectations on mobile services. Seeing the market direction that land-based systems have taken, MobileTel recognizes that it must reduce the cost of operations while improving services in order to meet these high profit level expectations.

Mobile telecommunications customers desire uninterrupted mobile telecommunication services regardless of their dialing location. The industry has experienced high levels of customer turnover due to its inability to achieve both price and service levels. MobileTel is no exception. To improve its coverage and service levels MobileTel is embarking on an ambitious capital project to expand its network 300% through investments in UMTS (Universal Mobile Telecommunications System) technology.

MobileTel must earn a return on this investment in assets by increasing customer loyalty (reducing customer turnover or churn rate), providing additional billable services available through the new technology, and by reducing its cost of operations per billable minute. The value density of its service offerings is about 75%. This means that on an average, customers are using about 75% of the available features such as roaming, messaging, call forwarding, and Internet access.

MilBase Ops

MilBase Ops is a military installation that supports military operational and training activities. In addition MilBase provides and maintains housing for members of the military and their families.

MilBase Ops receives funding through an annual budgeting process where recurring expenditures and capital projects must be justified. Although it is a not-for-profit entity, MilBase Ops still feels the cost pressures experienced by the commercial sector. Every three years MilBase Ops undergoes intense scrutiny to prove that it is indeed the most efficient organization (MEO). If MilBase Ops cannot show that they are the MEO, current base personnel may lose their jobs to an outside contractor who has qualified as the new MEO.

Mission readiness, asset stewardship, and overall infrastructure maintenance drive asset management and MRO supply chain decisions. Value density can be improved by minimizing base operational costs so that existing funding can be redirected to mission critical assets and activities.

Commander-in-Chief directives to act like a commercial business have caused a change in the financial reporting system. Financial audit findings indicated that "no opinion" could be rendered due to lack of accounting data integrity and traceability. Continued studies by Armed Forces chief financial officers have unearthed several incidences of potential fraud, waste, and abuse. MilBase Ops must implement both operational and information technology improvements to meet command directives.

TL Freight

TL Freight is a national provider of trucking services to multiple industries. Since the 1980 Motor Carrier Act that created a sweeping deregulation of the trucking industry, TL Freight has consistently pursued both business and technology solutions to reduce its cost of operations. To support multiple industries, custom trailers have been designed to haul bulk materials, specialty chemical products, and refrigerated foodstuffs. Acquisitions and mergers have added to the scope of its trucking services.

As operations have grown to include all of North America and international ports, the need to optimize asset utilization has become painfully apparent. TL Freight has estimated the excess capacity required to offset unplanned asset down-time and required Department of Transportation (DOT) maintenance to be nearly 350 trucks per day. A recent industry economic downturn has prompted TL Freight to begin active research into leading edge asset management technology to improve its cost of operations.

TL Freight generates revenue on a per mile basis. Their goal is to keep their revenue producing assets on the road. The customer value density is a function of the percentage of time a truck or trailer is under load moving product from its origination to its final destination on time, without material handling damage, lost shipments, or associated customer downtime.

Define the Management Strategy

Each of our sample companies faces typical market pressures and a common need to improve the availability and reliability of its assets. The underlying management strategy of the first DSC guiding principle was to achieve a clear understanding on how one's organization creates revenue or generates funding.

Why is this important to Strategic MRO? The answer may seem intuitively obvious. But if it is so obvious, why is it that most organizations cannot tell you what assets create how much revenue? Why is it that maintenance departments cannot correlate lost asset availability with its impact on revenue? Why is it that most industrial distributors do not know the amount of revenue that key customers lose when they are out of stock of a critical part? Why is it that original equipment manufacturers cannot tell you how much revenue their equipment generates for key customers?

The management strategy is clear. Begin the Strategic MRO intervention with a clear understanding of the organization's purpose. For most, this means producing a unit of value to the consumption requirements of the market and the profitability expectations of the shareholders.

As units of value are planned, designed, validated, launched, produced, sold, and eventually retired, this product lifecycle must be meshed with a similar asset lifecycle. We refer, of course, to the lifecycle of the facilities and production assets, which enable a company to produce units of value. The asset lifecycle activities must be planned and coordinated with product lifecycles to ensure that the lowest cost of operations can be achieved as products and services are consumed in the market.

Paul's Reflections

Paul closely observed the results of each of the teams within his executive forum. Even though his chemical company was not chosen as a case study, he felt confident that the lessons learned and the insights gathered would improve his thinking.

The discussions regarding only producing to consumption were challenging but not showstoppers. Paul knew his own company made money only if his specialty chemical products sold. Pressures to consign inventory made it impossible to sell his customers bulk shipments that vastly exceeded their weekly production requirements. He too had to figure out how to deploy assets to meet the ever more demanding requirements of the market.

The value density metrics really caught Paul's attention. What percentage of his company's product characteristics matched customer requirements? His engineering staff had added a special blending process at the end of the line because up-front processes were not capable of holding specifications. What were these specifications and were they necessary? He wondered how much it cost to keep this special blending process in operation. The cost of the equipment, the operators, the maintenance, and the facility space utilization had to be significant amounts. Was it really necessary? Paul came away from the executive forum meeting with a definite to-do for Monday morning.

Other participants were as enthused as Paul with the session's outcome. In fact, they unanimously voted to continue their investigation of the Demand Supply Compression methodology as the topics for upcoming meetings. The next guiding principle is: Connect the asset to the value stream. The team facilitators had the script...time to repeat it.

Chapter 6

Connect the Asset to the Value Stream

Executive Summary: All assets are not equal! Their criticality is based on their proximity to the value stream. As such assets can be classified as revenue producing or non-revenue producing assets. Connecting the asset to the value stream requires linking the product lifecycle to the asset lifecycle to drive investment decisions. Value stream analysis is an excellent methodology for identifying the performance requirements of revenue producing assets.

Paul started to get a sense of where Demand Supply Compression principles were trying to take his organization. Defining the value stream provided insight on the demand requirements created by his customers for the products and services his company produced.

Paul came to understand that connecting the asset to the value stream represents the supply side to the market-driven demand engine. If supply side assets do not perform to expectations the potential for lost revenue exists. Lost revenue occurs because of not having products and services available for sale or penalties for not delivering as promised. Paul also knew that repeated poor supply performance resulted in long-term negative revenue consequences for his business. In his world, lost contract bids typically meant three to five years before the next bid opportunity, and the competition was fierce.

At Paul's request his CFO had calculated the cost of a lost customer to the company. They estimated that a typical five-year, $10,000,000 contract resulted in $318,627 in net earnings. Paul knew that net earnings could be improved if he could just get operational costs under control and if he could only stop paying penalties for late deliveries. To date his plant's performance had cost his company a shot at supplying higher-margin products with several of their customers. These customers were not willing to take a risk on his company.

Paul was more than curious to know how the executive forum would respond to the second guiding principle of connecting the asset to the value stream as a discussion topic. The facilitators began the meeting by reviewing the efforts of the previous session. The executives who were participants in the forum liked the progress they had made thus far, but wanted to get to the meat of Strategic MRO.

Review Guiding Principle #2: Connect the Asset to the Value Stream

DSC's second principle—connect the asset to the value stream—focuses the organization's enterprise asset management strategies and operational priorities. At its core the principle attempts to classify asset criticality by its impact on revenue creation by the value stream. Figure 6.1 offers a recommended classification scheme for revenue and non–revenue producing assets.

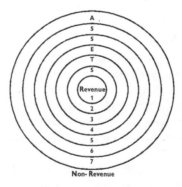

Figure 6.1 - Asset Criticality Classification

1. Assets required for conducting value stream functions that produce the unit of value. These might include mixers, lathes, distillation columns, milling machines, assembly robots, and others.
2. Assets required to ensure that revenue producing assets are powered or controlled. These include power plants, generators, engines, compressors, distributed control systems, manufacturing information systems, and others.
3. Assets required for order fulfillment functions such as sales orders, production planning, shipping, and accounting. These include computers, software, telephone systems, fax machines, and others.

4. Assets required for other core production or service functions such as material handling or warehousing. These might include trucks, conveyors, fork trucks, pipelines, and others.
5. Non-revenue producing assets required to protect revenue producing assets from inoperable conditions. These include buildings, structures, HVAC systems, sewage systems, and others.
6. Non-revenue producing assets required to conduct supporting business functions. These include computers, software, telephone systems, desks, chairs, tables, and others.
7. Non-revenue producing assets that impact quality of life. These include cafeteria equipment, vending machines, access roads, parking lots, playgrounds, child care facilities, and others.

Strategic MRO priorities suggest that taking care of revenue producing assets is always the highest priority. Class 1 assets represent pure revenue producing assets. Classes 2 through 4 assets are required to ensure the performance of revenue producing assets. Non-revenue producing assets always take second priority to revenue producing assets. Classes 5 through 7 provide a relative importance ranking for non-revenue producing assets.

More often than not assets function in series or tandem to produce the end product or service. Thus the interrelationships between assets must be fully understood in their operating context. Ideally all assets are tied together under the business purpose of the organization.

Review Future Perfect Precept

Priorities are based on the future perfect precept of investing only in assets that produce that which is consumed in the market. Theoretically asset investment should not exceed market risk. Market risk can be measured by the percentage of the units of value produced versus consumed in the market.

Risk, or exceptional costs, can be attributed to both over- and under production. Different industries face different market dynamics. The oil refinery has to cope with dynamic production rates; however the product contents rarely change, resulting in relatively stable asset requirements. On the other hand the discrete manufacturer faced with frequent product changes may experience a very dynamic asset structure.

The question becomes, what do we do with assets for which the organization has diminishing or no foreseeable future needs? Achieving this future perfect precept requires the organization to clearly understand the current and future asset status relative to the value stream. As the market changes so do the asset requirements.

As discussed in defining the value stream, asset investments must be optimized to produce the unit of value right the first time (form), at the right time (time), deliver it to the right location (place), at the right cost (possession) for an organization to be successful.

Asset availability should be tied to production schedules. Production schedules should be tied to customer demand. Customer demand should be a function of consumption patterns in the market. Consumption is a moving target over the life of a product or service. Future perfect would suggest that asset production capacity, availability, and timing of use would match consumption variation instantaneously. Further, asset investments would be optimized over the product lifecycle of the unit of value.

Determine Organizational Impact

Connecting the asset to the value stream requires the linkage of the product lifecycle to the asset lifecycle as shown in Figure 6.2.

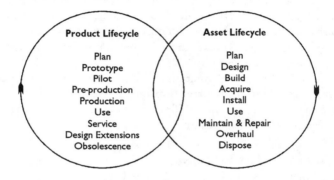

Figure 6.2 - Product Lifecycle Alignment with the Asset Lifecycle

Industry studies suggest that easily 80% of operational costs of assets are designed in. Similar studies suggest that 80% of improvement dollars are spent redesigning operations to achieve desired performance levels. The numerous unknowns in the design and performance of assets are costly and require constant executive and operational attention. However practiced, initial design activities establish where a company is located on the future perfect continuum. How close are you to future perfect? Perhaps more important, how close are you to your competition (see Figure 6.3)? If you are not the market leader, do you want to be?

Initial asset design requirements should be closely linked to the demand requirements that the asset must meet. Unfortunately, "closely linked" is not the order of the day. Excessive engineering safety factors, overly optimistic sales predictions, the compelling desire to have the latest and greatest technology, and "because I want it" often overrules the logic of sound asset investment principles. In summary, organizations need a value-based approach to asset design and investments. Uncoordinated initiatives whether they be technology purchases or busi-

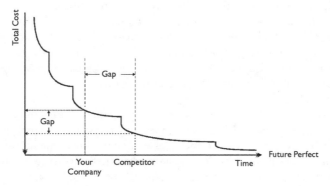

Figure 6.3 - Designed In Competitive Starting Point

ness practice improvements made in a disconnected manner seldom move an organization to the future perfect of the lowest total cost for the unit of value delivered in the marketplace.

Managing the asset lifecycle, done properly, requires combined effort from marketing, sales, engineering, purchasing, and operations. "Done properly" means matching asset capacity, availability, and timing of use to customer orders. What does not doing it properly result in?

- Excess asset investments to meet unrealized demand.
- Excess assets to overcome poor asset availability and quality.
- Lost sales due to unplanned asset downtime.
- Excess maintenance and repair costs associated with unplanned downtime.
- Obsolete assets or assets retired before the end of their useful life as a result of product lifecycle change.
- Extraordinary capital expenditures to move, replace, and overhaul assets to match unplanned capacity shifts.
- Excess MRO inventories.

Executive leadership should be aware of asset disconnects to the value stream so they can be planned for and minimized. Eliminating asset disconnects improves both top and bottom line performance.

Reflect on the Islands of Pain

Most executive forum members agreed that they did not have a cohesive asset management strategy. That *"the asset lifecycle is the least of our worries,"* was the cause of not having a strategy. They intuitively knew that having no strategy drove up costs.

The initial asset lifecycle activities of plan, design, build, acquire, and install are critical to achieving the lowest total cost of ownership for an asset. When these activities are conducted without due consideration being given to the product lifecycle factors and TCO, performance and costs can go awry. Particular attention should be given to this subject when outsourcing asset design, build, and installation to engineering, procurement, and construction (EPC) firms. Potential costly disconnects between EPCs, product lifecycles, and O&M (operations & maintenance) can move your starting point on the future perfect continuum further to the left.

During the initial alignment of the assets to the value stream, costly mistakes are made when one *operates as if all assets are exactly the same.* There must be a clear distinction between revenue producing assets and non-revenue producing assets. Assets that create the unit of value must be given first priority. This first priority means providing the best engineering talent, the best maintenance resources, the best supply chain specialists and the best operators.

Define Value Density Metrics

What should be the common high-level drivers (metrics) for eliminating islands of pain and moving the company toward a future perfect? The value density metrics for connecting the asset to the value stream are as follows:

Fixed asset turnover is the book value of real assets to revenue generated. Book value of real assets excludes current direct material inventories, receivables, cash, and cash equivalents. Real assets, then, consist primarily of structures and equipment. The goal is to maximize revenue produced for per dollar of asset investment.

Using book value of assets has the advantage that the information is easily available from the balance sheet. Therefore fixed asset turnover is a very good internal measure. However, as a comparative measure it is not that effective. Using this measure, organizations with new assets such as in the mobile telecom industry will compare poorly to the rail industry, for example, where most assets have been depreciated.

Industry statistics gathered from the 1997 U.S. Economic Census reveal the asset leverage ratio for the manufacturing sector (shown in Table 6.1.)

1997 U.S. Industry	Value of Shipments ($1,000)	Book Value of Asset ($1,000)	% Asset/Value Shipped	Fixed Asset Turnover
Manufacturing All	$ 3,834,700,920	$ 1,551,319,045	40%	$2.47
Paper	$ 150,295,890	$ 139,378,691	93%	$1.08
Chemical	$ 415,616,508	$ 246,033,140	59%	$1.69
Primary Metals	$ 168,117,728	$ 89,574,167	53%	$1.88
Plastics & Rubber	$ 159,161,346	$ 75,923,401	48%	$2.10
Petro & Coal Products	$ 177,393,098	$ 78,004,070	44%	$2.27
Fabricated Metals	$ 242,813,453	$ 90,925,758	37%	$2.67
Computer & Electronic Products	$ 439,381,300	$ 159,250,346	36%	$2.75
Machinery	$ 270,687,165	$ 83,792,229	31%	$3.23
Transportation Equipment	$ 575,306,996	$ 172,385,913	30%	$3.33
Food	$ 421,737,017	$ 119,140,412	28%	$3.54

Table 6.1 - U.S. Economic Census - Industry Segments

The U.S. Economic Census is taken every five years. Statistics are gathered for the following industry segments and can be found at the following website http://www.census.gov/epcd/www/econ97.html.

Return on assets (ROA) is the measure of earnings to booked value of assets. This metric takes into consideration all operational costs incurred to achieve the current profit level. Why is this metric important? Capital expenditures, maintenance expenditures, MRO supply expenditures, and outsourced services for structure and equipment increase operational costs. Increased cost reduces the return on assets. The higher the return on assets the higher the economic advantage in the market. Companies have become accustomed to fairly stable ROAs accepting annual capital and maintenance budgets as necessary evils. After a period of time the "evil" term is dropped.

Asset-based customer churn rate measures the impact of asset downtime on lost customers. Market studies suggest that continued dissatisfaction results in lost customers. Wisdom suggests that if you do not take care of the customer the competition will. Losing customers to the competition is known affectionately in some industries as a customer churn rate. For example, the automotive industry estimates that losing a customer means losing sales on at least five cars over that customer's lifetime. At $20,000 per car that's $100,000, with no inflation considered. As companies chronically fail to deliver due to poor asset performance, the risk of customer churn goes up.

Value generating asset value to total asset value reveals the percentage of asset investment that is used to create revenue for the organization. Future perfect would point to investing only in assets that create revenue. The goal is reduced investment on owned assets. Rid the company of assets that do not create revenue streams.

Asset contribution margin is the measure of earnings contribution for revenue producing assets. Asset contribution margin can be calculated both annually and over the life of the asset. This metric enables a company to investigate which assets are contributing in what percentages to revenue creation. In the absence of asset operational cost, revenue contributions can be established in terms of absolute monies gained for monies invested. Asset operational costs should be measured using TCO calculations on an annualized basis. Calculated over the life of the asset, a company can analyze shifting ratios of acquisition, possession, and disposal costs.

For example suppose first-year TCO ratios for Asset A are 7% purchase price, 3% acquisition, 85% possession, and 5% disposal and that they amount to total cost of ownership of $300,000 in year 1. Suppose revenue generated by Asset A in year 1 equals $600,000. Asset contribution based on planned production of 4,000 hours is $300,000 ÷ 4,000 hrs = $75/hr.

Now suppose first-year TCO ratios for a similar Asset B are 7% purchase price, 23% acquisition, 65% possession, and 5% disposal. In this case up-front engineering charges associated with early equipment management and product standardization have reduced possession costs. Overall TCO is calculated to be $250,000. Revenue generated by Asset B in year 1 is $600,000. Asset contribution based on planned production of 4,000 hours is $350,000 \div 4,000$ hrs = $87.50/hr. Asset B creates about 16% more contribution than does Asset A.

This metric is not common to industry, but is quite similar to contribution analysis conducted for products. Ultimately this value density metric enables a company to calculate the asset contribution with the goal of maximizing asset availability at the lowest TCO.

Non-revenue generating assets cash outlay ranks non-revenue generating assets according to strategic importance. Then it subsequently compares cash outlays per non-revenue generating asset value.

The goal of this value density metric is to establish spending priorities based on business revenue and cost impact. At 5% net earnings, $1 in savings is equivalent to $20 in revenue. How much money is flowing out of your organization toward non-revenue producing assets?

Asset criticality density ranks the book value of Class 1 revenue producing assets through Class 7 non-revenue producing assets as a percentage of total asset value. The future perfect goal is to invest only in assets that produce that which is consumed in the market. A company should seek to maximize the revenue contribution of Class 1 assets, while minimizing the cost impact of Class 2 through 7 assets.

Asset utilization in a future perfect world would suggest that assets be operated 24/7 during their useful lives and that their outputs be 100% consumed or utilized. This value density metric for revenue producing assets is constrained by two factors. The first is desired production levels required to meet demand requirements. The second is the fact that all physical assets in use wear, fail, and must be maintained. Therefore 100% uptime is usually not physically possible. Thus asset utilization must be balanced with production needs and the need to perform preventive and corrective maintenance.

Process industries often operate 24/7, knowing that asset performance will deteriorate over time to some lower performance limits. Planned plant shutdowns then restore the assets to desired upper performance specifications. Discrete manufacturing industries tend to run assets only when needed to conduct fabrication and assembly operations.

Asset performance efficiency is a metric used to determine if an asset is performing at design or rated operating levels. Performance efficiency is similar to asset utilization in that it is constrained by production needs and the need to perform maintenance. If the asset is part of a continuous or one-piece flow operation, then the asset may be purposefully operated at lower than rated levels to achieve line balancing. Right-sizing assets suggests that assets be sized to desired utilization and performance efficiency levels. Sometimes the largest capacity and fastest rate looks good in theory but results in underutilized assets running at less than optimal rates or overengineered assets that are more costly to maintain for the function supported.

First time through quality is a value density metric that gauges the ability of the asset to produce outputs to desired specifications the first time. Poor maintenance and operating equipment outside its rated parameters, out of specification conditions, and functional failures impact quality levels. One Fortune 500 manufacturing organization attributed 90% of its first time quality levels to poor asset maintenance practices.

Although not always the case, it is critical to know how asset functional failures impact product or service quality levels. When connecting the asset to the value stream, a company must balance utilization with performance efficiency and first time through quality. In Chapter 7 we will combine performance efficiency with first time through quality and asset availability to determine overall equipment effectiveness (OEE). Ultimately OEE is bounded by asset utilization requirements.

Identify Compression Strategies

In an ideal sense, properly connecting assets to the value stream can increase value in two ways. First we would strive for investments in assets that are perfectly synchronized with the production requirements of the market. Then we would invest in assets that would never fail and would always be physically available and capable for duty as required. Compression strategies include:

Target costing. The target costing methodology is a structured approach for establishing maximum product or service costs that can be incurred in the process of delivering these unit of value functional requirements. In the same sense that the target price defines what consumers will pay for a unit of value, the target cost specifies what cost can be incurred while still meeting target earnings goals.

Mathematically, target earnings = target pricing – target costing. In a very real sense this says that, given an earnings expectation and a price the market will tolerate, the organization must find a way to make the unit of value at the target cost. Throughout its lifecycle, as unit of value pricing pressures increase, there will be the need to constantly review and, where practical, reduce target costs to ensure that target earnings goals can be met in the future.

Value stream analysis. What activities and assets do we need to produce the unit of value? Information gained from quality function deployment activities or gained through analysis of existing operations enables us to quickly identify critical assets connected to the value stream. Value stream mapping is a graphic tool that works well in identifying revenue producing assets and their performance characteristics. As shown in Figure 6.4 the value stream map allows quick identification of key asset performance metrics such as availability, first time through quality, and overall equipment effectiveness. In addition, bottleneck operations that can seriously impact revenue creation when the particular assets are unavailable can be identified.

Right-sizing assets. This is an asset design and deployment philosophy. Assets should be designed to meet the value stream objectives of utilization, availability, performance efficiency, and first time through quality. Assets typically must work

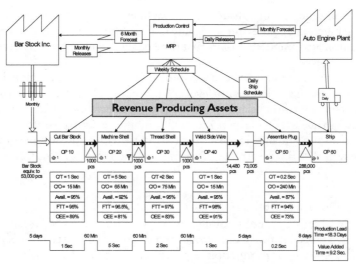

Figure 6.4 - Value Stream Analysis

in coordination with other assets. An analogy is streams that feed into rivers, rivers that feed into seas, and seas that feed into oceans. Water evaporates, clouds form, precipitation occurs, and the water flow begins again. In the end there is balance. Future perfect drives right-sizing assets to achieve synchronous flow among other assets to only produce that which is consumed in the market. Unfortunately our value stream asset design, deployment, and ultimate performance is far behind this future perfect precept.

Contract manufacturing. The need to achieve target costing objectives often requires leveraging another company's assets to provide purchased parts. In-house manufacturing processes often require the ownership of certain assets, which do not generate the desired contribution margin needed to justify their ownership. As an example consider a plastic injection molding machine that is needed only 20 hours per week to meet production volume. Not owning assets is a sure-fire way to reduce asset TCO. Many companies are adopting contract manufacturing models to reduce asset investments while retaining product R&D, brand management, design, sales and market, and distribution channel management.

Leased facilities and other outsourced functions. As we continue our focus on meeting target costing objectives, what do we do with assets that do not directly connect to the value stream? You guessed it. So have many others. If it doesn't make money for us let someone else make money with it. To this end, markets have continued to grow in outsourced property management, warehouse management, fleet management, logistics management, and MRO inventory management.

Many companies believe that they manage non-revenue generating assets better than outsourced asset service providers and, frankly, some do. This has resulted in companies turning what was previously operated as a cost center into a profit center and offering those services to the market. This movement comes primarily from large manufacturing concerns that conduct warehouse management, flow through facilities, and fleet management services for a group of manufacturers. This scheme reduces the cost of non-revenue producing assets across multiple entities.

Asset criticality classification. This is a compression strategy that provides a clear priority scheme for failure management actions based on asset criticality classification described previously in this chapter. The asset criticality classification emphasizes that all assets are not equal. Operating under the scarcity rule of "do not spend money if you do not absolutely have to," maintenance and supply resources must be applied first and foremost to Class 1 revenue producing assets. All other asset demands are responded to according to the relative importance of their impact on Class 1 assets. Notwithstanding safety, health, environmental, and catastrophic failures, the asset criticality provides the general guidelines to maximize asset availability and minimize asset support costs.

All organizations have Class 1 assets. But not all Class 1 assets command equal response urgency. Constraining operations typically are classified 1A assets. When these assets go down more than likely so does revenue. Revenue impact is dependent on the current capacity utilization of the Class 1 asset relative to the production schedule demands placed on it. This leads to further distinction of the Class 1 asset relative to its impact on revenue based on unplanned downtime.

Class 1B assets can be defined as those where unplanned downtime of four hours or less has no effect on revenue. Unplanned downtime is mitigated because the Class 1B asset is simply producing inventory, a redundant system takes over during unplanned downtime, or scheduling flexibility exists where no harm occurs. 1C assets simply extend the time frame to eight hours or one production shift. 1D assets should be reviewed for their usage if greater than eight hours of unplanned downtime can occur and no financial impact is felt by the organization.

The asset criticality classification should be performed to facilitate comparing statistics such as current maintenance costs per asset criticality class, current MRO inventory investments per asset criticality class, and current asset ownership cost per asset criticality class.

Availability modeling. Organizations analyze the demand requirements of critical assets to determine their required availability. 24 x 365 asset requirements exist within the public utility industry where uninterrupted services of electric power, gas, and water are necessary. For assets that aren't required to operate continuously, availability requirements would be a function of scheduled and unscheduled need. For redundant systems, availability is required during a functional failure of the primary asset. An example of availability target is 90:7:3, indicating 90% availability 7% planned downtime, and 3% unplanned downtime.

Availability modeling challenges organizations to understand "asset connectivity." Modeling these connections using simulation applications provides useful insight into asset dependency. Availability model results then become the performance target for the specific assets.

When modeling asset availability it is important to understand all reasons for or causes of asset downtime. With no redundant systems in play, asset availability is a function of reliability and maintainability. Often maintainability is cited as having the bigger impact on asset availability.

Develop Case Study Examples

Paul's executive forum teams were challenged by the future perfect precept of investing only in assets that produce only what is consumed in the market. They had not viewed their asset investments through this type of lens before. They did not have clear separation in their accounting practices to fully isolate revenue and non-revenue producing assets. Connecting the assets to the value stream was not as obvious as it sounded. As is often the case, they found the simplest questions are often the hardest to answer.

Superior Water

Superior Water has a network of over 7,500 miles of high pressure water mains with 2.7 million joints and connections. With 745,000 service connections Superior Water has significant impact on the quality of life of its 2 million customers, working across an area of 3,000 square miles.

The primary revenue generating assets of Superior Water's distribution division include pipelines, pumping stations, and meters. Primary non-revenue creating assets include service vehicles, office buildings, depots, and warehousing facilities. The book value of their assets is $174 million. With revenues of $150 million, the resultant fixed asset turnover is $0.86. New assets were being added daily through new service connections to commercial and consumer accounts.

Superior Water's water network assets are vital to the safety, stability, and growth of the communities it supplies. Revenues are impacted if the customer does not use or does not receive water. The executive forum team was amused at the company's efforts to educate the public about water conservation, knowing that this impacted the revenue stream. Given that people could not live without water, the goal was to provide this water at a reasonable rate such that the value was realized for both the consuming public and Superior Water. Price regulation meant that Superior Water was under constant pressure to reduce their cost of operations.

Often their assets did not help them achieve this low-cost position. Leakages resulted in lost revenues and delayed expansion opportunities, as the government regulator would not approve line extensions if leakage rates and water quality levels did not meet acceptable standards. The executive team reviewed the forecast of network expansion activities and determined that the highest payback for a

Strategic MRO initiative was not new revenue creation through leak reduction or improved water quality, but through reducing the cost to maintain existing assets. They had to find a way to cost-effectively service their existing asset structure and to replace those sections of the water network incurring high maintenance costs. The replacement plan construction costs had to be offset by a lower total cost of ownership.

Superior Water Compression Strategies

Target costing analysis. The Superior Water team recommended conducting a target costing analysis of its new line extensions and line replacements. Target costing models would provide a detailed view of the functional costs to deliver an uninterrupted source of water, desired flow rates, desired quality level, and accurate metering capabilities. The financial goal would be to drive future operational costs to a minimum through design changes, standardization of assets, process improvements, and contractor management. Target costing data would be composed of a mixture of newly gathered data and data from the company's past activity-based costing efforts.

EuroCar

The EuroCar team knew that the use of its assets represented its competitive advantage. A passerby would never suspect the level of asset sophistication that went into the fabrication and build of a finished vehicle. They would simply observe a steady stream of high-quality vehicles rolling off the assembly line destined for the dealerships or someone's home.

Over the last 20 years, the automotive market has refined manufacturing practices and expanded the limits of technology capabilities. Early cost accounting logic dictated that machine utilization was the true measure of efficiency and competitiveness. This logic would be sound if the consuming public bought every vehicle produced. The push mentality has long sense been challenged as both inefficient and wasteful. Today's pull systems are constrained by market consumption patterns. "Produce only that which is consumed in the market" is the driving force for EuroCar. This requires EuroCar to run multiple models of vehicles across the same assets. These assets must be able to quickly change over with minimum unplanned downtime, as each hour of downtime represents approximately $1.2 million in missed revenue generation.

Most of EuroCar's assets are revenue producing. Yet not all revenue producing assets are equally important. Operations and production planning knew the throughput (units of production per minute) of each operation. Their target line rate was 52 cars per hour. Some operations easily performed at this rate, others struggled. The ones that struggled affected the overall throughput of the assembly line. If the assets used in these constraining operations went down, everything stopped.

Two operations in the body shop and the paint shop were clearly constraining. The body shop consisted of several welding operations. Painting required micro-dusting of the body, priming, and finished coating. The EuroCar team agreed that if they could take all of their maintenance personnel and focus them on these two operations higher value would be realized.

EuroCar Compression Strategies

Asset criticality classification. EuroCar aligned with the seven classes of asset criticality presented by the facilitators. However, they felt that Class 1 assets needed to be further categorized by their impact on production objectives. Assembly line assets would be given the highest priority. Assets that produced parts to inventory would be given a lesser priority. 1A assets would be used to designate constraining operations where no downtime was acceptable, 1B assets were those where less than 4 hours of downtime was tolerable, and 1C assets were those where less than 8 hours of downtime was tolerable.

The EuroCar team believed that classifying assets would help set up the overall priority scheme for service response and inventory stocking practices. Nearly ten years ago they had moved to a process orientation as part of their "lean manufacturing" based production system. Their version of total productive maintenance focused on elimination of all unplanned downtime yet it did not provide guidance on establishing asset priority according to its impact on the revenue stream.

Everyone easily understood this new classification scheme. Everyone agreed that focusing on revenue producing assets was most important. The result sought was more efficient scheduling of resources based on asset priorities. With an emphasis on 5% cost reduction per year, this new focus on the value stream assets would create the costs savings desired. Plant leadership was pleased with the new focus.

Value stream analysis. The EuroCar team recognized the power of value stream analysis to aid in asset criticality classification. A value stream map was constructed showing the flow of operations from inbound components to the finished assembly. Data was collected regarding asset availability, first time through quality, and performance efficiency of the assets in the value stream. All constraining operations were clearly marked with a funnel symbol. Inventory stocking levels and locations were identified. Class 1A, B, C, and D labels were placed directly on the value stream maps created during the analysis.

Availability analysis. The EuroCar team completed its value stream analysis and then decided it needed to conduct an asset availability analysis to determine their targets. Not all assets needed to be available 100% of the time to meet production schedules. This provided confidence to the maintenance staff that through planning they had a shot at improving asset uptime during scheduled usage.

MobileTel

MobileTel requires a sizable infrastructure to handle nearly 1,550,000 hours of communication services every week. With approximately 42,000 geographically dispersed GSM (Global System for Mobile Communication) elements, revenue generation depends primarily on the elements' location, availability, and reliability. MobileTel's planned introduction of UMTS (Universal Mobile Telecommunications System) technology will dramatically increase the number of network elements. This increase is expected to be nearly 20% each year to a forecasted total of 120,000 elements. Elements are classified as A, B, or C depending on utilization. Class A elements experience utilization in excess of 85%; C elements less than 35%; and the rest are classified as Bs.

MobileTel had designed redundancy into their system, such that three elements supported each other in a single cell configuration. Theoretically, when one element went down, other elements picked up the transmission with no interruption of services. With greater than 30% of its revenue coming from transmissions going through A elements, the performance of A elements should have been the primary focus of MobileTel. But because A elements were already more than 85% utilized, when these elements went down there was no excess capacity to go to. Thus revenue went down as well.

Almost as an afterthought the MobileTel team recognized that they owned significant non-revenue producing assets including office buildings, service warehouses, and nearly 850 service vehicles. The cost of these assets was and is significant.

MobileTel Compression Strategies

Customer churn rate analysis. The MobileTel team was sensitive to an industry pattern of frequent customer turnover. Attractive incentive packages that included free mobile phones, no annual contracts, and discounted rates for peak periods during the first six months meant that some customer accounts could take a year to become profitable.

Churn rate was the industry jargon for losing customers to the competition. Churn was experienced from customers who frequently made long distance calls and conducted heavy data transmission as part of their business operations. MobileTel marketing estimated that these customers were contributing more than average to the revenue and were more likely to switch carriers if they experienced chronic problems. Because most of these customers were located in areas covered by A network elements they clearly felt the effects of the 30% downtime being experienced; 30% of 1.2 million hours is not insignificant.

MobileTel's research of international benchmarks established by customer satisfaction surveys indicated that 15% of customers that experienced bad service would switch providers. Based on the 1999 revenue of $4.8 billion, 30% downtime, 50% contribution to revenue and 15% churn, a potential $216 million of revenue was at risk because of downtime on A class network elements alone. Of all the teams present at the executive forum, MobileTel was the only one to connect asset availability to directly losing a customer. The message was powerful.

Asset criticality classification. Like EuroCar, the MobileTel team recognized that Class 1 revenue producing assets had different levels of importance. Thus their use of the A, B, and C element subclassifications for level 1 assets. The team recommended that the existing classification be combined with the seven asset criticality classifications to create a total asset stratification model. Expansion plans meant that more Class 1 assets would be added. The goal was to not grow a disproportionate amount of Class 2 through 7 assets in response.

MilBase Ops

MilBase Ops owns, operates, maintains, builds, restores, and protects military facilities and infrastructure. Their goal is effective mission performance at the lowest asset life cycle cost while housing, training, and equipping defense forces for potential deployment. MilBase Ops are stewards of the real property required to sustain national defense force readiness. With more than 500 square miles of land ranges, living quarters, and facilities, MilBase Ops has a set of highly geographically dispersed assets. Replacement cost for base assets has been estimated at $1.5 billion.

In connecting the assets to the value stream, MilBase Ops has defined two core missions that it must support. The prime mission is national defense. Tanks, armored personnel carriers, planes, helicopters, trucks, and all-terrain vehicles are examples of the national defense assets. In the commercial sector these assets would be defined as the revenue producing assets. In the defense sector they are called mission critical assets. Without these assets national defense would not exist.

In order to ensure defense readiness, combat personnel must be housed, trained, fed, medically supported, and transported. Administrative and operational personnel who have similar needs support combat personnel. Other resources requiring support are combat and noncombat personnel families, civilians employed to operate base businesses and provide needed services. Thus the second mission of MilBase Ops is to provide services necessary to secure combat readiness for combat personnel and provide for the personnel welfare of all other base resources and families. The assets required to achieve this second mission would be considered non-revenue producing assets in the private sector. They are called non-mission critical in the defense sector.

The MilBase Ops team was somewhat distressed by the classification of their assets as non-mission critical. But they did agree that an asset classification ranging from mission critical to non-mission critical made sense. They also agreed that first priority should be given to mission critical assets. As base caretakers they knew their assets did not warrant the same type of priority and funding as mission critical assets. Their support operation was rightfully perceived as a cost center. The less cost the better.

Command directives were clear. MilBase Ops must reduce operational costs by no less than 20% over the next three years while simultaneously improving base readiness and service levels. This would be no small feat and it would bring tremendous career consequences for those in charge.

The executive forum team struggled to develop an appropriate value density metric for MilBase Ops. Future perfect would suggest to only invest in assets that enable an organization to produce its unit of value. In this case, the unit of value was determined to be national defense. Therefore the financial or funding impact of non-mission critical assets must be minimized to achieve a future perfect goal of zero expenditure for non-mission critical assets. The executive forum team decided to use mission critical expenditures divided by all expenditures as the value density metric for MilBase Ops.

MilBase Ops Compression Strategies

Asset criticality classification. The MilBase Ops team believed that there was little or no flexibility in redeploying assets elsewhere or outsourcing assets, both real options available to the private sector. Their real goal was to begin a focused effort to streamline Strategic MRO labor, material, and equipment costs, while extending asset life. To establish a clear path forward the team recommended that assets be classified according to the seven categories recommended by their Strategic MRO facilitator.

Classification would define the priority of their mission objectives and tasks. This became quite a sensitive subject to the team members. The seven classes of assets seemed to be driven by revenue, which was mission critical to a private sector company, but not to the military.

Mission critical Class 1 assets were clearly the tanks, planes, and other combat equipment. They did have revenue producing assets such as such as base exchanges (stores) but clearly, these were not as critical as defense assets. Some team members argued that base exchanges were quality of life assets and belonged in Class 7 for all bases except remote bases where goods could only be gotten from one source.

Class 2 assets would have been fueling stations for both diesel and jet fuel. But how would they classify public utility power sources that were maintained through the use of local utility service personnel? The team agreed that lack of public utility based power would shut down much of the base's operations and computer systems, thus making it no less than a Class 3 asset.

Mission critical information systems that defense resources used while stationed at their base were designated Class 3. They had plenty of service vehicles, trucks, backhoes, and other equipment that they used to perform repairs to base assets and infrastructure. These were definitely Class 4.

The team struggled with placing service vehicles ahead of the buildings that protected assets and military and civilian personnel, which were Class 5 assets by the model's definition. But their facilitator informed them that just as assets are not all the same, neither are the functional failures. The facilitator assured them that further classification by failure would occur under the next principle of connecting demand to the asset. The team quickly understood that the combination of asset proximity and functional failure criticality would dictate service responses.

By continuing their categorization of assets, the MilBase Ops team recognized that they were establishing a practical classification of infrastructure that could be easily understood by all. Once understood the improvement process could begin in earnest.

Telephone systems were also a tough call for the team. They decided that these were a Class 3 asset. However, base pay phones were Class 6 assets. All agreed that the least of their worries were soda machines. These were clearly Class 7 assets. They were filled daily and the machine owners performed maintenance.

At the end of the exercise the MilBase Ops team recognized that they didn't have clear definitions on the priorities of assets relative to their mission. Because of this, they wondered just how much budget money they had appropriated to take care of Class 5 through 7 assets. The team was determined to find out.

TL Freight

The freight industry understands that higher rates of asset utilization win. Lane density is critical, and empty trailers or tractors without trailers mean no revenue is being generated. Unplanned asset downtime is critical if the tractor is under load. This delays the shipment and delays the opportunity to use the same asset for other customer orders.

To meet market demands TL Freight has invested in 32,000 trailers for hauling bulk materials, frozen goods, paper and paper products, and consumer products. Trailers are the revenue producing asset. However revenue is not generated unless the trailer moves under load from a source to a destination. Powering this movement are 7,500 TL Freight owned and operated tractors. An additional 2,500 carrier partners own and operate tractors. Other sources of trailer power are rail, air, and cargo ships.

To match its capacity and the capacity of its carrier partners to the customer needs, TL Freight uses complex scheduling algorithms automated through software. Planned maintenance, DOT inspections, and unplanned downtime must be accounted for in capacity planning. To overcome downtime associated with maintenance, TL Freight readily acknowledges that it must own an additional 150 tractors. In addition to the cost of these additional tractors, TL Freight has calculated that unplanned asset downtime has a potential revenue impact of nearly $36 million annually.

Non-revenue producing assets include 9 operating centers and 15 operating points offering fuel, maintenance, and driver support. TL Freight strategic plans include converting these into revenue producing assets by providing fee-based services to its carrier partners. It headquarters building is owned by TL Freight whereas its regional offices are leased facilities.

TL Freight Compression Strategies

Asset location tracking. Unlike the rest of the executive forum teams, TL Freight's assets moved. Their first priority was having information that instantaneously located assets such that asset shipment progress could be tracked and expedited, future loads planned, and maintenance scheduled. To accomplish this the TL Freight team decided to install a two-way satellite communications and tracking system. This was a significant investment that ultimately would be leveraged to improve efficiencies of its maintenance activities.

Asset criticality classification. It was clear that trailers were Class 1 assets. What was not clear was why tractors were Class 2 assets. By definition Class 2 consists of assets required to ensure that revenue producing assets are powered. Tractors power trailers. But so do railcars, ships, and planes. The highest priority had to be given to the functionality of the trailer. If it leaked, allowed for contamination, was immoveable, was unsafe or environmentally hazardous, revenue was severely impacted. TL Freight had not calculated how many additional trailers they had in inventory because of poor asset reliability. It never occurred to them. Their predominant focus was tractor performance. Now they realized that the Class 1 asset, the trailer, had to be in a certifiable operating condition first.

Define the Management Strategy

All of the teams felt that starting with an inventory of current assets was the best place to start. The seven asset criticality classes would categorize the assets. Book value, replacement value, revenue, and cost estimates would then be calculated per category. Incremental units of value would be identified for revenue producing assets with incremental contribution margins being generated by asset. Utilization, availability, performance efficiency, and first time through quality would be calculated for revenue producing assets.

The goal is to produce the ultimate unit of value at the lowest total cost. Beginning with non-revenue generating assets, the organizations' CEOs will challenge their financial staffs to determine if they should be in the asset owning business. Or does it make sense to lease them? Leasing may or not be inclusive of asset maintenance.

For revenue producing assets the teams recommended a thorough review of asset utilization and availability requirements using value stream analysis. Results of this analysis would drive make versus buy and asset right-sizing initiatives.

Paul's Reflections

Paul was fearful that the teams would feel like they were being sold another set of buzzwords…define the value stream…connect the asset to the value stream. But his fear was soon dispelled by the open and honest discussions each of the five teams was having. There was no need for false bravado among the members of the executive forum.

Until we reach future perfect, assets will be required to deliver units of value to the market. What Paul needed to know was simple. Was his executive team capable of making asset investment decisions that would move them toward the lowest total costs? Could they quantify the earnings contribution that revenue producing assets delivered? Had they established any investment and cost control strategies for non-revenue producing assets? The consistent answer was no, quickly followed by a "so what?" Often the egos of his staff got in the way of these straightforward notions. "We know this stuff already," they would tell him. But did they understand what to do with this knowledge?

Paul was tired of all the excuses his staff had given him. It was clear to him that his chemical company had wasted money on assets that met minor production capacity or specification needs. It was clear to him that the 83% availability of the bottleneck operation was simply accepted as the best it could be. It was also clear to Paul that, in many cases such as dust collection systems, drainage systems, and office renovations, costly overspecification based on some notion of improved performance with no hard data to support such claims had taken place.

Listening to the discussions of the teams inspired him to figure out what the next logical step in bolstering his lackluster return on assets would be. If, as was discussed, all assets are not the same, why was he spending vital dollars and resource time as if they were? He believed that the Demand Supply Compression guiding principle of connecting demand to the asset would provide additional insight.

Chapter 7

Connect Demand to the Asset

Executive Summary: If all assets are not equal then all failures are not equal. As an organization attempts to prevent or react to asset failures, demands are created. The principle of connecting demand to the asset should drive the organization to perform three core activities with extreme diligence. First: identify all assets by their criticality (asset criticality classification). Second: proactively identify deterioration or other factors that will likely lead to functional failures of critical assets (demand criticality clasification). Third: reactively capture functional failures, their causes, and solutions to inform clear decisions on whether to pursue cost-effective proactive strategies or continue cost-effective reactive strategies (demand response strategies).

P aul's leadership team had become leery of attending an operations meeting right after their fearless leader had attended another executive forum. They expected to receive news clippings, white papers, and websites to visit to so that they could become more informed on new business strategies. This meeting was slightly different in that Paul handed his leadership team notes from the EuroCar, MobileTel, MilBase Ops, Superior Water, and TL Freight case studies. Immediately the Strategic MRO initiative took on a different feel. Gone were the standard discussions on improving machine availability through improved maintenance. Now it was back to business basics. Paul was on a mission and his staff knew it. It was no longer business as usual.

The only normal aspects to this Monday's operational meeting were the financial and plant performance review. The leadership team sensed that Paul's initial confusion on what to do to improve earnings was replaced with a laser-like focus. He had a new perspective on company assets and his vision had sharpened. Paul discussed with his staff the fundamental difference between revenue and non-revenue producing assets. He challenged them to think about how much money they had invested in both types of assets. Then he cut to the chase. He mandated that all assets be classified by their impact on revenue creation. He explained to them that this was called an asset criticality classification. The discussion became quite lively as Paul reviewed the seven classes of assets used in the classification.

"Now," said Paul, "we need to know where we are spending our money by asset criticality. We need to understand asset utilization for Class 1 assets. We need to measure availability for all Class 1 through 4 assets." He reminded everyone that Class 1 through 4 represented revenue producing assets. "We need to..." and the list went on.

His staff was reeling from Paul's unending flow of consciousness. It was clear that, from this moment forward, all asset investments, improvement efforts, money, and resources would be required to have a singular focus on improving company earnings while providing a safe and conducive work environment for company associates. The priority of efforts would begin with an all-out effort to ensure revenue producing assets were available when needed, producing 100% quality product, operating at desired performance levels, and doing so at the lowest possible total cost of ownership. Non-revenue producing assets would be reviewed for cost minimization. If this meant leasing facilities, outsourcing facility management, standardizing on office equipment, and consolidating service agreements, then so be it. This new approach would allow Paul to manage assets as if they were separate portfolios.

The Strategic MRO journey had begun. Paul's staff worked diligently and with a renewed purpose. Paul looked forward to the next executive forum meeting. In that meeting they would be discussing the next DSC guiding principle of connecting demand to the asset. The members of Paul's staff, on the other hand, were not so sure they looked forward to Paul's attending that next meeting. He brought back so many new ideas that it made their collective heads hurt. But his staff grudgingly accepted the fact that these new ideas made sense. And the ideas were helping them focus their efforts to improve the company.

Review Guiding Principle #3: Connect Demand to the Asset

The executive forum met to discuss the third DSC principle: *connect demand to the asset.* This principle focuses the organization's efforts on the prevention, detection, and correction of asset failures that create demand. At the center of this guiding principle is the asset. The asset, a potential combination of physical components, control systems, power supplies, fluid mixtures, and the like, when connected with other assets enables the value stream to produce the desired unit of value. Certainly failure occurs at the component level, but the consequences are at the asset level. Asset performance impacts the effectiveness of the value stream.

What constitutes an asset failure? An asset failure has occurred any time an asset fails to perform to design intent. Failure detection, then, requires analysis of two components: design intent and a measurable indicator of performance. This definition of an asset failure reshapes current definitions and emphasizes the need for design intent specifications to be considered in developing asset performance metrics.

When does an asset failure create a demand? A demand is created when the asset owner determines that preventive or corrective actions must be taken to mitigate the loss of critical asset functions. Asset owner expectations can vary considerably from the design intent of the asset. Thus the interminable argument: If the asset is not running to our expectations is it a design issue or is corrective action needed?

Does deterioration constitute failure? Not necessarily. Assets tend to operate within a range of acceptable performance. Deterioration occurring within this range does not constitute a failure. All assets experience deterioration throughout their useful lives. This deterioration may decrease performance but until performance drops below some specified level, no failure has occurred. Natural deterioration does not necessarily constitute a design failure, a functional failure, or create a demand. When natural deterioration proceeds to a point that performance diminishes beyond acceptable levels then a functional failure is said to have occurred.

What do functional failures creating a reactive demand look like? They include:

- Spillage creating an unsafe working condition.
- A gas leak creating a catastrophic failure such as an explosion.
- A stoppage resulting from component failure.

What does proactive demand management look like? It includes:

- Routine inspections for loose bolts, worn components, lubrication condition, and others.
- Routine maintenance and replacement based on time. For example, replacement of filters every 6 months.
- Overhauls to bring the asset back to its "as new" performance levels.

Functional failures occur with and without warnings. Some are immediately obvious, others take hours, days, or weeks to discover.

Is response to demand always reactive? Yes, sort of. In theory, even proactive maintenance is reactive. In a proactive maintenance environment preemptive tasks are conducted because of past failure experiences or some statistical prediction thereof; therefore we are reacting to past bad experiences. The practitioner, however, views demand relative to the occurrence of the functional failure. Proactive maintenance is ahead of and reactive maintenance is after the functional failure occurrence.

Adherence to the principle of connecting demand to the asset allows for the prioritization of maintenance and improvement efforts designed to reduce demand costs per asset. Asset criticality classification used along with demand criticality classification helps guide the setting of failure management priorities within the organization. The future perfect goal is elimination of asset demand and related supply cost.

Review Future Perfect Precept

Connecting demand to the asset guides our thinking as we progress toward the future perfect objective to invest only in assets that never fail over their useful life. Specifically, the future perfect objective is to *prevent or eliminate all failures that create a demand*. Asset demand future perfect has several dimensions.

Asset lifecycle. When connecting the asset to the value stream the useful life of the asset might match perfectly with the product lifecycle as shown in Figure 7.1. In this scenario, as the product life ends, the asset is used up and can be disposed of where it will indeed return to mother earth, from whence it came.

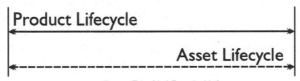

Figure 7.1 - PLC Equals ALC

Some suggest that the asset lifecycle should far exceed the product lifecycle as indicated in Figure 7.2. The asset should be used and reused until it is physically unable to function at a reasonable cost to the owner. At such time it is sold as used equipment or scrapped.

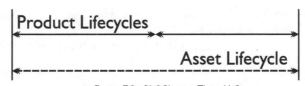

Figure 7.2 - PLC Shorter Than ALC

Failure occurs at the component level but the impact is felt at the asset level. Future perfect suggests the there should be perfect alignment of the product lifecycle and the asset lifecycle because this alignment may have the highest probability of not incurring component failure during the asset lifecycle as shown in Figure 7.3.

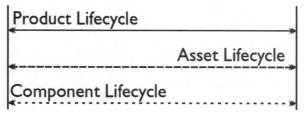

Figure 7.3 - PLC Equals ALC Equals CLC

Asset owner repair psychology varies according the intended useful life of the asset. If the asset useful life is long, the asset owner reasonably assumes that repair and component replacement will be inevitable. The asset owner takes measures to improve reliability to mitigate future downtime and repair costs. On the other hand, if the intended useful life is short, the asset owner expects to dispose of, exchange, or replace the asset. In either case there are significant costs incurred if the asset life is considerably less than intended.

In reality there is seldom a perfect alignment of product lifecycles, asset lifecycles, and component lifecycles. Most organizations do not attempt to understand or synchronize these cycles. It could easily be surmised that component lifecycles would be the shortest of the three but this is not always the case as shown in Figure 7.4.

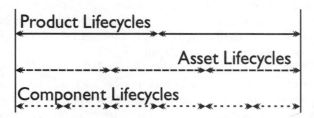

Figure 7.4 - PLC, ALC, and CLC Unequal

Perhaps the biggest contributing factor to these cycles getting out of sync is planned obsolescence. Today's societies have been conditioned to replace perfectly acceptable products with those that are newer, quicker, prettier, have more functions, or that are "guaranteed" to produce better products. This same phenomenon also occurs within the world of production and support assets. The availability of new technology offerings in the market is almost impossible to resist. Often planned and unplanned obsolescence leaves storerooms full of old parts and challenges maintenance resources to quickly unlearn old systems and learn new ones.

Asset reliability. When connecting assets to the value stream, the goal is to improve asset availability. Connecting demand to the asset seeks to improve asset reliability. Reliability is defined as the extent to which an asset yields the same results repeatedly over its useful life without interruptions. As asset reliability improves, availability improves. For revenue producing assets this means more trade potential. For all assets improved reliability drives possession cost down.

A broader industry perspective reveals significant progress has and continues to be made toward zero asset and component failure over their planned useful lives. Robust designs enable like assets to operate under a wide variety of operational conditions. Where environmental conditions dramatically impact asset reliability, controlled environments are being designed and installed. New materials, improved system designs, technology breakthroughs, error-proofed designs, and improved operator and maintenance resource skills all have extended component and asset life.

If desired asset reliability cannot be obtained then critical Class 1 through 4 (revenue producing) assets are reviewed for inclusion of redundant or backup systems to ensure uninterruptible operations. Similar redundant designs are performed for non-revenue producing assets but for a different reason. The prime driver for non-revenue producing assets is to reduce the total cost of ownership. Therefore design redundancies such as a light bank holding two lights allow one to fail without stopping operations. Subsequently the failed light replacement is scheduled based on resource availability, other tasks needing to be done in close proximity, and availability of supply.

Predicting demand. Future perfect strives for zero failure, yet failure is expected. Achieving future perfect requires understanding the phenomena of failure such that we can predict it, design it out, instantaneously recognize it when it occurs, instantaneously diagnose the cause, instantaneously restore the asset, and ultimately prevent it from happening again.

What a future, where failures are predictable and all causes of failure are eliminated! A future where all basic machine conditions such as cleanliness are always adhered to would be included in this notion of perfect. Also included are asset designs that match performance expectations, assets that are operated to design specifications, and environmental conditions that actually promote good asset health and well-being. The world in which we exist does not fully cooperate with the notion of future perfect.

Many studies have been conducted using techniques such as Weibull analysis, fault tree analysis (FTA), failure mode and effects analysis (FMEA), materials analysis, and process simulations to understand the failure phenomena. The component failure rate curve for a component's lifecycle shown in Figure 7.5 is known as a Bathtub Curve.

The Bathtub Curve demonstrates a phenomenon known as infant mortality. This is where a component exhibits a high rate of failure during the early stages of its life. To help ensure that such component failures are detected early, asset makers often subject components to a burn-in period where assets are exposed to power and environmental conditions over time. Component failure rates gradually decrease over time until a constant failure rate is attained. Eventually, the component enters the wear-out period of its life where failures increase dramatically.

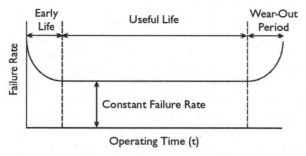

Figure 7.5 - Component Failure Rate - Bathtub Curve

Experts suggest that no fewer than six distinct failure patterns exist. The Bathtub Curve is but one of them. Examples of others include failure patterns where no infant mortality is present and those where no wear-out period is ever reached. Still other failure patterns include those where there is a steady, ever-increasing probability of failure the longer an asset is in use. And there are patterns where a gradual increase in failures is expected until a steady state is reached. Sometimes failure patterns vary considerably for the same materials, components, and assets depending on the context or environment in which they are functioning.

In addition to varying failure patterns, failure analysis studies from statistically significant populations sometimes challenge the rules of thumb about wear out. Wear out is the notion that every component has a finite acceptable performance level before deterioration creates a failure mode. Because many components never reached wear out during studies, the deterioration phenomena hypothesized can not be proven. What's an asset owner to do? Run to failure is one option that may or may not be appropriate.

In a future perfect world the asset owner is on a never-ending quest to understand the peculiarities of his or her assets within the context of the operating environment. Unfortunately many of the tools used to understand failure are perceived as time consuming, difficult to understand, and resource draining. So reacting to failure seems to be a lower cost alternative compared to investing in the resources and time needed to achieve improvement.

Asset configuration. Future perfect would also suggest that all like assets have like demand requirements. However, as assets are repaired and replaced, multiple asset structures or configurations begin emerging. If these asset structures become too varied and complex, operational costs increase. Operational cost increase is inevitable given the varying asset demand requirements.

Imagine if you will, the impact of running multiple computer operating systems such as DOS, Windows 3.11, Windows 98, Windows 2000, Windows NT, Windows XP, Unix, and Linux. What would the IT staff have to look like in both skill requirements and size? It could easily be 25% to 50% larger than need be. This is the impact of not achieving a future perfect state where all asset structures are the same.

Determine Organizational Impact

In a market-driven company it is clear that when a consumer consumes, demand is created. Defining the value stream and tying the asset to it enables the company to satisfy marketplace demands. Connecting demand to the asset has a completely different demand connotation to an organization. Simply put, when an asset consumes an expense is created. The organization pays for resources to inspect, adjust, repair, overhaul, replace, and dispose of assets. Most organizations experience asset demand costs well into the millions of dollars.

Demand management for the organization's unit of value means understanding the consumption patterns of product and services in the marketplace. Production processes are designed to produce and deliver products such that market demand can be met, no more, no less. The same concept applies to asset demand management. It is important to understand the consumption patterns of the assets so that these demands can be met. The one caveat of asset demand management: What we really want is for the demand to disappear!

Asset demands can be responded to both tactically and strategically. Tactically the organization employs resources, purchases parts, and utilizes special equipment to execute maintenance practices. Tactical maintenance is reactive in nature requiring good maintenance management *after* asset acquisition. Even proactive maintenance is reactive in response to the demand characteristics of the acquired asset. If an organization stays in the tactical mode it will miss the opportunity to plan for successful deployment of *lower demand* assets in the future. This planning for future asset deployment is the strategic response to asset demands.

What does strategic asset deployment look like? It includes assets designed with past failures in mind, assets designed to minimize maintenance support requirements, right-sizing assets to projected market demand, asset designs enabling quick service, and standardization of assets and components to achieve the lowest total cost of ownership. This list makes sense when you view asset demands strategically. Strategic MRO requires leadership vision. Strategic MRO also requires good maintenance management. Together they help create the absolute advantage a company seeks in the marketplace.

Organizational leadership and resources responsible for asset readiness must understand that assets create the demand, not people. When a person says a bearing or a drive belt is needed, what is really being said is that the asset needs these parts to perform to expectations. Organizations need to continuously challenge engineering and maintenance resources on their interpretation of asset needs.

Not knowing the asset, what performance is expected from it, how it functions, how it could and has failed, and what the consequences of these failures are can be quite expensive to an organization. With this knowledge a demand criticality classification can be structured. Using the demand criticality classification along with the asset criticality classification, the organization can begin to develop its asset failure management strategy.

What is the impact of not having an asset failure management strategy? Conservative estimates are:

- 10% of yearly capital budget spent on the unnecessary replacement of assets due to premature failure.
- 25% of maintenance labor overtime due to responding to less critical demands during normal work hours and thus displacing work on higher criticality assets.
- 30% excess MRO inventory due to fundamental lack of understanding of asset consumption patterns.
- 10% additional inventory because of lack of asset standards and no guidance on planned obsolescence decision making.
- 50% of improvement dollars spent to find solutions to poor asset designs that create excessive functional failures.

The future perfect objective is to invest only in assets that never fail over their useful life. If the asset never fails, no demand is created. No demand means no supply costs. The lesson is simple in theory but more difficult to implement.

Reflect on the Islands of Pain

The facilitators at Paul's executive forum reminded the teams that it was time to reflect on the islands of pain. The teams had come to enjoy this portion of the session because they had started to believe they could do something about the pains that plagued them daily.

The teams began by reviewing the pains associated with the *lowest acquisition cost wins out over the lowest total cost of ownership (TCO)*. They now understood how buying the cheapest or the newest asset, if not carefully balanced with goal of mitigating asset demand, leads to increased operational costs.

The forum teams quickly moved on to reemphasizing the notion that as *assets are not equal, neither are asset failures.* One team member shook his head as he recalled his last motivational speech to his maintenance staff… "Fix everything, fix it now, everything is important," and how this "go get them" mentality would improve relationships between the plant floor and maintenance. He now realized how this emotional pitch worked counter to his need to keep critical assets in play and manage the rest from a cost-benefit perspective. For example, the clear possibility existed of much-needed critical assets having to wait for resources working on less critical assets, resulting in a deterioration in the relationships between the plant floor and maintenance.

The teams began to appreciate the need to know their assets and their operating environment. How could they expect the *asset makers (OEM) to fully understand and predict equipment failure rates and spare parts requirements?* They also realized that *two assets are not necessarily better than one.*

Future perfect discussions made the need clear to invest only in assets that produce what is consumed in the market, thus requiring assets to be right-sized to the demand. They also realized that assets right-sized to meet demand made it that much more critical for Class 1 revenue producing assets to be available. Finally the teams noted that if strategies for failure prevention cannot be utilized then the cost of redundancy is usually less than the penalties of lost asset availability.

"*Who needs standards? All commodity MRO products perform the same,*" quickly started a discussion on the cost of not having standards and the fact that many components have varying demand profiles thus requiring different supply response. Lack of standards and lack of control over planned obsolescence is why many companies have ten or more computer operating systems instead of one.

Last, the executive forum teams summarized the need to have a clear strategy for proactive versus reactive maintenance based on asset criticality, demand criticality, frequency of demand, and overall demand costs. The belief that *condition-based monitoring (CBM) is too expensive* took on a new meaning. Critical revenue producing assets needed to be reviewed for the application of CBM techniques to detect deterioration or other factors that may contribute to inopportune failures. The executive forum members also noted that any asset that could seriously harm or put at risk their employee associates was also a worthy candidate for CBM.

Define Value Density Metrics

What should be the common high-level drivers (metrics) for eliminating islands of pain and moving the company towards a future perfect? The value density metrics for connecting demand to the asset are as follows:

Asset availability. This equals operating time divided by net available time. Operating time equals the net available time minus all other downtime (breakdowns, setups, adjustments, minor stoppages, meetings, and maintenance). Net available time equals total scheduled time minus contractually required downtime (paid lunches/breaks). Most would suggest that the goal is to have all assets available when they are needed 100% of the time.

100% asset availability, particularly for constraining operations, may mean that no time has been allocated for the kinds of asset preventive maintenance that require the asset to be out of service. Never taking an asset out of service may not make sense. To achieve this, a company may have to invest in unnecessary redundant systems. To keep an asset up 100% of the time usually reinforces the saying, you can pay me now or you can pay me later. Later is typically more expensive.

Steady state asset availability. This is a commonly used availability metric for assets that must be up 24/7. The computer industry refers to the "nines" rating scale for availability. For example a four-nine rating would experience 52.6 minutes of downtime per year. The "nines" and associated downtime have been calculated and listed in Table 7.1.

Availability %	Average Downtime per Year
99	3.65 days
99.9	8.76 hours
99.99	52.6 minutes
99.999	5.26 minutes
99.9999	30.00 seconds

Table 7.1 - Steady State Asset Availability Downtime Calculations

Overall equipment effectiveness (OEE). This is a percentage equal to the multiplication of three metrics. These are asset availability, first time through quality, and performance efficiency. First time through quality and performance efficiency were introduced in the previous chapter. As implied by its name OEE is a useful metric for equipment. The industry benchmark is 85%. This is equivalent to achieving almost 95% in all three metrics. At a minimum, OEE metrics should be applied to revenue producing Class 1 assets. If OEE can only be applied to one asset…make it the constraining operation.

Asset demand density. This is a series of demand percentages by asset criticality class. The percentages include failures by effect, failures by effect by impact on asset availability, failures by effect by frequency of occurrence, and failures by effect by cost impact. Other percentages by asset class include work order types, labor classification, labor time, labor source, and material source.

Ultimately, the goal is to begin stratifying asset data so that the financial impact of maintenance activities can be fairly allocated, agreed upon, and subsequently used to drive asset decisions such as continue to repair, overhaul, or replace. By adding labor and material information, the organization gains insight on what resources were required for maintenance activities by asset class. This enables an organization to establish direction on whether to use internal or external labor resources, set appropriate response time by asset class, and to understand failure types. It provides insight on whether repair materials should be stocked or simply purchased at the time of need.

Mean time between failure (MTBF). This is the average time interval (usually in hours) between consecutive component failures as shown in Figure 7.6. MTBF is equal to the sum of the mean time to failure (MTTF) and the mean time to restore (MTTR). Reliability is improved when the time interval spanning separate failures is extended.

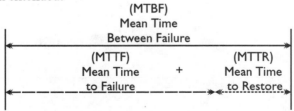

Figure 7. 6 - Mean Time Between Failure (MTBF) Components

There is a difference between the component MTBF and the asset MTBF. Asset MTBF can be extended through redundant systems such that a component failure does not impact asset functioning. Extending asset MTBF does not necessarily extend component MTBF.

Mean time between interruptions (MTBI). This refers to a temporary system outage that does not require repairs. These outages are usually caused elsewhere and simply require the asset to be restarted, reset, or rebooted. Interruptions usually do not necessitate asset repair but they do cause asset downtime, thus negatively impacting asset availability.

Equipment/component standardization density. This is the percentage of assets and components that have been standardized. This metric is usually applied to currently used assets. To do this a company enumerates the variety of its currently used asset configurations by asset maker, age, or revision levels. A natural outcome of this value density metric is a sense of direction on where potential savings could occur in both labor and materials required to support diverse assets.

Maintenance prevention density. This is the percentage of maintenance work orders dedicated to maintenance prevention. Maintenance prevention strategies extend component life by design. The purpose of this value density metric is to focus an organization on root cause failure analysis. This root cause analysis usually results in maintenance prevention solutions and the number of maintenance prevention work orders increases relative to reactive maintenance work orders. This metric must be balanced by the cost to conduct asset reengineering efforts versus continued maintenance costs.

Asset demand costs to replacement costs ratio. This is a measure of actual expenses incurred for an asset versus the replacement cost and projected operating costs of a replacement asset. As shown in Figure 7.7, costs are allocated per asset. Other factors such as energy costs, percentage of commodity versus engineered components, compliance to asset and component standards, predicted spares requirements, and number of operators required should be considered in a replacement decision. Ranked asset demand cost to replacement ratios guide asset repair, overhaul, and replace decisions.

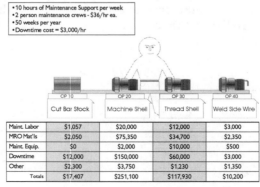

• 10 hours of Maintenance Support per week
• 2 person maintenance crews - $36/hr ea.
• 50 weeks per year
• Downtime cost = $3,000/hr

	OP 10 Cut Bar Stock	OP 20 Machine Shell	OP 30 Thread Shell	OP 40 Weld Side Wire
Maint. Labor	$1,057	$20,000	$12,000	$3,000
MRO Mat'ls	$2,050	$75,350	$34,700	$2,350
Maint. Equip.	$0	$2,000	$10,000	$500
Downtime	$12,000	$150,000	$60,000	$3,000
Other	$2,300	$3,750	$1,230	$1,350
Totals	$17,407	$251,100	$117,930	$10,200

Figure 7.7 - Demand Costs Per Asset

Identify Compression Strategies

Clearly assets are required to conduct and support value stream activities. The cost of these assets is directly related to demand created by the asset. Asset demand is created when an asset requires resources to restore it to desired operating conditions. Compression strategies for eliminating or reducing asset demands are as follows.

Total productive maintenance (TPM). This is a holistic maintenance management strategy encompassing both asset design and maintenance activities, and supported by several compression tools. The goal of TPM is to maximize overall equipment effectiveness (see OEE value density metric described previously). Improving OEE requires an organization to establish a comprehensive preventative maintenance plan covering the life of an asset. Involve all departments that plan for, use, and maintain assets. Involve all levels of associates from executive level management to front-line workers. And try to motivate OEE improvement through autonomous maintenance and small group activities.

TPM is an excellent umbrella program for combining value stream and maintenance objectives. Any asset downtime that impacts the value stream should be addressed. This includes setup time, lack of materials, and poor quality, as well as equipment functional failures. TPM is traditionally a component of a larger initiative such as lean manufacturing.

Reliability centered maintenance (RCM). This is a systematic consideration of asset functions, the way functions can fail, and a priority-based consideration of safety and economics that identifies applicable and effective planned maintenance (PM) tasks. The goal of RCM is to reduce maintenance costs by focusing on the most important functions of the asset and avoiding or removing maintenance actions that are not strictly necessary. RCM is a systematic process for developing a PM program. It is based on the assumption that the inherent reliability of the equipment is a function of the design, component quality, and appropriate maintenance activities. An effective PM program will ensure that the inherent reliability is realized.

RCM has made its way into the standards of major industries for assuring asset reliability through design. The RCM philosophy and approach is both logical and powerful. However, the tools required to complete a RCM study are both tedious and resource-intensive. This can cause management to discount RCM efforts as too expensive for the payback. This notwithstanding, for those who have completed RCM studies and implemented its core practices, the payback has been significant.

Zero breakdown maintenance. This is a practical four-phase process designed to eliminate asset breakdowns. The phases are:

- Phase 1 – Reduce variation in failure intervals.
- Phase 2 – Lengthen equipment life.
- Phase 3 – Periodically restore deterioration.
- Phase 4 – Predict equipment life from its conditions.

These four phases, published by the Japan Institute of Plant Maintenance, provide a practical approach to implementing each of the following six zero-breakdown strategies:

1. Eliminate accelerated deterioration by establishing basic equipment conditions.
2. Eliminate accelerated deterioration by complying with conditions of use.
3. Restore equipment to its optimal condition by restoring deterioration.
4. Restore processes to their optimal condition by abolishing environments that cause accelerated deterioration.
5. Lengthen equipment lifetimes by correcting design weaknesses.
6. Eliminate unexpected failures by improving operating and maintenance skills.

Zero breakdown maintenance has not received the industry recognition of TPM and RCM; however it provides a powerful and practical roadmap for minimizing asset demands.

Demand lead time analysis. Demand lead time is defined as the time from when a demand is first suspected or recognized until the time it is effectively communicated to the source of supply. Demand lead time can be divided into two categories: predictive maintenance and reactive maintenance.

Predictive maintenance (P_dM) provides the longest demand lead time between when a demand is suspected to the time when the asset needs to be restored prior to an occurrence of a failure. Autonomous maintenance (AM), where the operator or user participates in maintenance inspections, can also provide insights on failure before they occur. Preventive maintenance (PM) can check for potential failures as well. Often AM provides an earlier warning of impending failure than does PM, especially when the asset is not on an inspection schedule.

Failure occurrence does not always translate into failure detection. AM provides the quickest detection for obvious failures. PM provides adequate detection depending on the frequency of inspections.

In all cases the demand lead time for Corrective maintenance (CM) is by far the shortest. Figure 7.8 shows the relationship between various maintenance strategies and their general impact on extending demand lead time.

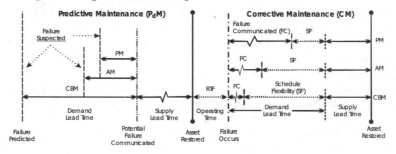

Figure 7.8 - Maintenance Practices Impact on Demand Lead Time

Extending demand lead time provides the asset owner, service providers, and asset makers the greatest opportunity to optimize resources, operations, and logistics to meet service requirement while striving for the lowest total costs. Whether to pursue predictive versus corrective maintenance strategies should be a function of the asset's demand criticality.

Design reliability analyses. These are a collection of methods designed to identify potential component failures so that asset reliability may be improved. These techniques are used during asset concept design, prototype, pilot, build, and qualify phases. They include Weibull analysis, fault tree analysis, failure mode effect, and criticality analysis and simulation.

Weibull analysis matches historical failure and repair data to appropriate Weibull distributions. These distributions represent the failure or repair characteristics of a given failure mode and may be assigned to failure models that are attached to blocks in a reliability block diagram or events in a fault tree diagram. The Weibull distribution is used in the calculation of the Bathtub Curve for failure probabilities.

Fault tree analysis is a deductive, top–down method of analyzing asset design and performance. It involves specifying a top functional failure to analyze (such as a machine stoppage), followed by identifying all of the associated elements in the system that could cause that top event to occur. Fault trees provide a convenient symbolic representation of the combination of events resulting in the occurrence of the top event. Events and gates in fault tree analysis are represented by symbols. Fault tree analyses are generally performed graphically using a logical structure of AND and OR gates.

Failure mode effects and criticality analysis (FMECA) is a procedure for identifying potential failure modes in a system and classifying them according to their severity values. A FMECA has two main parts. The first identifies failure modes and their effects (failure mode and effects analysis or FMEA). The second ranks failure modes according to the combination of severity and the probability of that failure mode occurring (criticality analysis). The automotive industry in its SAE J1739 standard has customized the FMEA for machines (MFMEA).

Simulation allows an organization to design and validate assets without disturbing value stream processes. By creating a virtual copy of the asset environment, one can experiment with different asset configurations and decide on the best scenario for each operation. The impacts of varying asset reliabilities on capacity, asset availability, and cost of operations can be explored. Simulation results can be used to make asset right–sizing, redundant system, and component selection decisions.

Asset makers and asset owners have conducted design reliability analyses for years. The results are self-evident...assets are lasting longer and failing less f requently.

Asset condition assessment. This is the practice of reviewing an asset's condition to determine its fitness for use. This assessment is conducted throughout the lifecycle of the asset. The asset condition assessment reviews several factors in order to establish asset investment strategies. These factors include:

- Safety and environmental risks.
- Structural integrity for buildings and other structures.
- Current performance issues such as operating rates and output quality.
- Current cost profile including direct operating costs and indirect maintenance costs.
- Historical maintenance and repair activities by asset and component and their actual costs.
- Planned maintenance and estimated cost of labor, materials, and special equipment.
- Planned capital expenditures such as overhaul, major modifications, or replacement and the projected costs.
- Economic life comparison to intended useful life; further compared to the asset life expectancy based on current asset conditions and planned maintenance and capital improvement activities.
- Certifications activities and their associated cost as required by industry regulations, applicable laws, or contractual obligations.
- Asset valuation to include depreciation, replacement value, market or salvage value, and future earnings.

The results of the asset condition assessment are used by the asset owner to make asset repair, modification, or replace decisions based on the total costs (direct and indirect) to operate and maintain an asset to availability and performance expectations.

Early equipment management. This is an element of TPM requiring the participation of asset makers, service providers, and owners to increase overall return on assets. Early equipment management efforts take place during the early phases of the asset lifecycle. These phases include design, prototype, pilot, and pre-production. Early equipment management activities include other compression strategies such as design reliability analysis, maintenance prevention, demand criticality analysis of existing equipment, and asset standardization. Early equipment management is a program management model where the goal is to learn from the past and not repeat costly design decisions.

Early equipment management is strategic in nature and requires leadership vision to capture knowledge from existing operations to prevent functional failures in the future. Traditionally organizations have failed miserably at developing long-term corporate memory, and then retrieving it at times of need. Early equipment management makes sense for those who must continually invest in assets in support of their value stream.

Maintenance prevention. This is a subset strategy to early equipment management that focuses on the initial design of equipment to reduce the amount of maintenance required. Maintenance prevention activities rely on information gained from past failures to prevent failures "by design" in the future. Examples include the use of sealed versus lubricated bearings, adding seals to eliminate contamination, error proofing designs to eliminate asset assembly and installation errors, and selecting longer life components to match or exceed asset useful life objectives.

Accelerated deterioration elimination. Artificial causes such as contamination, lack of basic equipment maintenance, and operating or using assets outside of their design limits accelerate deterioration. Natural deterioration is a gradual form of deterioration due to such factors as normal wear and use of the asset.

Unfortunately, we do not always run our machines in ideal conditions and the way we operate and maintain them can cause accelerated deterioration. Contamination, improper lubrication, and inappropriate preventive maintenance account for most incidences of accelerated deterioration. Examples include:

- *Loose parts.* A loose bolt was not tightened. Excessive vibration not only dislodged the bolt but also caused excessive wear on a plastic part retainer. The loose bolt fell into the indexing unit causing the asset to stop. The worn plastic part retainer caused part misalignment that resulted in the production of defects.

- *Contamination in belts.* If dirt gets on belts it causes them to wear out quickly. The life expectancy of a belt is based on it being properly maintained. Preventive maintenance intervals were set based on this planned life. The belt failed before the first check due to excessive contamination.

A combination of TPM, RCM, and Zero Breakdown Maintenance strategies eliminates or greatly reduces accelerated deterioration. Figure 7.9 shows the relationship between time to failure and accelerated and natural deterioration.

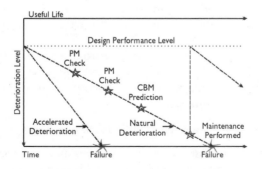

Figure 7.9 - Accelerated versus Natural Deterioration

Infrastructure, equipment, and component standardization. The result of some of the pathological thinking in the "Strategic MRO" world (such as changing asset makes and models for small price breaks) results in large numbers of different asset makes and models inside the same plant. This not only increases the number of asset types to be managed, it also increases the need for specialized skills, material buffers, and special tools.

Asset and component standardization significantly reduces the number of alternatives from which an engineer, maintenance, construction, or purchasing resources may choose. These simplifications streamline sourcing and purchase order administration. Standardization can occur at five distinct levels. These are:

- Standardization within an operating unit.
- Standardization within a company.
- Standardization between MRO, services, and capital project purchases.
- Standardization within a buying community.
- Standardization within one's industry.

The asset and product standardization process requires significant teamwork from multiple disciplines, alliance members, and manufacturers. The product standardization team should be both cross-functional and inter-organizational. Members should represent engineering, maintenance, construction, purchasing, quality assurance, and sales disciplines from alliance and distributor organizations.
Typical standardization team efforts include:

- Asset inventory to record the major types of assets owned or leased and their associated cost of ownership.
- MRO component commodity group analysis to determine the variety and quantity of component held.
- Standards analysis to determine if asset and product standards exist and the content of those standards.
- Inventory analysis to determine the current usage of MRO components.
- Product analysis to determine which products among alternatives has the lowest TCO for the desired application(s).
- Standard selection and development to ensure that existing or new standards are documented.
- Protocol for addition/subtraction to standards used to improve communication of changes and to aid in configuration management.
- Compliance measures and reporting use to ensure standards are being adhered to throughout the organization.

What are the MRO component standardization technology considerations?

- Computerized document management systems should be considered for control and dissemination of product standards. Linking document management to product data management (PDM) technology enables engineering, procurement, maintenance, and construction personnel to view machine or process prints on-line while simultaneously accessing related MRO product standards with one click of the mouse.

- Database linkage to electronic catalog technology enables the management of product standards.
- Standardized product descriptions ensure data integrity necessary for effective procurement, order entry, and inventory replenishment activities and avoids part number proliferation.
- ERP, EAM, and other sourcing technology should flag and alert nonconformance to product standards.
- Similarly, distributor electronic catalogs should filter offerings to reflect designated customer standards. When an order is placed, only those standards (products or manufacturers) are viewable by the distributor sales force and the asset owner, thus minimizing the chance for error.

The asset owner may build in system controls to ensure purchasing compliance to standards or it may require alliance members to develop system controls to allow only standard items to be sold. With these system checks and balances in place, the standard procurement process may be bypassed, allowing engineering and field resources to conduct procurement activities directly with supply sources.

Commodity configuration management. This is used where engineering is encouraged to use existing MRO supply chains and commodities rather than engineered items when developing new designs. If, in an organization's list of potential maintenance or repair items, there are a substantial number of engineered or hard to obtain items, two things will occur. First, the inventory of critical spares will magically grow. Second, the length of unplanned downtime will increase as well.

For example a company we once visited had specified specialty valves to reduce emissions. This was easily justified because of state and federal emission requirements and a shattering explosion believed to have been caused by a leaky valve. As cost cutting pressures hit the plants, inquiries into why current valve costs were double what they would be if commodity values were used were made. This led to a review of commodity valve performance. Rigorous testing indicated that today's commodity valve outperformed yesterday's specialty valve. The company saved in excess of $6,000,000 in their first year.

Commodity configuration management suggests that existing supply chains help reduce the cost of inventory investments and reduce the length of unplanned downtime. Commodity configuration reduces the requirements for a specialized workforce. It also reduces the need to keep hard-to-find items in stock and interpret engineering drawings and specifications for rarely used items. Balance all of this with the fact that an engineered item may well be worth the effort and expense if it does not fail or it fails substantially less than a commodity item.

Design for serviceability. This is a strategy where engineers design assets so that they can be easily monitored and quickly serviced. This helps to reduce unplanned downtime. The goal is to quickly restore the asset to its desired performance level.

Component repair is conducted off-line. Design for serviceability follows the same principles as quick changeover used in lean manufacturing systems.

Design for serviceability is supported by modular maintenance designs. Modular designs enable quick disconnect of entire modules or subassemblies to reduce equipment downtime. For example, modular design will allow the entire motor unit with motor mounts and quick disconnect wires to be removed and replaced in its entirety. Motor modules are then repaired off-line and placed back into stores as a critical spare. Another example is the use of carpet squares so that only damaged sections of carpet need to be replaced.

Demand criticality classification. Not all assets are equal, not all failures are equal, and not all failures create a demand. The demand criticality classification is a business leader's version of a failure mode and effects analysis (FMEA) that can be implemented using enterprise asset management (EAM) technology. Failure management policies are derived from both predicted and actual classification of asset demands based on the failure effect, availability impact, failure frequency, and cost impact of occurrence. Demand criticality classification consists of the following elements.

- *Asset criticality classification.* The demand criticality classification begins with the classification of assets by their position relative to the value stream (refer to Chapter 6).
- *Failure effect type.* Asset failures should be categorized according to a logical hierarchy based on their operational effect. The logic is based on first achieving safety then ensuring the asset is performing to expectations. Failure effect types are shown below.

    1. Asset condition creates unsafe or hazardous work environment (highest priority).
    2. Asset unavailable for use.
    3. Asset does not produce a quality output.
    4. Asset does not perform to design or operational efficiencies.
    5. Asset use drives up cost of operations (lowest priority).

- *Availability impact.* The lost availability effect of any functional failure can range from no effect to catastrophic impact on asset availability. The demand criticality analysis uses expected mean time to restore (MTTR) or work order estimates of time to restore to quantify the effect of lost availability for different type of failures.

As shown in Figure 7.10, "no effect" implies that asset availability is not impacted. Insignificant is less than 4 hours, significant is between 4 to 8 hours (one production shift), very significant is 4 to 24 hours (one production day), catastrophic is greater than 24 hours. Some would argue that catastrophic should be greater than a week or even a month. Remember availability is dependent on the need or schedule for use. If an asset is not required or scheduled for use for long periods of time then the lost availability impact is diminished.

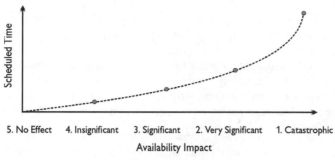

Figure 7.10 - Failure Impact on Asset Availability

- *Failure frequency.* Frequency of occurrence determines if the failure is chronic or sporadic. Mean time to failure (MTTF) estimates are a good starting point when establishing failure frequency. Past work order history provides the last known date of the failure if MTTF data is not kept.

  A simple frequency classification (see below) is used for failure frequency. Sporadic and chronic are used to describe both the repetitiveness and the potential inability to eliminate the failure. Sporadic failures indicate a failure that is sudden and which often has significant impact on asset availability, quality levels, and performance efficiencies. Chronic failures are usually less significant but usually occur more frequently. Often these chronic failures have been gradually accepted as the norm but their cumulative effect on total cost can be quite significant.

  1. Chronic – Daily.
  2. Chronic – Weekly.
  3. Chronic – Monthly.
  4. Sporadic – Quarterly.
  5. Sporadic – Yearly or greater.

- *Cost impact.* The last element of the demand criticality classification is the cost impact of the failure. Cost estimates can be derived from work order estimates of labor, materials, and special equipment needed restore the asset to availability after the failure. Cost impacts are expressed as a percentage of asset replacement value. For chronic failures cumulative costs over a period of one year are expressed as a percentage of asset replacement value.

  1. Catastrophic – greater than 75% to 100% of the asset replacement value.
  2. Very Significant – 50% to 75% of the asset replacement value.
  3. Significant – between 10% to 50% of the asset replacement value.
  4. Insignificant – between 5% to 10% of the asset replacement value.
  5. No effect – less than 5% of the asset replacement value.

The demand criticality classification facilitates the calculation of asset demand densities (refer to value density metrics). The classification of demand criticality allows asset owners to objectively make decisions regarding predictive versus reactive maintenance, asset repair, overhaul, and replacement. This classification also helps in establishing priority of work orders for planning and scheduling labor and material resources. Ultimately the demand criticality classification logic implies that an asset is only functioning correctly if it is safe to use, available to use, produces what it supposed to, at its expected rate, and doesn't turn into a giant money pit.

Location failure analysis. Many organizations extend the notion of connecting demand to the asset to a second dimension. Demand can be connected to the asset residing in a particular location within the plant or even a geographic territory. This is done because two pieces of exactly the same equipment installed at different locations in a plant may indeed create different levels of demand for wear parts and consumables.

This differing level of demand for wear parts and consumables is usually because the equipment at different locations is used to do different tasks. For example a plant may use two pumps that are the same except that they are installed in different locations. One runs only sporadically and pumps only clean fluid. The other runs continuously and always pumps dirty fluid. The latter will likely require more parts and labor to maintain.

Tracking demand by asset in a location usually requires the use of a enterprise asset management (EAM) system. A properly configured EAM system will allow the definition of the asset, perhaps a piece of equipment, and that asset's components, which include wear parts, consumables, and all other structural pieces and components. The EAM system will also allow the asset to be assigned to a location within the plant. Once this is done for all assets, demand for parts and labor can be tracked for the equipment at a location level.

Once assets are assigned to locations and demand associated with assets in those locations, demand profiles of assets by revenue (mission critical) and non-revenue (non-mission critical) status can be developed. This can be extended to projections of demand costs for new equipment, facilities, and other assets. These projections can then be compared to actual demand costs realized in the future so that projections can be fine-tuned.

Standardized failure codes. These are used to assist data collection efforts. Failure codes must give the organization a first hint as to the source of the problem so they can direct their attention accordingly. For example, during the initial asset warranty period it is important to distinguish between material defects and improper operations. Material defects are just cause for a warranty claim while the improper operation is just cause for operator training.

Traditional failure causes that can be coded at a high level are listed in Table 7.2. Detailed codes can be established to narrowly define reasons based on experience. If "other" or "unknown" is the largest category, then much work remains to be done in designing and implementing an effective failure code scheme.

Failure Source	Code	Failure Code Description
Design (D)	D1	Faulty Design
Build (B)	B1	Material Defects
	B2	Fabrication or Processing errors
	B3	Assembly or Installation errors
Use (U)	U1	Off-design or unintended service conditions
	U2	Improper Operations
Maintain (M)	M1	Maintenance Deficiencies
	M2	Natural Deterioration
	M3	Accelerated Deterioration

Table 7.2 - Failure Codes

Develop Case Study Examples

The executive forum teams found the concept of connecting demand to the asset confusing at first. Demand was a term that they had always used for quantifying the needs of their customers. The principles of Demand Supply Compression clearly stated that similar assets created similar demand. The forum members soon realized that they should think of their assets as the customer of the supply chain.

Each team went back to its breakout area to discuss how this principle applied to their organization and their case study company. They were asked to define what actions they would take to improve their knowledge of asset demand requirements. They were also asked to think about what actions should be taken to reduce the cost impact of asset demand.

Superior Water

A goal of Superior Water is to invest only in assets that never fail over their useful life. While the planned life of the network was infinite, in reality, the water supply network's asset performance declined over time. Thus asset maintenance, repair, and replacement were inevitable. The network was susceptible to both sporadic and chronic failures. Sporadic failures included lines being punctured by other service providers such as road construction, telephone, gas utility, and electric utility crews. An emergency call system was already in place and shared by all public utilities and government services. Chronic problems of poor water quality and leakage presented most of the need for maintenance services.

Superior Water's asset database did not keep complete records of asset failures other than descriptions on work orders. Mean time between failure (MTBF) and Mean time to repair/restore (MTTR) was indirectly calculated by time recorded on work orders. But a quick analysis indicated that the work order did not track the actual downtime period of the asset. Any downtime information captured started with the recording the time of the complaint in the call center database. This system was not integrated with the work order system. No formal system was used to log the actual completion time of the maintenance work order.

Work orders were used to track internal and contract labor costs and a separate system was used to track inventory usage. However these two systems were not integrated. At the end of the day the Superior Water team realized it had no accurate way of determining demand or supply lead time and no accurate compilation of costs (labor, material, and equipment) per revenue and non-revenue producing asset. Inconsistent and incomplete asset data could not be easily stratified into sporadic and chronic problems. This lack of information was quite disturbing to the Superior Water team.

Superior Water Compression Strategies

Zero breakdown maintenance. The Superior Water team's goal was to drastically reduce water distribution network maintenance requirements. They liked the approach discussed in the zero breakdown maintenance strategy as it began with understanding existing asset failures and then proceeded in a logical fashion to develop priorities for line replacement activities based on known water quality and hydraulic problems. Ongoing line replacement activities were designed to restore assets to their optimal condition.

The Superior Water team also knew that they needed to understand the environments in which their network operated. This required the skills of seasoned experts and the use of a geographic information system (GIS) to isolate failure patterns by location. The team believed that they could lengthen the life of the network by correcting known design weaknesses. The team also suspected that they could eliminate unexpected failures by improving maintenance skills. This was a challenge because many of Superior Water's maintenance activities had been outsourced.

Design Reliability Analysis. The Superior Water team knew of simulation programs that could model water flow, water turbidity, and overall line hydraulics. They thought, however, that the expense of these modeling activities outweighed the benefits. As an alternative to simulation, the team decided that they would incorporate hydraulic study information to test asset reliability and availability. They would also use this information to establish the order of replacement work and to eliminate unnecessary replacements. The goal of the design reliability analysis for the Water Main Replacement Program was to improve water pressure and to prevent leaks.

The Superior Water team was also aware of a potential problem with lead leaching. The toxic effects of lead on humans were well understood. By the early 1900s, lead piping was no longer used in new plumbing and water systems. However a number of older residences had lead service lines or plumbing systems containing lead solder. The team decided to conduct a corrosion control study to determine what the causes of lead leaching might be and how they could be avoided. The goal was to determine how to minimize lead in the water system. The study revealed several alternative solutions, none of which where available to Superior Water. Superior Water concluded that it should protect its consumers from lead by accelerating the replacement of lead service lines in the water distribution system.

In addition to the hydraulic and corrosion control studies, the Superior Water team knew that tracking installation, repair, and replacement data associated with critical components such as main sections of pipe, valves, regulators, and meters was needed. This data would allow the Superior Water engineering department to determine MTBF statistics. These statistics could then be used to establish product standards based on the lowest total cost of ownership. The goal here was to increase asset reliability thus reducing the need for repair.

Maintenance prevention. With over 7,500 miles of network, Superior Water had learned the advantages flushing water mains twice a year. Flushing was accomplished by opening fire hydrants. The purpose of flushing is to remove sediment and mineral deposits that settle on the bottom of the water mains. The team recognized this as a form of maintenance prevention that would ultimately prevent a water quality problem. A better maintenance prevention strategy, the team realized, was keeping the sediment and mineral properties out of the network to begin with. They decided to conduct an analysis of various discharges to determine where they had excessive build-up. They would then use these results coupled with their knowledge of hydraulics, soil mechanics, and other factors to determine if sediment and mineral deposits could be prevented.

Commodity configuration management. Superior Water had a legacy water distribution system. Parts of the distribution network infrastructure were installed in the early 1900s. Because of this Superior knew that the network components varied significantly by manufacturer, model number, and age. This variation certainly added to the amount of MRO inventory carried. As is often the case where diverse MRO inventories exist, many of the items carried on the books could not be physically located when needed.

The Superior Water team invited its six major distributors in for individual meetings to review current water distribution network configurations. The objective of the meetings was to determine if any opportunities existed to standardize on commodity products instead of the engineered items currently used in the distribution network. Ultimately Superior knew that they would have to incorporate these new commodity standards into line replacement activities.

Location failure analysis. The team recommended that a geographic information system (GIS) be used to implement an asset location hierarchy. When interfaced with asset management technology, patterns of failures could then be discerned by location. The belief was that certain sections of the network experienced higher failure rates than others. This belief came from the locations recorded on work orders. Certainly as entire network sections were replaced the expectations would be that their maintenance costs would be less, but without data...who knew?

Standardized failure codes. The Superior Water team also recommended that, where practical, a standard list of failure codes be used to categorize failure modes.

When failure codes were integrated with the GIS system the team expected to be able to systematically discern failure patterns.

Finally the team addressed costs per asset. Connecting repair work orders, with associated labor, material, and equipment costs, to the asset would enable Superior Water to understand costs, timing, and effectiveness of maintenance activities. The goal was to create a demand and cost profile per asset and asset location.

EuroCar

EuroCar had a history of collecting data. Databases sprouted up everywhere. One team member said he definitely related to the DRIP (data rich/information poor) description used by the team facilitator. But the problem, the team realized, was that the data that had been collected did not reveal total cost per asset. Early attempts to achieve the 5% cost reduction mandated by management were driven by budget controls: buy less and use fewer resources. The team now realized that the asset caused demand not people. Just hoping to spend less or use less resources glossed over the root cause...why were assets needing service to begin with?

EuroCar had always tracked the number of work orders for each plant area. However they had never tied these maintenance and repair costs back to specific assets. Nothing in their systems prompted EuroCar to repair, overhaul, or replace an asset based on cost. When asked if they could provide asset failures by revenue and non-revenue producing criticality classifications the answer was a resounding no. EuroCar did know the number of work orders completed last year, the average time for work order completion, and the relative percentages of preventive, predictive, and corrective maintenance work orders.

EuroCar soon discovered these were measures of activities, not results. What were the results they were looking for? How many failures occurred, to what assets, and at what costs to the organization? How many sporadic versus chronic failures were reported, corrected, and prevented for Class 1 through 4 assets? How much money was being spent on Class 5 through 7 assets at a premium or to the disadvantage of Class 1 through 4 assets? Their disjointed set of databases did not reveal this information.

EuroCar Compression Strategy

TPM. EuroCar had already developed a *EuroCar Production System* which contained total productive maintenance as its core strategy for asset improvement. By EuroCar's definition, total productive maintenance (TPM) is a team-based method to continuously improve overall equipment effectiveness (OEE) and supporting processes within a work area. In the EuroCar Production System initiative, TPM methodologies helped focus and accelerate equipment improvements required to support one-piece flow, quick changeover, load balancing, and first time through quality levels.

The EuroCar team reported that efforts were already underway to implement the seven elements of autonomous maintenance (AM). These included:

1. Initial cleaning – which reduces contamination, increases familiarity with equipment and work area, and uncovers hidden defects.
2. Preventive cleaning measures – where sources of contamination are identified, isolated, and controlled, including leaks, process excess, and material from the external environment.
3. Development of cleaning and lubrication standards—combining inspections for cleanliness with lubrication checks so that they can both be performed as efficiently as possible.
4. General inspection – to include tightening, adjustments, minor calibrations and inspection of subsystems: hydraulic, pneumatic, and electrical.
5. Autonomous inspection – where responsibility is transferred to the operator for lubrication, cleaning, and general inspection. This included training for operators on their systems as well in the technical aspects of the inspections.
6. Process discipline – which required the improvement of methods and procedures to enable efficiency and repeatability. Improvement goals included reduced setup times, decreased manufacturing cycle times, standardized procedures for handling materials, reduction of work in progress inventory, and institutionalizing of visual control and inspection methods.
7. Independent autonomous maintenance (AM) – where self-sustaining improvement was the objective.

Demand lead time analysis. The EuroCar team knew that, in the past, they had taken care of every problem that had occurred. This left their maintenance staff scrambling. They wanted to move toward a more planned approach to maintenance. They were taken by the notion of increasing demand lead time. This fit well with their EPS initiative.

The team began a historical analysis of work orders by maintenance type. These types were predictive maintenance (P_dM), autonomous maintenance (AM), preventive maintenance (PM), and corrective maintenance (CM). The results were revealing.

About 1% of work orders were for P_dM, 2% for AM initiatives, 35% for PM activities, and 62% for CM. Since each work order creates a work transaction, the EuroCar team knew that this amount of CM work could only lead to poor planning. Poor planning resulted in excessive labor overtime, poor staff utilization, and excess material purchases.

System Integration. The EuroCar team felt their first step was to integrate computer systems to create real time data capturing, reporting of failures and associated failure modes, and overall failure costs. Mindful of the importance of Class 1 assets, the team needed failure data to guide their investments in redundant systems, condition based monitoring, predictive maintenance, autonomous maintenance, maintenance prevention, and early equipment activities that were core to their total productive maintenance efforts. The bottom line was that they needed "line of sight" data on assets costs if they were to have a chance of reducing those costs.

The team reviewed several commercial off-the-shelf (COTS) software solutions and determined that most computerized maintenance management system (CMMS) packages provided the ability to record failure data by asset. This data included failure codes, mean time between failure (MTBF), and probable causes and could be used to guide diagnostic efforts.

Only one company had developed reports that placed these failures in the context of business impact. This included calculating total cost per asset, providing guidance on repair, overhaul, and replacement decisions, and highlighting component lives that statistically outperformed the rest.

In addition, the failure analysis module of this company's CMMS provided insight on employee and skilled trade effectiveness as a function of asset downtime. For example, the software could report on instances where multiple work orders were issued against the same asset for the same repair, enabling plant leadership to schedule appropriate maintenance training and development sessions.

The EuroCar case study showed the executive forum members that a plethora of software suppliers existed in the market. The message for software suppliers, one executive forum members can understand, and must be: You must truly understand global best practices, understand your client's business needs, and continue to help those clients after software acquisition to achieve definable measures of success. Asset and MRO supply chain problems have actually changed little over time. So you software providers must stop acting as if this is a new subject requiring a new gimmick.

In the end, EuroCar selected the software provider who best understood the needs of their business. This provider was well respected in the market as a financially solid company with an unblinking eye on the mission of assets and the MRO supply chain, one who challenged current thinking, and was a technology shaper, not an after-the-fact adopter. And most important, the software provider, through their alliances weith skilled professionals who worked in partnership with them, felt confident that they could achieve the desired results.

Maintenance prevention and early equipment management. EuroCar understood the impact of poor lubrication especially in conveyor operations. If they could eliminate all bearing lubrication requirements, their problems would be greatly diminished. Their strategy to do this was twofold. First replace lubed bearings with sealed bearings during repair operations if technically feasible. Second, early equipment management activities would require all new equipment designs to use sealed bearings.

Once they had the bearing lubrication problem solved, they focused their attention on motors and motor controls. What they found was quite revealing. Motor controls often failed not by design but because of large power fluctuations during line startup activities. Maintenance prevention meant eliminating the power fluctuations so that repairing the motor controls would be virtually eliminated.

Demand criticality classifications. The EuroCar team was intrigued with the business leader's version of the failure mode and effects analysis (FMEA). EuroCar was required to complete process and machine FMEAs during preproduction approval activities. Many great ideas and improvements occurred as a result. What they were looking for was a way to streamline FMEA information and integrate it into their overall maintenance strategy on a daily basis. With the procurement of EAM software they had the system tool to do it. They just needed to structure the demand criticality classification to set maintenance priorities, and provide asset cost data so that repair, overhaul, and replacement decisions could be made in real time.

The demand criticality classification allowed EuroCar to use the principles of Strategic MRO and TPM to systematically reduce asset demands while improving resource effectiveness. They found that the secret to making this work was focusing first on the asset classification, then on the failure effect type, and finally on the availability impact. Frequency and total costs would be captured after the fact in order to drive TPM improvement initiatives.

EuroCar would eventually repeat the demand lead time analysis but this time they would analyze work orders by asset class. From their perspective Class 1, revenue producing assets, were the prime targets for implementing predictive maintenance. Too much reactive maintenance for Class 1 assets meant availability suffered. However, they decided reactive maintenance was the appropriate strategy for Class 7 assets.

MobileTel

The MobileTel team gathered data from several sources to develop asset demand profiles. To everyone's amazement they had experienced nearly 1.2 million hours of downtime during the pervious twelve months. The team recalled from previous discussions that nearly 30% of downtime was recorded on A sites. Further analysis revealed that 35% of all work orders were for A network elements, 58% for Bs, and 7% for Cs. What was not known was the nature of the failures. Handwritten notes on work orders indicated most were PCB (printed circuit board) failures, however no further analysis was ever completed.

MobileTel estimated the cost of asset demand by aggregating labor, materials, vehicle, measurement tools, and overhead at nearly $63 million. For 42,000 elements the average demand cost per element was $1,500. Labor alone contributed in excess of 56% of the cost.

MobileTel estimated that maintenance support for their GSM network would ultimately stabilize and decrease. The larger UMTS network was projected to experience failures similar to the GSM network when it was new. Asset demand requirements were projected to go up substantially.

MobileTel Compression Strategies

Reliability centered maintenance. Clearly the MobileTel team relied on the engineering and design skills of its equipment providers to achieve uptime goals. The uptime goal was a steady state system with five-nine capabilities. Quite an aggressive goal, considering that a 99.999% uptime meant only 5.26 minutes per year of downtime was acceptable. The only way they felt they could achieve this level of reliability was to pursue a disciplined approach to understanding and improving the factors that impact element reliability. They choose the RCM methodology to guide their efforts. They knew that this method was used by the aviation industry to achieve high reliability rates for its fleets of aircraft.

Early burn-in failures (infant mortalities) were becoming a thing of the past, yet PCB (printed circuit board) failures remained significant. They suspected that field technician practices might be the dominant cause. What they did not want to do was confront people with the past, but to focus on how failures could be eliminated in the future. By focusing on the seven basic questions of RCM they believed the issues and the solutions would be revealed. The questions posed to their engineering resources and the field technicians were:

1. What are the functions and associated performance standards of the asset in its present operating context?
2. In what way does it fail to fulfill its functions?
3. What causes each functional failure?
4. What happens when each failure occurs?
5. What impact does each failure have?
6. What can be done to predict or prevent each failure?
7. What should be done if a suitable proactive task cannot be found?

Design reliability analysis. The MobileTel team suspected the performance promises made by their UMTS technology providers might be exaggerated. The team had always thought that the UMTS failure rates would be the same as experienced with the GSM network. The question arose as to why they were not investing in a new system more reliable than the old system? They already knew that their maintenance costs were excessive. How would this new technology, with the same reliability as the old system, reduce these costs while improving availability?

The team requested that their engineering team and the technology providers (asset makers) conduct various design reliability analyses. Although time consuming, results produced could be easily applied across the UMTS network. Basic fault tree and FMEA studies were reviewed. Failure estimates were used to derive budget numbers for revenue and operational costs. These budgets would guide the construction rate of the UMTS network. MobileTel could not afford to replace its existing system with a less reliable one. In fact, MobileTel really needed to replace the existing system with a much more reliable one.

Value density metrics. The MobileTel team was immediately struck by their lack of metrics to indicate asset performance and maintenance effectiveness. They kept rudimentary metrics such as billable minutes per cell, cell availability, and cell utilization. What they did not know was the maintenance costs for each element, whether elements were experiencing sporadic or chronic failures, the source of the failures, and the associated causes.

The data currently available could not be easily combined to show what the actual cost per asset was and each asset's impact on the revenue stream. The team recommended that metrics be established to track failures by asset, asset contribution margin based on all-in costs and revenue generation, and mean time between failure for critical functional components that rendered a cell nonfunctional. They then recommended that a demand criticality classification be done and integrated into their EAM technology to set maintenance priorities.

Demand criticality classification. A MobileTel team was assembled to complete the asset classification, failure effect types, and availability impact estimates. They would not be able to develop failure frequencies at the component or asset level until they completed the installation of their new EAM system and subsequently recorded failure data.

MobileTel needed the demand criticality classification to provide direction on how to reduce maintenance costs. They needed a clear priority system to guide technician activities. What assets failures needed proactive maintenance considerations? What failures could be allowed and responded to at a future date based on maximizing technician utilization? Their work had just begun. They felt the combination of RCM studies and the practical application of the demand criticality classification in the EAM system was the correct combination of smart thinking and smart doing.

Location failure analysis. MobileTel was not sure if failures were a function of location. They knew that certain locations experienced higher usage rates but they had not conducted a correlation analysis to connect usage to failure for electronic components. It seemed that failure was random. The team knew that technicians were assigned to regions and that a study of failures by regions might yield differences in failure and maintenance patterns. The team also believed that remote sites would suffer longer downtimes. If this were not the case, what did this imply about the effectiveness of crew scheduling as considerable travel was involved in servicing remote sites? Location failure analysis was worth a shot. The team suspected that important patterns might be revealed. They also knew that they needed EAM technology to help them gather the necessary data.

Standard failure codes. The MobileTel team was ecstatic over the standardization of failure codes. This would become critically important as multiple UMTS sites became functional. Design, build, installation, use, and maintain failure codes fit the bill. A considerable amount of money was being spent on the network expansion. Warranty claims, dispute resolution, burn-in failures, startup errors, and unfamiliarity with new equipment were a fact of life for capital projects. The team felt that capturing failure information right from the start would provide invaluable insights for failure prevention for each subsequent installation.

MilBase Ops

"Invest only in assets that never fail" needed to be restated for MilBase Ops. This restatement was: Invest only in assets that can be forever repainted, repaired, cleaned and waxed, but never replaced. Buildings and monuments continued to stand the test of time, housing many inhabitants throughout the years, each filled with their own rich history.

Asset values were not seen in terms of book value less depreciation but as assets that would simply cost X amount to replace. Some of these seemed almost irreplaceable because of their place or role in military history.

Every asset had to be in proper working order and in accordance with proper military appearance. Given that all financial incentives pointed to living in base housing, buying from base exchanges, and using base facilities, there was no competitive incentive to improve assets to attract new or better paying customers as experienced in the private sector.

The policy of utilizing all assets until they failed meant that the heating systems ranged from hot water, to steam, to gas, and electric. The result was that each heating system had a unique set of components dating back, in some cases, 50 years or more. Lack of standards and upgrade policies resulted in the demand for special maintenance skills, special inventory requirements, special repair facilities, and special tooling.

Only recently has the most efficient organization (MEO) analysis enlightened base leadership to the fact that the cost of labor can only be reduced if demand created by the asset is designed or redesigned out. Clearly, legacy systems create legacy labor and materials requirements. The only way to reduce tomorrow's labor and material cost is to spend on standardized and reliable assets today.

MilBase Ops Compression Strategies

TPM, Zero Based Maintenance, and RCM. The MilBase Ops team, not to be outdone by any of the other executive forum participants, chose all three methodologies as their umbrella asset improvement strategy. In the past, MilBase Ops had tried elements of all of these methodologies. They had more military standards and best practices documents than any organization in the world...yet they could not perform basic asset management and MRO supply chain management functions as inexpensively as outside service providers.

Because of recent cutbacks in staff, they needed now, more than ever, the autonomous maintenance (AM) practices inherent to total productive maintenance. The users of base assets needed to be coached and trained on the principles of asset stewardship. They needed to view maintaining assets as if they were the owners and not the government. Basic checklists could be provided for routine maintenance inspections. A base website was established for reporting maintenance issues and giving tips on proper care of facilities, appliances, lawns, and equipment.

RCM made perfect sense for critical assets where reliability was paramount. An example was the base information technology center where computer assets needed to be available around the clock. Another area where RCM principles would apply was hazardous waste, defined as any solid waste, or combination of solid wastes which, because of its quantity, concentration, or physical, chemical, or infectious characteristics may cause or significantly contribute to an increase in mortality or an increase in serious, irreversible, or incapacitating reversible illness.

Zero breakdown maintenance made sense for all other assets that were being maintained by the base staff and contractors. The use of an EAM system was absolutely necessary for failure data collection and analysis.

Early equipment management. The expected life for most base property was 30 years. Yet every day new construction and maintenance activities brought new assets and new asset configurations into the mix of property. The MilBase Ops team felt that an early equipment management team should be established to review the impact of past failures on new equipment and infrastructure material selections. The team also wanted to review purchasing practices. Even though an approved supplier list existed, the variety of equipment and materials bought seemed to expand year after year. The goal was to extend asset life. Even a one-year extension in average asset life translated into substantial savings.

Infrastructure, equipment, and component standardization. In determining where to standardize, the MilBase Ops team decided to understand first what the price of having multiple standards was. The team decided to review historical failure patterns to determine if standardization would have been a benefit. The benefits they sought were reduced labor and material expenses.

Beginning with roads, the team discovered clear failure patterns at points of tracked vehicle crossings. They found that certain materials and designs did indeed last longer. Designs varied by subsoil conditions. The decision was clear. Contractor crews would no longer repair tracked vehicle crossings. They would replace them when they deteriorated to the point where passenger vehicle damage could occur. Only the new standardized design would be used. The replacement project was estimated to take nearly two years to complete based on estimated failure rates.

The next area of focus was the standardization of heating and ventilation systems. The base commander's office noted that they were proud owners of no less than 175 different systems. When the team reviewed the inventory levels in the HVAC repair shop they were not surprised to find piles and piles of parts, some dating back to 1962. No less than 15 different manufacturers' products had been used over the years, each having their own special connections and power requirements. Tracking warranty claims was near impossible with the existing maintenance management system.

The MilBase Ops team recommended that they adopt HVAC standards based on the size and use of the building. These standards would be integrated with purchasing standards and would be negotiated in the next contractor bid cycle coming up next year. They knew they would have to fight the government's lowest price bid policy by showing the benefit of standardizing on more reliable systems, requiring less parts and service.

The team recognized that certain MRO products seemed to be used in large quantities. You guessed it...valves. Butterfly, gate, globe, plug, check...in homes, in sprinkler systems, in water systems, in sewage treatment, in storage tanks... ¼", ½", up to 16"... bronze, copper, cast iron, cast steel, forged steel, stainless...butt weld, socket weld, flanged in, screwed in, press fit, ... the descriptions were endless. Could they standardize and reduce inventory?

The team brought in two distributors to discuss these issues. One distributor was primarily known for plumbing applications and the other for industrial applications. The answer from both regarding standardization was a unanimous yes. What was the estimated savings for standardizing? Both distributors provided analyses indicating no less than a 15% price reduction and contended that improved valve specifications should extend replacement valve life by 25%. This would have the effect of reducing overall valve purchases nearly 2.5% each year for the next 10 years.

Demand criticality classification. The MilBase Ops team, like EuroCar, pondered the business leader's version of failure mode and effects analysis. Under tremendous pressure to reduce costs, the team knew the benefits of FMEA from past efforts. Institutionalizing a form of FMEA through EAM technology made sense. The demand criticality classification would be applied to the asset criticality classification already established. The team wanted to send a clear message to base occupants: The assets you occupy, even though they are non-mission critical, will be maintained as carefully and efficiently are the planes, armored vehicles, and weapon systems. Their challenge was simple, be the first base that actually freed up budget dollars to be redistributed to front line defense assets.

Location failure analysis. The MilBase Ops team definitely knew that asset location when matched with asset user would reveal failure patterns. These patterns might be transient given the nature of rotating military deployments and assignments. What they wanted was real-time identification of failure patterns that were 1) unique to the asset, 2) unique to the asset user, and 3) unique to the specific environmental conditions of the location itself. They had already established a location hierarchy in their EAM technology by adding asset configuration information and current asset user so they could begin developing the failure patterns they sought.

Standardized failure codes. The MilBase team discovered that standardized failure codes already existed. The list was longer than the Mississippi River, making it impossible for maintenance people to easily apply the failure codes to the job. In this case simpler was better. Their plan was to create a multi-tier failure code scheme that could be accessed through pull-down menus to build the failure descriptions. With the EAM system they could access records based on higher level failure codes and then sort if need be.

TL Freight

The TL Freight team's focus was strictly on their revenue producing assets. There was no need to pursue facility maintenance strategies until they improved trailer and tractor reliability. End of discussion!

The team acknowledged the tractors and trailers on the road created significant demand. So much demand that considerable monies had been invested in numerous service centers, emergency maintenance services, warranty tracking, tire management programs, fuel management programs, and global positioning systems to locate downed assets.

The team presented no less than 26 major tractor and trailers systems from which demand could originate. Sample systems included:

- Engine.
- Air intake.
- Engine cooling and radiator.
- Clutch.
- Frame and frame components.
- Suspension.
- Wheels and tires.
- Drive line.
- Fuel system.
- Exhaust.
- Doors.
- Windshield wipers and washers.
- Seats and restraint system.
- Trailer frame and components.

The team noted that tractors and trailers should be greased on a weekly basis. And fluid changes should be conducted at the following recommended intervals.

- Engine oil: 250 hours.
- Automatic transmission: 500 hours.
- Standard transmission: 1,000 hours.
- Rear differentials: 600 hours.
- Power steering: 1,000 hours.
- Antifreeze: 1,000 hours.
- Hydraulic oil: 1,000 hours.

If these were not enough do not forget the tires. The team was not sure whether they bought more petroleum products in the form of fuel and oil or in the form of rubber tires. Any tire, they agreed, no matter how well constructed, may fail in use as a result of punctures, impact damage, improper inflation, overloading, or other conditions resulting from use, or misuse. Tire failure may create a risk of property damage, serious personal injury, or death.

With 7,500 tractors and 32,000 trailers, preventing and reacting to asset demands was a real challenge.

TL Freight Compression Strategies

TPM and zero breakdown maintenance. The focus on asset availability was primary for the TL Freight team. They knew the secret to their success was having the right tractor and trailer combination ready to go, and go, and go, based on customer demands. TPM had the singular focus on making revenue producing assets more available. It also focused attention on the vehicle operator's responsibility to perform routine maintenance functions through autonomous maintenance practices. Zero breakdown maintenance would become a subset strategy where failures would be captured, analyzed and, where practical, prevented.

Up to this point, TL Freight departments all had programs in place to extend asset life and reduce operating costs, yet none of the programs were coordinated in a centralized way. It was hit and miss. The team decided that a set of TPM strategies needed to be developed and deployed in a systematic manner.

Early equipment management. The first coordinated effort the team recommended was early equipment management. It only made sense to track known tractor and trailer failures and to work with primary vehicle suppliers to seek improvements. By performing their own maintenance at service centers, TL Freight was confident that they knew more about good vehicle design than did the manufacturers themselves.

The tractor manufacturers listened to field feedback. They announced that their newly improved front suspension reduced maintenance by eliminating components that traditionally have required frequent and costly maintenance. Their leaf springs utilize maintenance-free front and rear bushings. Their axle clamp group with four-sided clamping pressure eliminates the need for retorquing and the knuckle design's easy disassembly eliminates the need for king pin removal. And finally their knuckles use high-quality, low-friction bushings and thrust washers with integrated seals for maximum service life.

The TL Freight team identified additional examples of early equipment management success. Examples include adding oil coolers to the hydraulic system, power steering system, and the automatic transmission. These add-ons often doubled or even tripled the life of some components.

TL Freight had always worked in partnership with their tractor and trailer suppliers. Early equipment management processes would add structure to their efforts. With clear definable goals to eliminate asset failures, partnership efforts took on a renewed life.

Accelerated deterioration elimination. Another element, accelerated deterioration elimination, was certainly part and parcel of early equipment management. However, the team recognized it also extended into the area of asset maintenance and use. Efforts to reduce accelerated deterioration existed but needed more focus. This meant an all-out effort to elevate all tractors and trailers to a standard-ized condition of road worthiness.

Accelerated deterioration elimination also called for measures to ensure that equipment was operated within design standards, that the slightest hint of some-thing not sounding right, excessive vibration, or oil pressure changes be reported so that preemptive maintenance decisions could be made. Everyone in the busi-ness understood the extreme pressure to meet delivery windows. Sometimes this pressure was more perceived than real, resulting in drivers pushing their vehicles to the limit.

Demand criticality classification. The TL Freight team knew that properly maintained drivers and equipment meant improved performance. Yet not all failures were equally important and equally urgent. For example a failure of the AM/FM radio was not as important as a failure to the brake system. Depending on the volume of work or the mood of the operating center dispatcher, work priori-ties were juggled. A good mood could suddenly turn sour when a real emergency showed up and the shop was full of mundane repairs.

The TL Freight team reflected on the demand criticality classification as a possible way to establish consistent work priorities. It was a given that trailers were Class 1 assets and tractors were Class 2 assets. This meant tractors and trailers were given the highest priority because they impacted revenue generation. Starting with the 27 major subsystems of a tractor-trailer combination, they begin to clas-sify failures by type: Type 1, impacts driver safety; Type 2, impacts vehicle oper-ability; and so on.

The team felt that they could estimate frequency based on existing failure data and that cost impact could be easily calculated based on repair standards that ex-isted in their current accounting system.

The demand criticality classification could also be tied to an advance notifica-tion system, which up-linked information from either the engine ECM or the driver communication center to a satellite and then to the nearest operations center. The demand criticality classification would be applied to this advance information and a work management system would provide the dispatcher with an optimal repair plan. The repair plan might require the driver to keep on truck-ing or to stop for immediate maintenance. In either case, the problem would be logged by asset. More critical demands would be addressed immediately and less critical demands would be addressed during scheduled maintenance.

Define the Management Strategy

It became clear to the members of the executive forum that all failures and all demands must be connected to the asset! Not to a location, not to a work order, not to a purchase order, not to a warranty claim...to the asset. Thus the principle of connecting demand to the asset should drive the organization to perform three core activities with extreme diligence.

The first activity was described earlier: Identify all assets by their criticality. The second activity is to proactively identify deterioration or other factors that will likely lead to functional failures of critical assets. Use this information to prevent functional failures at the lowest total cost to the organization. The third activity is to reactively capture functional failures, their causes, and solutions so that the organization can make clear decisions on whether to pursue cost effective proactive strategies or continue cost–effective reactive strategies.

Numerous compression strategies and tools exist to improve asset reliability. Umbrella programs such as TPM, RCM, and zero breakdown maintenance are excellent for creating organizational focus. Yet none of these strategies addresses the whole of the Strategic MRO challenge. Thus the development of the Demand Supply Compression decision support methodology contained in this text.

The demand lead time analysis as performed by EuroCar provides insight on an organization's current deployment of proactive and reactive maintenance practices. Combined with the asset criticality classification, organizations can now measure their ability to apply cost effective maintenance strategies to both revenue and non–revenue producing assets.

The design failure analysis provides a preemptive strike on failures before they strike operations at the most inopportune times. Every leader understands the cost leverage of preventing failure in design versus redesign efforts driven by asset failure while in use.

So the goal is the elimination of failures. Clearly, lack of asset failure data is costly, thus the need to deploy effective early equipment management and maintenance prevention activities. Both of these should be formalized and built into the overall Strategic MRO initiative.

As organizations begin to accumulate assets, the shapes, sizes, brands, models, and configurations begin to vary wildly if not controlled. Asset standardization and commodity configuration management are strategies used to reduce configuration variation. The organizational impact of asset and component proliferation is simply increased labor, increased MRO inventory, and increased asset downtime.

Design for serviceability recognizes the need for assets to be inspected, adjusted, and repaired on a regular basis. Too often, asset design builds in an obstacle course that the maintenance technicians or operators must traverse while doing their jobs. Each obstacle represents time and time represents money.

Perhaps the biggest breakthrough in connecting demand to the asset is to understand that not all assets are the same and neither are their associated functional failures. The demand criticality classification was designed to support a business–person's objective to prioritize efforts and reduce maintenance costs while keeping critical assets in play and less critical assets performing to expectations. Instead of sophisticated FMEA software, the demand criticality classification can be integrated with COTS (commercial off–the–shelf) EAM technology giving the asset owner real–time control of work management functions.

In both the short and long term, organizations must establish a continuous improvement process for preventing functional failures and reducing their impact. Location failure analysis and standardized failure codes, when associated with the asset, provide a great data stratification approach that will pay dividends by shortening analysis cycles.

The next chapter discusses the DSC principle of connecting supply to demand. That chapter will present additional tools and technology to further compress waste and non-value adding activities out of the Strategic MRO process.

Paul's Reflections

Paul had left the previous executive forum session feeling pumped. He left this session with a headache. He never realized how unstructured his organization's approach was to asset design, build, and installation. He had no umbrella strategy for asset management.

This was his first exposure to total productive maintenance. He had heard of and actually used FMEAs early in his engineering career. Now their ugly heads were popping up again. Ugly for him, because it meant long hours, testy discussions, customer sign-offs, and documents that were eventually filed and never looked at again. He knew technology had advanced, making the development and improvement of FMEAs easier, but he still wasn't convinced that he could afford to do an all-out RCM campaign.

Paul had never heard of zero breakdown maintenance. He knew the Japanese manufacturers were focused on perfection and had developed similar approaches for defects and automation. He liked the approach but wondered how it could appeal to his workforce. His staff might think it was too simplistic.

Unlike the other executive forum teams, his company faced annual maintenance shutdowns or "turnarounds" as they were called. These were normal events in his industry. In any continuous process manufacturing, refinery, or chemical plant, "turnarounds" represent a major component of a process unit's downtime. Determining the appropriate turnaround strategy (frequency and scope of work) is a key factor in determining long-term reliability, cost competitiveness, and overall process safety.

Paul's challenge was twofold: 1) optimize daily maintenance requirements, which amount to patch work until the big shutdown, to keep the plant running and 2) use turnaround activities to drive improvements in asset reliability by preventing future failures and minimizing performance deterioration throughout the remainder of the year.

He wanted to structure his organizational efforts to better understand the phenomena of failure. It was easy for his operations staff to rattle off block, leak, cracking, rupture, corrosion, seizure, fatigue, slack, wear, distortion, burning, short-circuiting, faulty insulation, wire breaks, misoperation, current leaks, and overheating as failure modes. He needed clearer insights on these failures, their frequency, and subsequent impact on operations.

This led Paul, like other executive forum members, to seek more insightful design reliability analysis tools. Now his engineering and maintenance staff needed to become proficient in using them. A standardized failure coding system was a good start, but he was tired of everyone knowing the problem, but nobody knowing the solution.

He believed that early equipment management and maintenance prevention strategies needed to be built into his turnaround activities. Paul was concerned with the number of standby assets in existence. This was sure sign of poor asset reliability. Maybe he should require his staff and the usual cast of contractors to evaluate each major process modification relative to extended reliability, commodity product content, adherence to standards, and improved serviceability capabilities. These requirements would be in addition to normal goals of process simplification, de-bottlenecking, safety and environmental hazard reduction, and energy reduction initiatives.

He would also use the shutdown period to begin his asset database. As the DSC facilitators kept reinforcing, all demands must be connected to the asset! Not to a location, not to a work order, not to a purchase order, not to a warranty claim, to the asset. And without a doubt he would initiate the elements of the demand criticality classification and build it into his EAM technology.

What next, he thought. If this is what must be done to combat excessive asset demand…what will be needed to improve the effectiveness and efficiency of supply? What started out as a mundane subject, back to business basics, was now taking a profound turn. He commiserated with other members of the executive forum. How could they have let their assets take control of their world, quickly, relentlessly, and with nary a sound? Until BANG…the assets are in charge and we are reacting!

Chapter 8

Connect Supply to Demand: Labor

Executive Summary: Supply has three primary components: labor, materials, and special equipment. Predicting demand such that supply can be planned, acquired, and dispatched so that an asset is restored to its desired condition is a fundamental challenge to asset owners. Providing the most effective supply response to demand has often been left to common sense approaches. Many of these approaches lack well-defined implementation strategies. While it might appear that using asset criticality and demand criticality to determine a proper supply response is complicated, in reality there are only a handful of supply responses. Consistently applying the correct response is important because the right supply response uses scarce resources in the most effective and efficient manner. Continuing, an asset owner uses supply tactically to keep assets performing to expectations. Strategically, the asset owner uses information about supply activities to drive asset lifecycle improvements. The functional future perfect goal is to spend the precise amount needed to keep an asset performing to expectations.

Paul sensed uneasiness in his organization when he introduced the principle of connecting demand to the asset. He explained that assets create the demand for labor, components, and special equipment/tools. Connecting these demand costs to the asset would give them the insight they needed to guide their Strategic MRO activities as a business.

Paul explained that their first business task was to put together a Strategic MRO budget for the next year. "Simple!" said the controller. "We will simply take what was spent last year for maintenance labor and materials and add 3% to it. The 3% should cover wage and price increases. So," said the controller, "there you have it." Paul shook his head in disbelief. Paul did not really want to discourage his team but his next statement seemed to have that effect. "So," Paul stated, "what you are telling me is that we do not know what our budget should be, just what it is!" His staff's response was...Silence!

"Here is our new direction," Paul said. "We are going to implement a zero-based budget for Strategic MRO. This means that our operating budget starts with no authorized funds. In a zero-based budget, each activity to be funded must be justified every time a new budget is prepared. The bottom line is that we must justify every resource including labor, materials, and special equipment we use to maintain our assets."

Paul then outlined plans to begin developing reports that would provide insight on whether assets were working for or against performance and cost objectives. He proposed using the next fiscal quarter to fully understand what the budget should be based on asset demand. "Then we will recalculate our budget on a quarterly basis," he said. "Let's stay focused. Remember our share prices are floundering, our cash flow is slowing, and our assets keep eating our proverbial lunch."

Paul had to get a handle on where his company's money was going. He knew the asset created the demand. But he did not know the effectiveness and cost efficiency of supply.

Paul knew that this meeting had increased the pressure on his leadership team. He was not naïve enough to expect his leadership team to magically gather their wits, develop a unified plan, and succinctly step forward under a new direction.

This chapter is devoted to the labor component of supply. Chapter 9 addresses the materials component of supply. We split these components because the challenges facing asset owners as they attempt to satisfy asset demands are both broad and deep. Further, more than 200 better and best practices are available to provide high-level guidance for supply improvements. Some of the discussions in this chapter will be repeated in Chapter 9. This is done so that each of these chapters on supply is comprehensive and stands on its own.

Review DSC Guiding Principle #4: Connect Supply to Demand—Labor

The fourth DSC principle: *connect supply to demand* focuses an organization's efforts on achieving asset management objectives through improving supply capabilities and performance. The operating premise is that for every asset demand there is a necessary source of supply. This source of supply must be fully known, understood, and managed to achieve business objectives and the lowest total cost of ownership for existing assets.

Supply defined. Supply consists of labor, materials, and special equipment or tools needed to respond to asset demand.

Labor consists of all human resources required to maintain asset performance. Most asset owners limit their labor discussions to maintenance resources. However, from a Strategic MRO perspective, labor includes engineering, procurement, operations quality, storeroom, facilities, accounting, and supervisory resources to the extent that they relate to maintaining assets. All of these labor resources must be skilled and working in coordination with each other to drive both short- and long-term enterprise asset and MRO supply chain management objectives.

Materials required for maintaining and repairing assets are the second element of supply. Bearings, belts, blowers, bolts, and bulbs are only a few of the MRO supplies that begin with the letter "b." By the time most organizations get to "m" they have described nearly 25,000 SKUs (stock keeping units). Why so many? Because asset owners do not have a strategy for spares, repairs, and consumable items.

Special equipment/tools comprise the working assets of those involved in the maintenance of assets. Welding machines, meters, test units, computers, and many other types of equipment and tools need to be used for standard maintenance and repair tasks. Using the right wrench for the job is critical but often overlooked. Countless tales exist that illustrate the needless waste of time spent searching for equipment and tools while revenue producing assets remain idle. Sometimes just the opposite occurs. Universal tools are used that ultimately do more damage than good, thus reducing component and asset life.

Optimizing demand fulfillment. What, when, where, and how asset demand is fulfilled, and by whom, must be continually analyzed, understood, and streamlined. Given that not all assets are the same thus the need for a asset criticality classification, refer to Chapter 6. Further that not all failures or demands are the same thus the need for a demand criticality classification, refer to Chapter 7. The next implication is not all responses to demands need be the same, thus the need for a demand response strategy. Let's quickly review two examples.

Consider a Class 1 asset that creates a demand with a Failure Type of 1 safety, catastrophic availability impact, sporadic failure frequency, and significant cost impact. The supply response will likely be to immediately provide all needed resources to react to the asset demand (remember that asset demands are failures of some type) so that the asset can be restored to operational readiness as soon as possible. In fact, this combination of asset criticality and demand criticality would probably lend itself to condition-based monitoring to facilitate early recognition and prevention of this type of failure.

To contrast the above example, consider the same Class 1 asset. For this example, however, suppose the demand created by the asset has a Failure Type of 5 (asset use drives up cost of operations), no availability impact, sporadic failure frequency, and no cost impact. The supply response could easily be to do nothing until it is time for regularly scheduled maintenance for the asset.

At the risk of being tedious, we will repeat ourselves: *The combination of asset criticality class and demand criticality dictates the proper supply response.*

While it might appear that considering all of the factors associated with asset criticality and demand criticality to determine the proper supply response is complicated, it turns out that, in reality, there are only a handful of supply responses. The real trick is to make sure that the right one is used consistently. This is important because the right supply response uses scarce resources in the most effective and efficient manner. A full understanding of asset criticality and demand criticality results in always providing the correct supply response.

Tactics vs. strategy relating to supply chain activities. Tactically, an asset owner uses supply to keep assets performing to expectations. The asset owner must develop specific processes for the execution of labor tasks.

For example, consider hazardous liquids leaking from a pump, a functional failure caused by a corroded pump seal. The subsequent questions that must be asked and answered in a systematic way include:

- What seal failed?
- Where is a replacement seal located? Is it in the storeroom, in the maintenance crib, in a repair vehicle, in a point of use (free issue) store, in the distributor's inventory, or in the seal manufacturer's inventory?
- When does the repair need to occur? Now or in the future?
- Who needs to conduct the repair? A skilled technician? A contract service provider? The original equipment manufacturer?
- How is the repair to be accomplished? On-line or off-line? Special instructions? Special equipment?
- How can the asset owner gain from the knowledge of this failure and the subsequent response?

These high-level questions elicit additional questions, answers to which help effectively and efficiently connect supply to demand.

Strategically the asset owner uses information about supply activities to drive asset lifecycle improvements. Clearly, as the complexity of demand grows due to the use of new equipment and controls technology, new materials, new production practices, and new facility designs, so grows the complexity of the supply chain. And it seems that the demand-supply complexities will continue to grow in the future.

Review Future Perfect Precept

The connect supply to demand principle guides our thinking as we progress toward the future perfect precept to achieve zero total cost of ownership (TCO) for all assets.

Earlier we discussed future perfect in a world where assets never failed over their useful life. Because future perfect is a long way away for most companies, we initially strive for assets that are as reliable as possible, failures that are predictable, and asset configurations that are as nearly the same as possible. All of these future perfect objectives are achieved through perfection in asset deign, build, and installation. In connecting supply to demand, the asset owner has now installed the asset and is using it within the constraints and conditions of the environment.

Assuming future perfect has not been achieved during the asset planning, design, and build stages of the asset lifecycle, the next best solution is to achieve future perfect for the remainder of the lifecycle. What remains? The asset owner must strive for the future perfect objective of zero total cost of ownership through improving and optimizing supply activities. TCO is comprised of four main elements: the purchase price, acquisition, possession, and disposal of assets.

- *Purchase Price.* Includes all one-time and recurring monies paid for an asset, MRO supplies, or services.
- *Acquisition Cost.* Includes all costs associated with generating and processing an order and its related paperwork. Acquisition costs are the sum of the ordering, transporting, handling, and all initial inventory investments and include the costs of outside services associated with the acquisition of an asset.
- *Possession Cost.* Includes all direct and indirect costs associated with the installation, use, maintenance, and repair of the asset throughout its useful life. Examples of possession costs are inventory, conversion, scrap, warranty, training, downtime, and opportunity costs.

   Possession costs for MRO inventory include the cost of receipt, storage, and issuance. Examples are inventory carrying costs, cost to install MRO item, quality inspections, returns, calibration, repair, and others.

   Possession costs for outsourced services include all costs associated with the performance of the service not included in the purchase price. Examples include performance reviews, inspection of work quality, dispute resolution, training, systems, and others.
- *Disposal Cost.* All costs incurred when an asset reaches the end of its usable life, net of amounts received from the sale of the equipment (salvage value) and associated MRO supplies. Examples of end-of-life costs are administrative, operations labor, cleanup, inspections, permits, and other termination costs.

Future Perfect TCO

Purchase price future perfect. Future perfect suggests that the asset purchase or lease price would be recovered by real revenue and savings generated at its first moment of use. Some would argue that this is an impossible achievement. Again, future perfect is a directional compass and is simply an extension of industry behavior that attempts to recover asset investments as quickly as possible. This recovery results from right-sizing assets to value stream requirements; compressing asset design, build, installation, and startup times; and minimizing asset direct and indirect costs.

Acquisition costs future perfect. The future perfect goal is zero costs. In essence, this means there would be zero resource requirements for a buy-sell transaction. With the advent of EDI, e-commerce, electronic RFIs, RFPs, RFQ, automated bid evaluations, sourcing moved to operations, machine sensors checking inventory and ordering materials with no human intervention, the future perfect path is being paved to zero acquisition costs. The goal is simple: instantaneously define what you need, locate where to get it, get it, and pay for it.

Possession cost future perfect. Possession, by definition, means that monies have been invested. Ostensibly, opportunity costs were considered and, after the investment, the monies spent are sunk. But what is opportunity cost? Opportunity cost is defined as the advantage foregone as the result of the acceptance of an alternative. It is measured as the benefits that would result from the next best alternative use of the same resources that were rejected in favor of the one accepted.

Opportunity costs result from constraints on both resources and income. In a future perfect world the acquired asset is the best alternative in the market for its intended use. Further, for all other possible expenditures, the asset investment in question provides the highest possible return. Sunk costs are costs that have already been incurred and cannot be recovered regardless of future events.

Therefore future perfect for possession costs seeks to minimize investments in assets, MRO supplies, operations and maintenance resources, and other support resources given all other available options. The functional future perfect goal is to spend less and get more of what is required to keep the asset performing to expectations. Not simply spend less to get more.

Moving to future perfect is already happening! Here are a few examples:

- Designing assets that fail less often.
- Designing assets that can be serviced faster.
- Outsourcing skilled technicians based on demand.
- Buying MRO supplies to complete specific work order requirements.

For future perfect enthusiasts, the future model for mechanical assets is a biological model. In the biological model the asset conducts self-diagnosis and makes the appropriate self-adjustment to prevent failure, much like an immune system. Ultimately this biological model could be extended to the asset that repairs itself should a failure occur. We are not there yet. But if this is not where industry is headed, then where?

Disposal costs future perfect. Future perfect for the estimated value of an asset at the end of its useful life is zero. Even better would be an asset that, at the end of its useful life, would be worth exactly what its replacement costs new. Even more, the asset should impart no negative outcomes on society through its disposal, and disposal cost should be zero. This supports "greening" strategies that counter industrial activities which often emphasize:

- Dependence on nonrenewable resources for energy and material.
- No limit to how much is taken or used.
- Little concern for safety and environmental concerns, beyond that regulated.
- Little to no accountability for an asset beyond its sale and use.

Future perfect envisions assets that resist deterioration throughout their useful lives. Thus the asset could be sold to another asset owner at the current market-based replacement value.

Future Perfect Supply Response

Supply lead time, capacity, and availability. Future perfect for the lowest possible supply cost has to be balanced with the asset availability requirements. Thus the supply lead time, capacity, and availability must match the need for the asset to produce "units of value." Supply availability and capacity are constrained by lead time. In other words, as lead time grows longer supply resources are occupied longer and thus are not available for other tasks. Future perfect supply would have zero lead time, enabling infinite availability and capacity.

Zero supply lead time. Lead time is comprised of cycle time, batch delays, and process delays. Cycle time is the actual time it takes to conduct an activity. An example of cycle time is the time to repair a pump. Batch delays are created when information, MRO supplies, and resources sit idle waiting for other resources required for completing an activity. An example of a typical batch delay is when work orders pile up during the day and are not scheduled until the next day.

Process delays exist when resources are delayed between executions of multiple activities. Examples of process delays include work requests waiting for upper management approval and maintenance crews waiting dispatch directions between work orders.

The future prefect goal is that no batch and process delays exist. This implies there would be a continuous stream of information and activities maximizing supply utilization to meet demand requirements. Although probably physically impossible, the cycle time future perfect goal is zero as well.

Industry is moving toward future perfect. Improved special equipment, modular maintenance designs, and advanced diagnostic tools reduce activity cycle times. Near elimination of batch delays is being achieved through real-time system integration of CBM (condition-based monitoring), EAM (enterprise asset management), and ERP (enterprise resource planning) technology. Work orders are requested, approved, and instantaneously communicated to technicians. Mobile (remote working) technology sends information to maintenance resources to reduce process delays between activities. Automated workflow technology routes requests through the appropriate approval authority to reduce administrative process delays.

100% supply capacity. Capacity has two distinct dimensions that must be addressed for demand to be satisfied. The first is an individual's mental or physical ability to provide the appropriate supply response to a demand. The second is the more classic definition of capacity: the maximum number of tasks that can be accommodated by a given system. We have moved toward future perfect when demand utilizes resources, which minimize task cycle time. Further, future perfect would suggest that there is an infinite quantity of resources available to satisfy demand requirements.

Some would argue that the future perfect resource, be it a technician, an engineer, or an administrator, has the skills to accomplish any task. This provides the ultimate in flexibility in allocating resources to a task. This future perfect notion does indeed include the goal of creating multi-function workers.

If future perfect cannot be achieved with the multi-function worker, then the next best future perfect is the instantaneous identification of skills required to provide the appropriate supply response and the instantaneous identification of the right resource. In this scenario, future perfect is achieved when there is an exact match of resource skills to the task. In addition future perfect suggests that all resources should be fully utilized throughout the work period.

Maximizing the number of tasks that can be accommodated requires a future perfect world where no downtime is experienced during tasks. It also requires materials and special equipment to instantaneously appear at the job site as required by the resource. Further, future perfect requires that 100% of the resource's time be spent conducting the maintenance or repair task and that no downtime is experienced due to transit time or adverse environmental conditions. Again, this future perfect may seem unachievable but this is what the goal should be.

Large quantities of resources are needed if asset demands occur simultaneously and are equally urgent. Most companies have experienced conflict with resource priorities. Resource conflict challenges managers to prioritize tasks. Many an organization has wished that they had more resources. In future perfect world, resources would exactly match the criticality of the task. Can this happen in reality? Maybe not, but remember, future perfect is a journey in the right direction

100% supply availability. Achieving future perfect requires 100% availability of resources that are present and ready for immediate use. Where capacity is a function of skills and quantity, availability is a function of time. Capacity must be made available to meet demand requirements 100% of the time in order for future perfect to be achieved. 100% availability requires the future perfect ability to predict demand, prioritize these demands by criticality, and schedule the right resource, with the right skills to complete the task, when the task needs to be conducted, and keep the resource 100% employed. Are we moving toward this future perfect? No doubt!

Determine Organizational Impact

Asset owners must spend money to keep their assets in play. How much is necessary? What is the minimum amount that can be spent without putting the company at risk? How much risk is too much? Can we be too conservative with risk and spend too much?

The bottom line is that asset owners spend plenty on supply. For illustrative purposes, the 1997 Economic Census indicated that the book asset value in the manufacturing sector was $1,551,319,045,000.

The manufacturing sector spent:

- Capital expenditures – $151,510,757,000 or 9.8% of book asset value.
- Outside services to repair and maintain facilities – $5,966,006,000 or 0.4% of the book asset value.
- Outside services to repair and maintain equipment – $27,926,648,00 or 1.8% of the book asset value.
- Retirements – $46,658,714,000 or 3% of the book asset value.

These statistics do not capture the costs of internal resources required to repair and maintain both structures and equipment. Nor do these statistics capture the cost of "waste" in asset management practices. Can we assume that all capital expenditures were necessary? Can we say that all structural and equipment failures were inevitable and could not have been prevented? Can we assume that all assets were retired because they reached the end of their useful life? Even a 1% improvement in asset management practices could result in savings in excess of $1.5 billion.

Demand created by assets can appear overwhelming to organizations. How can one predict 100% of asset functional failures in time to effectively coordinate supply activities? The pressures of supply quickly mount up. Idle revenue-producing assets impact the top line. High maintenance non–revenue producing assets impact the bottom line. Clearly unmanaged supply is extremely costly. Idle or misdirected labor, excess inventory, and specialty tools increase costs rapidly. How costly?

- Conservative industry estimates are that 10% extra maintenance staff exists due to poor planning practices, unnecessary PM tasks, and not involving asset operators in autonomous maintenance.
- 25% extra administrative staff exists due to lack of EAM system integration.
- 5% of capacity is lost due to poorly managed maintenance practices.

Determining organizational impact of poor enterprise asset management and MRO supply chain management practices is not an easy proposition. Four components are necessary. The first is a "neutral, unbiased" capturing of current state practices. Second is fundamental knowledge of better and best practices. Third is financial acumen. Fourth is a practical path forward for implementing better practices and achieving targeted cost objectives.

Asset owners have a challenge before them. Before we discuss better and best practices associated with compression strategies, let's briefly review some of those challenges, also known as islands of pain.

Reflect on the Islands of Pain

Islands of pain were becoming all too real to the members of the executive forum. Reluctantly they had admitted that the assets were running the show. Now they found themselves unsure that they were handling supply effectively. Their two months of Strategic MRO discussions had seemed like a year. This mundane subject had consumed their thoughts and actions. Barely recalling their initial discussions, the facilitators took the team back in time to discuss the islands of pain. They warned their teams that the list was long.

The first island of pain was perplexing to team members. As business leaders they were charged with investing and managing the financial aspects of their businesses. Yet the *lack of basic understanding of costs and realization of cost savings* was real and pervasive throughout their rank and file. Fundamental cost drivers such as *80% of MRO costs are designed and redesigned in* was not well understood. Also misunderstood was the notion that performance could be improved by *investing in more maintenance resources to solve their problems* without looking at the underlying generation functions. And many continued to run assets as if there was no tomorrow. *No time for planned maintenance or downtime when we are building to stock anyway* seemed quite comical upon reflection.

No clearer indication of their lack of understanding of cost factors existed than the prevailing logic that *internally supplied functions have no cost to us.* Counter intuitively, they *managed labor utilization instead of TCO,* thinking that keeping their resources busy was the most effective use of their capital.

Improving TCO suggests that the asset should be the center of the cost analysis. For revenue generating assets revenue and costs are usually a function of production availability. *Not integrating production and maintenance planning* means TCO goes up not down.

Define Value Density Metrics

The executive forum members were getting a firm grasp of value density metrics. The goal was to squeeze out waste and non-value adding activities, and to maximize use of time and labor. All of which adds up to money saved. They were reminded of the facilitator's wisdom…when a consumer consumes it's a demand; when a producer consumes it's an expense. A closer look at value density metrics revealed a surprisingly simple approach that expresses every activity in terms of it value contribution. The teams sought to apply value density metrics to the Strategic MRO supply components.

Lead Time Value Density Metrics. These focus on extending demand lead time and decreasing supply lead time. By improving one or both lead times, resource scheduling flexibility is increased and overall costs decrease.

- *Demand lead time* is defined as the time from when a failure is known or suspected to when it is reported. This data can be captured at the time of the maintenance investigation by noting when the failure or potential failure was first noticed.
- *Supply lead time* is the time from when a demand was known until the demand was satisfied. This metric can be considerably different than mean time to restore, as it captures both administrative and maintenance activity time required to satisfy a demand.
- *Mean time to restore* is the average time to correct a failure and return the equipment to a condition where it can perform its intended function; the sum of all repair time (elapsed time, not necessarily total labor hours) incurred during a specified period (including equipment and process test time, but not including maintenance delay), divided by the number of failures during that period.
- *Maintenance response time to request date* measures the percentage of maintenance tasks that were performed no later than the request date. Some asset owners may choose to set no-earlier-than dates to bracket time requirements. This metric is similar to on-time delivery except applied to labor versus materials.
- *System disconnects* is a measure of how many real-time system connections exist out of total system connections for completion of supply tasks. This metric provides insight on the level of information system integration that a company has enabled its resources with. Every disconnect adds either batch or process delays.

Skills Metrics. These focus on improving inherent labor skills and their utilization. By improving labor skills improved scheduling flexibility is achieved, demands are satisfied right the first time more often, and overall labor effectiveness is improved.

- *Multi-skilling* measures the total number of certifiable skills per labor resource as a percentage all available definable skills. This metric can then be averaged across all resources that perform maintenance tasks.
- *Skills density* is a measure of actual resource skills as a percentage of the skills required by craft or certification level.
- *Skill density per work order* is a measure of work orders that required a definable skill that was unique to a specific craft. For example, suppose a particular work order required both an electrician and a pipe fitter. The skill density of this work order would be two. The goal is to reduce the number of "craft" specific skills per work order through multi-skilling.

Maintenance Task Effectiveness. This focuses on improving the effectiveness of maintenance tasks; to do right things right. By improving maintenance task effectiveness reductions are made in supply lead time, rework, and total costs.

- *First time through quality* measures the ability of the maintenance resource to perform work order tasks right the first time. This measure is at the work order level. Some organizations may attempt to perform task level audits of labor performance during certification and re-certification periods.
- *Performance to standards* is a measure of the ability to meet time standards for definable maintenance tasks. This is a common measure for repair shops where certain repairs are routinely experienced. Performance to standards should not be confused with wrench time, where actual diagnostic and repair time is measured. Most standards include time to source materials, retrieve materials, travel time, and put-away activities.
- *Wrench time is* the percentage of total operating time (time spent conducting actual inspection, diagnostic, repair, and overhaul activities. Wrench time is therefore a measure of meaningful skills utilization to restore an asset.

Total Costs. These focus on improving the "hard cost" expenditures incurred in the maintenance and repair of assets. Total costs include all internal and external resources required to perform maintenance and repair tasks.

- *Labor costs per asset criticality class* measures the cumulative costs by revenue and non-revenue producing asset class. This metric provides insight on streamlining labor costs per asset availability requirements. It also gives clear indications of costly assets that may need to be overhauled or replaced. Further, the asset owner can begin to realistically compare internal costs to pricing proposed by outside resources.
- *Overtime costs per asset criticality class* measures cumulative overtime charges by revenue and non-revenue producing asset classes. The overtime metrics become more valuable when stratified by asset criticality. Insight gained is useful in determining if overtime monies are being spent on non-critical assets. The opposite case is where money is being spent on non-critical assets during normal work hours thus increasing overtime hours on critical assets. Further analysis might reveal a mismatch in timing of demand occurrence and supply availability. Ultimately this insight is used to improve planning and scheduling activities driven by demand criticality, thus reducing total overtime costs.
- *Hard cost labor savings* is a specific measure of the cumulative "hard cost" savings gained through specific improvement initiatives. These numbers are used to justify investments in assets and asset management technology.
- *Maintenance activity based cost* calculates the total organizational costs to complete maintenance work orders. Using activity costing techniques an asset owner allocates engineering, procurement, facilities, maintenance, operations, storeroom, and accounting costs to maintenance. The next step is to identify and implement improvement strategies that target specific cost reduction areas. Many organizations have calculated cost per MRO purchase order or cost per work order. If the number of purchase orders or work orders varies significantly, wildly fluctuating cost per purchase order or work order can

occur. It is better to measure actual costs and seek to control and ultimately drive down these costs.

- *Outsourced service expenditure* is a measure of the total monies spent on outside resources as a percentage of total labor expenditures. The total labor spend can be strictly the cost of internal maintenance department resources and overhead or the total maintenance activity based cost as defined previously. This measure aids in justifying outsourcing non–core competency functions.
- *Work type costs* is a measure of costs broken out by proactive and reactive maintenance work types. Work types are stratified by asset criticality class, failure type, and proactive versus reactive maintenance. The goal is to reduce costs by focusing efforts on shifting work types from reactive to proactive, by improving scheduling of work types thus improving labor utilization, and by seeking ways to decrease work type frequencies without causing asset performance problems.

Smart Planning and Scheduling. These value density metrics focus on improving the maintenance planning and scheduling activities. Improved planning and scheduling consistently results in increased asset availability, improved labor utilization, and reduced operational costs.

- *Planned work order density* measures the ratio of planned to unplanned work orders by asset criticality class. The key is analyzing this ratio by asset criticality class while taking into consideration the associated availability requirements. Higher percentages are expected where predictive maintenance practices are necessitated by high asset availability requirements. Lower percentages are normal for assets where run–to–failure strategies are being applied.
- *Schedule adherence* measures not only the ability to complete tasks in the allotted time, but in the predetermined sequence. The first objective is to improve task estimation for improved future scheduling. The second objective is to improve labor utilization by improving the sequence of work. Sequencing helps minimize waiting and travel time.
- *Work geographic density* is a measure widely used by asset owners whose assets are geographically dispersed. This measure reveals occurrences of multiple crews doing similar work in the same geographic region where one crew could have completed all tasks with the minimum of travel or wait times.
- *Opportunity maintenance* measures the number of maintenance tasks that were conducted due to unexpected downtime. This is different than scheduling busy work given resource availability. Opportunity maintenance is important when assets must run 24/7.
- *Production scheduling coordination* measures the percentage of maintenance work orders that were coordinated with production planning and scheduling so as not to reduce asset availability. This metric is designed to build a spirit of cooperation between maintenance and operations and to reduce costs of idle maintenance and operations resources due to poor planning coordination.

- *Configuration management* measures the percentage of work orders where documentation, forms, plan or work instructions did not match the actual asset configuration. This metric should be supported by statistics that indicate where additional time was required because of the lack of accurate documentation. Recorded labor costs should be apportioned and reported to provide a complete picture of the cost of poor configuration management.
- *Strategy effectiveness ratio* is a measure of identifiable assets that have an associated demand response strategy. These strategies are condition-based monitoring, autonomous maintenance, planned maintenance, and run to failure. The objective is to have a plan for every asset. With this metric in place, operations, engineering, and maintenance resources can begin to evaluate the effectiveness of each strategy. Further stratifying by asset criticality class ensures that the strategy being applied is based on real need or impact on the value stream.
- *Maintenance activities to failure ratios* is a measure of maintenance activities to failures discovered or created through maintenance activities. A combination of metrics aid in determining the occurrence and frequency of planned maintenance activities. These include:

    —The number of failures detected during planned maintenance activities as a percentage of all planned maintenance events.
    —The number of work requests originating from asset failures that are specifically addressed on planned maintenance schedules as a percentage of total work orders performed.
    —The average number of planned maintenance inspection events between failure detection.
    —The number of nonplanned maintenance failures occurring on the same asset where planned maintenance is performed.

Identify Compression Strategies—Labor

Demand comes from assets. Supply responds to demand. Supply has three primary demand such that supply can be planned, acquired, and dispatched so that an asset is restored to its desired condition is a fundamental challenge to asset owners. Providing the most effective supply response to demand has often been left to common sense approaches. Many of these approaches lack well defined implementation strategies.

Strategic MRO—Labor Management

Eliminating waste and non-value adding activity in the labor component of supply requires a multi-faceted approach. Each facet is important. Each needs to work together with others to achieve the desired service levels at the lowest total cost. These approaches are:

- Demand driven maintenance.
- Demand response strategies.
- Supply lead time reduction.
- Smart planning and scheduling.
- Opportunity maintenance.
- Work type management.
- Multi-skilling.
- Accelerated diagnostics and treatment.
- Maintenance practices compliance.
- Configuration management.

Demand Driven Maintenance – In demand driven maintenance the demand criticality classification guides the maintenance supply response. Refer to Chapter 7 for more detail on the demand criticality classification scheme. Briefly, the components of the demand criticality classification are as follows.

- Asset criticality classification – classifies assets by their position relative to the value stream, from revenue to non-revenue producing assets.
- Failure types – defines failure types by their impact on the functioning of the asset within its operating context. Failure types range from unsafe or hazardous conditions to high cost operating conditions.
- Availability impact – stratifies the failure's impact on the availability requirements of the asset. Asset availability requirements are established through availability modeling. Availability impact varies from catastrophic to no effect.
- Frequency – uses either predictive or actual mean time between failure data to determine the frequency of asset functional failures. Frequencies span the range from chronic, or daily to sporadic, yearly, or greater.
- Cost impact – projects or captures actual indirect costs associated with the asset failure. Similar to availability impact, cost impacts vary from catastrophic to no effect.

As stated previously, demand criticality classification enables asset owners to objectively decide regarding predictive versus reactive maintenance, asset repair, overhaul, and replacement by using COTS (commercial, off-the-shelf) EAM technology. This classification also helps establish priority of work orders for planning and scheduling labor and material resources. Ultimately the demand criticality classification logic implies that an asset is functioning correctly only if it is safe to use, available to use, produces what it supposed to, at its expected rate, and does not turn into a giant money pit.

Demand driven maintenance is not designed to replace the logic of reliability centered maintenance (RCM) or become a substitute for failure mode and effect analysis (FMEA). It does, however, guide decisions regarding failure response strategies by asset criticality class (1 through 7). The goal is to optimize asset management activities by recognizing that bottom line performance is important, all assets are not equal, and all failures are not equal.

Demand Response Strategies – organizational responses to asset demands created by prevention or detection of functional failures have been analyzed, discussed, probed, prodded, and debated for decades. In the simplest of terms, the asset owner either responds to the implication of a failure proactively or the reality of a failure reactively. The asset owner has one more option…do nothing at all. Failure detection ranges from hidden to self-evident. Figure 8.1, originally introduced as Maintenance Practices Impact on Demand Lead, will now be used to illustrate our discussion of various demand response strategies.

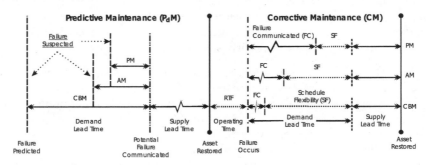

Figure 8.1 - Demand Response Strategies

Proactive strategies are conscious efforts by the asset owner to seek out potential conditions that can, with some level of surety, cause a functional failure. With this knowledge the asset owner can estimate the expected timing of the failure and its associated consequences in terms of asset criticality, failure type, availability impact, and cost.

Under the heading of *predictive maintenance (P$_d$M)*, multiple discovery techniques are used to predict failure. These are:

Condition Based Monitoring (CBM). This is also known as condition monitoring, is based on the premise that most failures forewarn of their occurrence. This failure warning can be detected either through real-time or event driven analysis. The analysis can be performed through automated instrumentation, human senses, or a combination thereof. There are numerous CBM techniques including vibration analysis, particle analysis, chemical analysis, electrical analysis, materials analysis, and thermo analysis.

It should be noted that virtually every equipment and component manufacturer is seeking to build intelligence into its products in the form of self-diagnostics. Man-machine interface (MMI) technology seeks to aid in the interpretation of potential failure modes and communicates these to asset users or other control systems.

An ounce of prevention is certainly worth its weight in gold. However, the asset criticality classification is based on the principle that not all assets are equally important. From a business perspective, revenue producing assets should be the target for CBM and MMI applications. Failures resulting in catastrophic safety or environmental failures must also be considered.

Condition based monitoring offers the longest demand lead time and thus the best opportunity to optimize supply performance and costs.

Autonomous maintenance (AM). This is a form of predictive maintenance in which the asset user observes asset conditions they feel will lead to failures. The asset user observes potential failure conditions in real-time while they are using the asset. They then take the initiative to prevent the failure themselves or alert others, depending on the type of impending failure.

Autonomous maintenance also extends demand lead time, thus improving the ability of supply to respond in a cost-effective manner.

Planned maintenance (PM). This is a form of predictive maintenance if used to observe potential failure conditions. Unfortunately, or in some cases, fortunately, many PM tasks have been relegated to simple replacement activities based on time or number of cycles.

Time-based maintenance. After a fixed time, a component is serviced or over-hauled independent of the wear of the component at that time. Time-based preventive maintenance is a common technique used to improve resource utilization, as all preventive activities can be planned beforehand. A classical example is oil replacement after a certain machine running time. Unfortunately, improved resource utilization doesn't necessarily translate to a real asset need, thus driving up asset TCO.

Meter-based maintenance. After a fixed number of asset run cycles the component is serviced or overhauled independent of the wear of the component at that time. Cycles could be based on start-ups and shut-downs, on-offs, rotations, distance, or number of parts processed. This is similar to time-based maintenance except that the schedule is not locked in beforehand. A maintenance planner can review past usage to determine an expected service period. Again the component could be repaired well in advance of an actual failure mode. This grace period is noted by a dotted line in the demand response strategies shown in Figure 8-1.

Planned maintenance also extends demand lead time based on known times and calculated cycles such that supply response can be more efficiently planned and executed. The tradeoff is premature completion of repair or replacement activities.

During economic downturn it is common for companies to adopt a 100% run-to-failure maintenance strategy. This is an extreme response to short term cost reduction as some failures are obvious and easy to predict and thus worthy of planned maintenance.

There is merit, however, to using shock treatment on one's PM schedule. The first step is to reduce frequency of all PM tasks by 50%. Then using the logic of zero-based budgeting, engineering, operations, and maintenance resources must justify keeping frequencies at their previous levels. This exercise should be repeated yearly until the optimal PM frequencies are established based on experience. This is known as "monitor and adjust based on reality."

Reactive strategies are just that. The failure has occurred. The only question is one of how and when to react.

Under the heading of *corrective maintenance (CM)*, multiple discovery techniques are used to identify actual failures. These are:

Autonomous maintenance (AM). This is a form of corrective maintenance where the asset user observes actual failure conditions. Asset users typically observe failures real-time. They either take the initiative to fix the failure themselves or alert others to perform the repair depending on the failure type.

Autonomous maintenance improves the probability that the asset will be restored in the shortest possible time. Its only downside is that empowered asset users may feel that every failure must be reacted to immediately. Logic would state that fixing a flat tire certainly has a higher sense of urgency than replacing a broken knob on the radio. This is why the demand criticality classification is a necessary method for reaching consensus on priorities of work.

Planned maintenance (PM). This is a form of corrective maintenance if used to seek out and identify failure conditions. In essence, the maintenance technician is on a failure finding mission. This approach is often legislated and more attention is paid to compliance than to the actual need to restore the asset based on business needs. An example of an extreme case is where a public utility mandated that all L-P regulators and valves be subject to teardown and inspection activities. The problem was that the literal translation was to tear down, then inspect. This approach created more failures. The policy was changed to inspect and teardown based on leak detection readings.

Run-to-failure maintenance (RTF). This is a form of corrective maintenance where the clear policy is to let the asset or a component thereof fail. Some maintenance experts deny that this is a legitimate option of an asset owner. The demand criticality classification would suggest that a run-to-failure decision is an appropriate maintenance strategy, particularly for non-revenue generating assets where the overall failure impact is insignificant. For example do not replace perfectly good light bulbs just because they may fail. This can be extended to carpeting, toilets, soda machines, and many others.

When using a run-to-failure strategy it is useful if the asset can alert users, maintenance technicians, or the casual observer that a failed condition exits. Fault signals such as warnings lights and buzzers are common. On a recent factory tour the plant manager pointed out a number of yellow flashing lights alerting observers that failure conditions existed. At another location the plant manager revealed that when a fault condition occurred it triggered the playing of different musical renditions, from Mozart to Led Zeppelin in the maintenance department to indicate the department where the fault had occurred.

As previously discussed, all maintenance strategies are theoretically reactive. Common sense suggests that predictive strategies extend demand lead time and thus provide the asset owner with the best opportunity to respond cost effectively. Reactive strategies on the other hand require the asset owner to exercise wisdom on what failures need response, when, and by whom.

Common sense suggests that proactive and reactive maintenance tasks must be optimized based on business impact. Some would suggest that all asset failures must be predictable, predicted, and prevented. This is indeed future perfect. However, if an asset owner could just begin with instituting clear policies on what demand response strategy is to be taken based on demand criticality, great progress will have been achieved.

The use of *demand response strategies* requires company leadership to determine whether predictive or corrective maintenance tasks are best suited for a given asset and budget. Each asset is assigned *pursuit* and *primary response* strategies.

For instance, a distillation column as a Class 1 revenue producing asset may have a pursuit strategy to apply condition based monitoring techniques where practical and planned maintenance as the primary response strategy. For a broaching operation, the pursuit strategy might be autonomous maintenance with the primary response strategy being planned maintenance. For an HVAC system the pursuit strategy might be planned maintenance and its primary response strategy as run to failure.

A pursuit strategy is a future perfect goal that may be restricted by the limits of practicality. These limits include limited technology to perform condition based monitoring or the inability of an asset operator to perform maintenance functions in support of autonomous maintenance.

In the above examples of Class 1 assets the primary response strategy is planned maintenance where time-based or cycle-based inspections and repairs are performed. For non-revenue generating assets one should pursue planned maintenance, but like other strategies it must be justified based on practicality. Changing filters on an HVAC system is one thing, but checking every electrical connection, all bearings, and the structural integrity of the blower may be overkill. Thus the HVAC system has a pursuit strategy of planned maintenance and a primary response strategy of run to failure.

Supply Lead Time Reduction – represents the time it takes for supply to respond to the demand plus the time to restore the asset to its desired functional state. In connecting demand to the asset the goal is to extend demand lead time. In the case of connecting supply to demand the goal is to shorten supply lead time and align the timing of supply activities with demand requirements. Refer to Figure 8.1 to see how supply lead times are impacted by predictive and corrective maintenance practices.

Recall that lead time consists of cycle time plus batch and process delays (refer to zero lead time future perfect). A typical supply lead time scenario is depicted in Figure 8.2. The first process delay experienced by supply is systemic. This is the time from when the demand is first predicted or known to when it is communicated to supply. Supply is at an information disadvantage and will more than likely have to react under pressure when informed of the failure. The next delay occurs when work requests accumulate in someone's in-basket waiting in a batch until they are sorted, and evaluated for need, priority, and resource and material availability. Then the work requests experience a process delay as they await approval. Additional process delays may include time spent waiting for purchased materials or the availability of outside contractors. Then the actual work occurs.

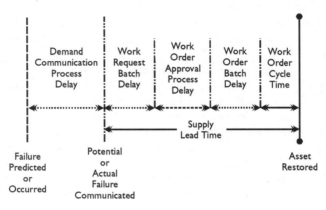

Figure 8.2 Typical Supply Lead Time Components

Further examination of the actual work performed reveals more value and non-value added activities. For a typical electro-mechanical repair, time is spent in diagnostics, identifying material needs, retrieving materials, preparing or dismantling the asset for repair, removing the component in question, repairing, or replacing the component, reassembling the asset, and finally testing to ensure that the asset is functioning properly.

Improving supply lead time begins with an all-out effort to eliminate batch and process delays. Typically, batch delays are eliminated through the use of integrated EAM applications and remote working technologies. Process delays are minimized through automated work flow applications. Where possible, work order requests, purchase requests, and inventory inquiries should be automatically routed to those with authority to issue those approvals. When the approval authority is not available automated workflow technology either re-routes or sends the request to an alternate approval authority.

A standard work combination chart typically used by industrial engineering is an excellent tool to analyze cycle time components of the work order. The standard work combination chart considers factors such as diagnostic, manual, automated, walking, and waiting times. Supply cycle time, which necessarily includes diagnostic time, is also known as wrench time. It is fairly typical that actual wrench time for a typical work order ranges from 20% to 25% of the actual reported work time. It is easy to see why 75% to 80% of a technician's workday is not spent conducting actual repairs. When one reviews the entire supply lead time components from a value adding and non-value adding activities perspective, the percentages get measurably worse. We have seen value adding wrench times of less than 5% of the entire supply lead time.

Smart Planning and Scheduling – the demand criticality analysis drives smart planning and scheduling activities. From a business perspective planning is a proactive activity that focuses on future efforts by asset class. Scheduling is a near-term activity that looks at current demands and schedules the appropriate supply response.

Smart planning suggests that planning is smart thing to do. If smart planning is done with business objectives in mind it is a powerful means for assuring asset reliability and availability while reducing total cost of ownership.

Smart planning begins with establishing asset management goals for both revenue and non-revenue assets. These goals are supported by specific target budgets based on asset classes. Smart planning should identify asset repair, overhaul, and replacement objectives. Smart planning requires enterprise asset management technology that can capture asset level information throughout the course of a planning period. Thus dependence on "personal knowledge" is slowly replaced with captured "corporate knowledge." There should be a plan for every asset.

Plans should be further divided into subplans for the resources required. These include labor, materials, and special equipment if needed. Much like project planning, resource requirements and loading are evaluated. Estimates are compiled by commodity for projected MRO supply expenditures and any special equipment needs. Smart planning should include planned outages or shutdowns to complete major repairs and perform opportunity maintenance. Refer to opportunity maintenance compression strategy.

Smart scheduling is based on demand criticality classification, supply lead time, capacity, availability, and total cost of ownership as identified in the future perfect discussion, with the goal of achieving the lowest total cost of ownership. Enterprise asset management technology for scheduling is essential for complex or sizeable maintenance operations. What is logically done in the mind of a good scheduler or dispatcher must be systematized. What are the basics of smart scheduling? To steal a popular phrase, every supply response must begin with the end in mind.

Knowing how long it takes to mobilize supply resources and conduct maintenance tasks is an essential ingredient of smart scheduling. Standard job plans for preventive maintenance tasks where supply lead times can be reasonably estimated support planning and scheduling purposes. Tracking actual task time is critical to keeping these standards accurate.

What skills are required for the given task and how many tasks are scheduled needing these skills must be known or estimated to understand *capacity* restraints. Capacity planning is a common practice for asset owners who produce products for industrial and consumer markets. It is almost completely overlooked for asset management activities. Normally, crew supervisors take responsibility for capacity planning. They must figure out what jobs can be done by what resource. This figuring is either done the night before or the morning of the planned maintenance day. The goal is to begin moving capacity planning activities further out in time.

Perhaps the toughest component of scheduling is coordinating resource availability. Jobs do not always go on schedule. Not every resource has the skills needed to do the job. Not every job is located in close proximity to the previous job. Not every job requires the same materials. For some jobs we do not know what we need until we get to the site. Not every maintenance resource desires to work overtime if needed to get the job done.

All of these and more have the possibility of creating availability conflict. And if a priority conflict exists, what is the judgment call of the crew supervisor going to be? Do the easy jobs first? Make sure the tough ones are started first thing so that overtime is minimized? What are the scheduling rules? Is does not take much imagination to understand how lack of smart planning and scheduling processes drives exceptionally high costs.

There are those who want to take smart planning and scheduling to the next level. To do this, planning and scheduling of maintenance, overhaul, and replacement activities must be coordinated with the asset availability per its value stream requirements. Many have struggled with the dilemma of whether to keep the asset running to meet production schedule requirements or take it down to perform necessary maintenance tasks. Coordinating is a necessary and beneficial task for asset-intensive industries that must maximize asset availability to meet business objectives.

Achieving the lowest total cost of ownership through smart planning and scheduling often requires a different perspective on the use of labor resources. Maintenance has traditionally been a "craft" process whose workers usually have had great latitude in how they employ work methods and standards, and how they pace themselves. The absence of smart planning and scheduling often results in work being performed because equipment is available, not because it is needed.

Smart scheduling attempts to manage these unique resources such that their utilization matches the business needs of the asset owner. Just like it is not always the right strategy to run an asset 100% of the time, it is the contention of smart scheduling that the goal is not 100% utilization of a resource just for the sake of using a resource. Filling up the day with low-priority work to achieve a high work order completion percentage is often nonsensical. A combination of internal and external resources is often the best strategy for "paying" for the right resource at the right time. This combination does not have highly skilled welders inspecting valves just to keep them busy.

Using a total cost of ownership filter for evaluating labor utilization often spotlights significant schedule disconnects between demand and supply response. For example, a homeowner arriving at home during the evening detects most public gas leaks. People to repair gas leaks are available during normal work hours. Responding to after-hours gas leaks either requires overtime or simply turning off the gas until it can be repaired the next day, leaving the customer without service. To complicate the matter, a typical gas utility is often restricted from completing major repairs during normal commute times in the morning and evening. To alleviate this problem, split shifts were developed to better align supply with demand. These mismatches between demand and supply occur in virtually every industry.

Opportunity Maintenance – can be illustrated by listening in on a surgeon talking to a patient in post-op...while we are in fixing your heart we decided to take care of that spot on your lungs. You were sleeping and you did not complain. Sure, your pulse went up and you lost an extra pint of blood...but hey we saved you the cost of going in for second time.

Asset owners often take advantage of unplanned asset downtime to repair other ailing functions of lesser consequence. They must weigh the cost of these repairs as if they were an individual event to determine their need. Just fixing things to fix things, even if the opportunity presents itself, implies the possibility of spending money unwisely. For companies who must engage assets 24/7/365, opportunity maintenance makes a great deal of sense. Typically minor repairs are made to keep the asset functioning, until a planned or unplanned shutdown occurs.

Work Type Management – It is both practical and insightful for supply activities to be classified by work types. This gives leadership a broader perspective on how maintenance activities are being managed. If costs are being captured by work type, asset owners can determine whether money is being spent appropriately on both internal and external resources.

Work types can be classified as proactive versus reactive for revenue and non-revenue producing assets. This can yield a business case for correct staffing levels. Some have suggested that work types should also be coded to reflect skill required, so that better insight is gained on whether an asset owner needs more or less of a skill type. Others create work types based on the departments requesting the work or by the location of the asset. Just remember that it is the asset in a location creating the demand, not the person or the departmental budget being charged for the work. Work types should, at a minimum, reflect the cause of the action taken for a particular asset. The asset causes the money to be expended.

Work types can be developed for proactive and reactive activities by asset criticality class and failure type. For example in reviewing Table 8.1, an A1F1P work type is a compliance-driven maintenance activity on a critical revenue producing

Asset Criticality Classification	Failure Type	Proactive v. Reactive
A1 - Assets required for conducting value stream functions that produce the unit of value. A2 - Assets required to ensure that revenue producing assets are powered or controlled. A3 - Asset required for order fulfillment functions. A4 - Assets required for supporting core production or service functions. A5 - Non-revenue producing assets required to gain access to and protect revenue producing assets from inoperable conditions. A6 - Non-revenue producing assets required to conduct supporting business functions. A7 - Non-revenue producing assets that impact quality of life.	F1 - Asset condition creates unsafe or hazardous work environment (highest priority). F2 - Asset unavailable for use. F3 - Asset does not produce a quality output. F5 - Asset does not perform to design or operational efficiencies. F6 - Asset use drives up cost of operations (lowest priority).	(P) Proactive (R) Reactive

Table 8.1 Work Type Classifications

asset. There is probably nothing worse than an A7F1C work type, meaning that the compliance money is being spent on the least critical assets of an organization.

An organization can also apply straightforward Pareto analysis to work type frequency and costs to gain a better appreciation of their folly or their professional efforts. Wisdom suggests that hope and despair come from the same measure; it is just a matter of interpretation.

Multi-Skilling – moves an organization toward achieving the future perfect resource, whether it is a technician, an engineer, or an administrator, who has the skills to accomplish any task. This provides the ultimate in flexibility in allocating resources to a task to meet smart planning and scheduling objectives. Multi-skilling is accomplished through a process of training maintenance, asset users, and other support employees in specific skills that cross the traditional trade or craft lines.

A typical example is the changeout of a motorized pump. Traditionally, a changeout could require an electrician to disconnect the motor leads and a pipe fitter to disconnect the pump flange connections and physically replace the pump. The electrician would then return to the job, and reconnect the motor leads. The pipe fitter would, at this point, be able to test the pump's operability. A single multi-skilled resource could conceivably do both tasks.

An outcome of multi-skilling is the utilization of the minimum number of resources to conduct any job. Additional resources are added to accelerate job completion, not because additional skills are required. Often skilled trade distinctions require close job scheduling based on the sequence of the job and labor skill requirement. If the loss of our example pump created downtime for a revenue producing asset, both individuals would remain at the job site, performing only their particular functions.

Multi-skilling requires that individuals receive additional training beyond the normal skills required for their craft. The pipe fitter would be trained in the proper disconnecting and reconnecting of the motor leads. The electrician, in turn, would be trained in proper pump orientation, and flange disassembly and reassembly, as well as alignment methods. After this training, either individual would be qualified to perform the entire job alone.

A typical skills breakdown by work order reveals that the majority of the maintenance and repair tasks do not required a particular craft skill. An example is removing and replacing bolts. In fact, there are many overlapping skills. In an autonomous maintenance environment multi-skilling would extend to asset users who would be trained to perform simple but necessary maintenance tasks. What occurs in the general context of work management is a shifting of lesser skilled tasks to operators and a sharing of common technical tasks among skilled trades. The advantage to the company that promotes multi-skilling is the ease of scheduling work, the freeing up of resources, and improved wrench time per work order. This advantage is often shared with the worker who receives incremental pay increases for knowledge gained.

Accelerated Diagnostics and Treatment – Maintenance and medical activities are similar. Symptoms are observed or communicated. They are then diagnosed to determine the possible problem. Prognosis is rendered relative to the severity of the problem. Based on both the diagnosis and the prognosis, treatment is recommended and applied. Then symptoms are monitored to determine if a favorable result is achieved. If not, it is back to the doctor. Each of the functions of symptom identification, diagnosis, prognosis, treatment, and follow-up must be flawlessly executed if the asset is to remain healthy or return to health in the shortest possible time. A somewhat less pleasant task is making disposal or replacement decisions knowing that an asset is terminally ill or the required treatment is too costly.

Diagnostics begin once symptoms are brought to the attention of something or someone. The "something" might be sensors or man-machine interfaces (MMI) that support condition based monitoring applications.

The "someone" might be asset users, maintenance resources, control room personnel, asset service providers, or asset makers. Through remote monitoring techniques asset symptoms can be scrutinized from virtually anywhere in the world. Once symptoms are recognized the next step is accelerating diagnostics. This is the analysis of the cause or nature of the condition, situation, or problem. Diagnostic technology is not new and continues to get better, often taking away the fun of the Sherlock Holmes- or Colombo-type investigation. Diagnostics can be quite time consuming, much to the disadvantage of revenue producing assets. If technology cannot be deployed, then human skills must be sharpened to accelerate diagnostic activities.

Knowledge resides in two places: in the minds of humans and in the environment. For example a yellow traffic light alerts us to slow down and be prepared to stop...most of us anyway. This is knowledge contained in the environment thus saving us from having to think about our next action. A smart workplace attempts to retain knowledge of symptoms and their possible causes in the work environment so that the proper diagnosis is arrived at quickly. Then the correct treatment can be applied quickly. What does a smart workplace look like? It includes handheld technology connected to sensors providing alerts to possible failures, and asset-specific EAM checklists providing records of past similar symptoms or physical checklists of instructions posted on or near the asset that list common symptoms and their causes. A smart workplace accelerates diagnostics.

Demand criticality analysis aids the asset owner in determining the severity of the failure or prognosis. Based on the asset criticality class (revenue versus non-revenue), the failure type, the impact of the failure on asset availability, the frequency of the failure and the cost of treatment, the asset owner can choose among several options. These include ignoring the symptoms, applying a bandage, stitching the wound, opting for minor surgery, or conducting a full-blown transplant.

Treatment is accelerated by the use of asset artificial intelligence. Upon the detection of an error or fault condition, the asset itself conducts self-adjustments or resets itself, much like today's computer applications that automatically send error messages to a log for later review and then reboot.

Accelerated treatment requiring human intervention is much more time consuming if the asset is not designed to be quickly serviced, or the component is not modular, thereby allowing for quick disconnects and reconnects. Treatment is further delayed if the human resource does not have ready access to materials and special equipment. Finally treatment is time consuming and costly if the doctor, in our case the maintenance technician, knows not what they are doing.

A smart workplace aids in providing treatment guidance by posting visual or electronic repair instructions. Perhaps the most exciting proposition for asset owners is that asset makers continue to error proof and modularize their designs, making adjustments, repairs, and replacements as simple as "disconnect red, blue, and green connectors; push button; remove board; snap in; and reconnect using same color scheme."

Follow-up to ensure that the treatment was successful is also a potentially time consuming challenge. Intrusive maintenance, by design, increases the probability of infant mortality failures and other unintended failures. Virtually all maintenance supervisors track how many times the same asset was visited in a short period of time for the same or other failures. This is a ready indication of the quality of the diagnosis and treatment.

Accelerated diagnostics and treatment is an exercise in problem solving involving the fundamentals of root cause analysis, containment actions, and eventually a permanent solution. The better an asset owner is at this function the lower the total cost of asset ownership will be.

Maintenance Practices Compliance – requires monitoring to ensure that maintenance practices are adhered to. Most asset owners are satisfied if the demand is satisfied. And, for most routine maintenance, this is perhaps as far as one should pursue the issue. So where should an organization focus its compliance activities? The obvious answer is safety and environmentally legislated activities, given the penalties for noncompliance. The next obvious focus is where will noncompliance negatively impact the business objectives of the organization? If repeated failures of revenue producing assets are caused by not adhering to acceptable diagnostic and treatment practices, then compliance checking is a must. This means the asset owner must bear the additional cost of prevention and inspection activities to avert the penalties of repeated failures.

For those organizations that aspire to such standards as ISO 9000, API, NQA-1, and others, the compliance measures must be established. An asset owning organization must be mindful of "overdetailing" compliance expectations, such that the cost of compliance exceeds the benefits of such programs. There are numerous examples where profit margins were squeezed by self-imposed or fanciful compliance standards.

The next area requiring "near absolute" compliance is the capturing of data relative to an asset. A wise organization understands the power of information. It further understands the challenge of determining what data to collect and whether that data will reveal important trends. Strategic MRO cuts to the chase by focusing on asset-centric data.

Without asset-centric data, an asset owner does not have the information needed to accelerate performance improvement and cost reduction. If this message is not clear, it is worth repeating. The asset creates the demand. The demand creates the need for supply and supply costs money.

Other than assets, there are two other sources of demand. These are people and the customers of the asset owner. The premise of Strategic MRO is that demand requirements for personal protective equipment, gloves, special tooling, and like items can be allocated to assets or to the product or service being produced. Everything can and should first be allocated to the products or the assets. Then asset costs should be allocated to appropriate products. When an organization determines that a product cost must be reduced to remain competitive, it knows what its cost factors are and can begin immediate improvement activities. This requires a disciplined approach to data collection and compliance.

Configuration Management - is a system that manages the technical information related to all assets (structural, equipment, and mobile), ensuring that information is available, correct, current, and usable.

The four pillars of configuration management are:

- Configuration identification – a numbered or alphanumeric coding system for identifying all assets.
- Configuration description – a name and description of the asset.
- Configuration change management – the process by which changes are authorized and coordinated.
- Configuration auditing – methods employed to verify compliance to configuration management policies and procedures.

Configuration identification and description data can be easily maintained with EAM technology using asset breakdown structures. The EAM technology enables asset owners to codify the following:

Assets. By configuration identification number, asset name, and description. Metadata includes asset criticality, location, primary functions, brand, age, and other items.

Documents. By type, number, and revision level; examples include specifications, schematics, drawings, bills of material, maintenance plans, and manuals.

Forms. Examples include problem reports, enterprise change requests (ECR), enterprise change notices (ECN), document change records (DCR) and work authorizations such as purchase orders, work orders, modification orders and others.

Records. These are comprised of completed forms and referenced documents. Records include evidence that the work was authorized and that the intended results were achieved.

Configuration change management must be perceived as an important part of the engineering and maintenance functions. To ensure the success of configuration management, identify the changes to the plant configuration as early as possible. Since modifications are the biggest cause of configuration changes, the configuration change management procedures should be integrated into modification procedures.

Configuration auditing requires a commitment to keep records updated and an information system that will record changes as they occur, even if the maintenance resources fail to do so.

Characteristics of a good configuration management system are as follows:

- It identifies configuration changes before changes are made to the physical plant.
- It updates information linked to the plant. Information like:
    —Drawings.
    —Location breakdown structure (LBS).
    —Equipment records and specifications.
    —Inventory records.
    —Maintenance program.
    —Personnel responsibilities.
    —Risk assessment.
    —Training manuals.
    —Legal requirements.

Lack of configuration management has cost employee lives, has resulted in materials being purchased for assets that have long since been removed or modified, and increases work difficulties. This extends supply lead time and increases total costs.

Develop Case Study Examples

Finally the light bulbs were going on! The great "Aha...now I understand!" had been achieved. The executive forum teams knew that total costs of ownership could be broken neatly into four components. Purchase price, acquisition, possession, and disposal. Not paying attention to initial asset design and specification requirements during acquisition activities could drive up possession costs. Poor acquisition processes could be overcome tactically only through a series of redesigns of both the asset and the supply chain to reduce these costs. If the early equipment maintenance prevention philosophies were used, subsequent acquisitions would not repeat the same mistakes. Given their current reality the executive forum teams focused on the here and now. What should and could they do to improve Strategic MRO supply labor practices?

Superior Water

The Superior Water team knew that executive leadership had already determined that they would outsource labor requirements to two contractors. Each contractor was awarded a geographic territory based on location and the number of qualified resources.

But now, due to the recent discussions on connecting supply to demand, various compression strategies, and value density metrics, the Superior Water team wondered what the real motivations were for outsourcing labor. Did we choose contractors simply to shift costs? Do these contractors have work management methods better than our methods? Do the contractors have a demand criticality classification and a smart planning and scheduling process? Do they use multi-skilled resources? What worried team members most was their inability to answer these questions. It seems price was the most significant selection criteria. They now understood the potential error of their ways.

What the Superior Water team did know was that they kept a veritable army of inspectors on staff to make sure the contractors did the job, and did it right. So much for trust, so much for reducing lead time, so much for developing a continuous improvement environment under a shared future perfect vision. Nonetheless the Superior Water team addressed the labor issue with a renewed sense of purpose.

Superior Water Compression Strategies

The Superior Water team quickly rattled off numerous compression strategies, but quickly surmised that there was little structure to their efforts. Going back to the basics seemed a great place to start.

Demand Driven Maintenance. The team began to refocus their maintenance strategy under a formal "program" that was driven by demand and business objectives. Earlier they had adopted the zero breakdown maintenance strategy to move toward a reliable system. Now they needed to add a second component that allowed them to optimize labor resources. They were challenged by the fact that they had outsourced the physical repair of assets while maintaining inspection activities in-house.

The decision to deploy resources varied considerably by inspector and contractor. The team felt that establishing standards for asset criticality classification, failure types, availability impact, frequency of failures, and costs would diminish the impact of disjointed priority setting. The demand driven maintenance standards would be required to be incorporated into the enterprise asset management (EAM) technology for internal and external resources. It was preferable that the contractors be on the same EAM system. However, if this was not economically feasible, systems would have to be integrated to achieve real time information flow with the newly established demand driven priority system.

Demand Response Strategies. The team, after being prompted by the facilitators, agreed to review current maintenance practices from the perspective of a simple proactive versus reactive strategy. The team also decided to review current maintenance practices by asset criticality to determine if there was opportunity to eliminate or streamline inspection activities.

Remarkably, the team found that inspection activities were both proactive and reactive in nature. Proactive inspections were conducted by internal resources to ensure compliance with regulations and as a part of asset condition assessments. Because of this they saw no overriding need to keep sending internal inspectors out in a reactive mode. The delays caused by these reactive inspections were costly and sent the wrong message to the customer.

The team found that a field inspector was not needed for nearly 80% of the work types. The better process would be to electronically transmit incident information in real time to the contract services planner. Upon assignment of the crew and work priority, the planner would dispatch the crew telephonically and/ or electronically. Then the incident verification would occur and repairs would be made. For simple inspections where no immediate work was needed, the team felt that meter readers and water quality inspectors could perform these tasks within a given geographic region to reduce labor costs.

A concern expressed by upper level management related to whether there was indeed legitimate work to be done or were the contractors simply creating revenue for themselves? Do we send out nearly 24 internal resources to ensure that work was actually needed, or just have the contractor perform the task? The cost was nearly $3.0 million to ensure that the contractors did only legitimate repairs. This was 3.3% of the total outsourced labor cost. Executive leadership decided to trust in the demand driven maintenance strategy to control labor costs. They would then use analysis of failures and contractor repair efforts to drive zero breakdown initiatives.

Supply Lead Time Reduction. The team readily admitted that there were substantial batch and process delays in their work management system. The recommendation for better practices included the integration of the call center technology with the work order system. A best practice suggested by one team member was the elimination of the call center altogether by simply adding telephony technology. This technology would direct calls to the correct depot by region, and customer profile information would be displayed automatically. The depot administration would have to key in information only once. Work orders would be automatically raised with customer information embedded and routed in real time to the contractor. Contractor progress and job completion reports would be transmitted electronically using mobile computing and job status could be posted to a website or communicated telephonically to the customer.

Smart Planning and Scheduling. Given today's handheld technology capabilities the team felt an improved response time could be achieved by the immediate and continuous assignment of work orders to the crew. This was accomplished by using scheduling software technology based on demand criticality logic. Smart scheduling would include the real time reporting of crew job status while at the site. New jobs would be automatically assigned to crews based on reshuffled priorities, availability of supplies and special equipment, maximizing work content, and minimizing travel time.

In the haste of getting crews out, supervision did not always organize jobs by location. Thus, the largest effect smart planning had on crew efficiency was planning jobs by geographic density. It was common to find multiple crews, each working on tasks taking two hours or less to complete, all within a five-mile radius of each other on the same day. These same crews would then experience an average of one hour travel time to the next job. The smart planning tool would allocate jobs by proximity, criticality, and estimated length of time including travel. Crews were then given assignments using a logical job order that minimized crew downtime.

Perhaps the most obvious compression strategy was the hardest to see. The team recognized that Superior Water had adopted standard work hours for its inspectors and contract suppliers. Similarly it had negotiated the same hours for its call center. And, of course, their material suppliers were open only during standard business hours. The problem was that residential customers discovered nearly 60% of all leaks and poor water quality incidents. These discoveries usually took place between the hours of 3:00 PM and 7:30 PM. Given an average work order completion time of 2.5 hours, it was easy to see why most jobs were not started until the next day. If they were worked on the same day they automatically resulted in overtime. This was a high-cost option but to an irate customer without water it was a necessary option.

The Superior Water team recommended that a split shift be utilized. They found that the 3:00 PM to 7:30 PM time frame could be covered with a 1:00 PM to 10:00 PM shift. A small number of crews would handle only emergency or high priority work orders. Crews would rotate through the split shift to ensure fairness in work hours and family time. What work was not completed would be automatically assigned to a new crew through smart scheduling technology. Leadership at Superior Water knew that some of its employees had grown accustomed to the overtime component of their pay...this would not be an easy change to make.

Maintenance Practices Compliance. As a regulated industry, Superior Water was under constant scrutiny not to endanger public welfare through improper or inadequate maintenance practices. Electronic job plans were generated and made available to crews at the worksite through handheld technology. These job plans were supported by electronic links to specifications, blueprints, safety, and material standards. As jobs were completed the crew leader electronically checked off the individual tasks in the job's work instructions. The crew leader was also able to electronically submit any changes made to the job plan for future review and potential incorporation.

Configuration Management. Superior Water had invested heavily in GIS (geographic information system) technology to capture knowledge about its network assets. The team wanted to make sure that, when work was completed, site information about the network was cross-checked against the GIS system to ensuring accurate information. This process would be perceived as burdensome at first because so many changes had been made to the network over the years and no one knew the exact configuration. The leadership knew that the long-term benefits of GIS information capturing and analysis would pay off through increased network reliability. Everyone involved would just have to suffer through the process of improving the initial data accuracy and then enforce the collection of information as part of the normal work order process.

EuroCar

Like all of the executive forum teams, EuroCar realized that supply not only consisted of materials but of labor and equipment as well. They had devised nearly 20 work types used for setting priorities. Examples include reactive immediate (RI) work, reactive deferred (RD) work, maintenance support (MS), and preventive maintenance (PM) work. Last year RI work was in excess of 35% of their efforts, RD 15%, MS 12%, and PM 30%. The team agreed that the addition of the seven level asset classifications provided the umbrella logic for their priority of work.

The EuroCar team certainly sympathized with the MilBase Ops team when it came to a diverse set of assets to support. MilBase Ops's assets were diverse because they were literally operating a city. On the other hand planned obsolescence, a critical part of EuroCar's continuous improvement efforts, drove its asset diversity. Major equipment reconfiguration occurred every other year. Each new configuration generated different asset demand profiles, thus a different failure management strategy. Each new drive shaft, motor, controller, hydraulic system, welding arm, and deionization system required new skills of their maintenance staff. Constant training meant time away from maintenance activities.

Paying attention to detail was always a hallmark of EuroCar process engineering. Yet hindsight indicated that gauges were often located out of the line of sight. Simple adjustments required difficult and time consuming machine teardowns. Reaching lubrication points required body maneuvers not possible by human beings and special tools abounded thanks in large part to a dedicated tool shop and creative maintenance personnel.

The EuroCar team knew that inefficiencies existed in their engineering, maintenance, and purchasing practices. They had tried several ways of accurately predicting the time needed to complete work orders, but their accuracy was always questioned. They had worked diligently to calculate the cost of a purchase order. They even tracked every process design change that affected part quality as part of their ISO 9000:2000 requirements. So why had they not gotten the performance and costs results they were looking for? Then the breakthrough occurred. Why fight the tenets of lean manufacturing?

What insights did EuroCar have that Superior Water, MobileTel, MilBase Ops, and TL Freight did not? Simply put, EuroCar had the ability to learn from the principles of just-in-time manufacturing, quick response manufacturing, time-based competition, Kanban systems, quick changeover, and error proofing. Even now, when the EuroCar team mentioned lean manufacturing, all eyes glazed over in the other executive forum teams.

The purpose of the executive forum was to learn from other industry best practices so that they could be applied, however modified, to elevate the performance within one's own company. Why did the other executives resist learning about lean manufacturing? Had they become educated beyond their ability to learn?

The EuroCar team marched ahead. Their manufacturing operations focused on production planning methods to build only what was consumed. The plan was simple. Build vehicles just in time for the market. Stop building inventory ahead of sales. This meant that equipment had to be flexible and responsive to changes in schedules. How could these same principles apply to maintenance practices?

EuroCar Compression Strategies

Demand Driven Maintenance. The EuroCar team was looking for a term they could use to distinguish their efforts from the corporate endeavor called total productive maintenance (TPM). Demand driven maintenance allowed them to adjust their collective thinking to focusing on assets by their criticality classification, failure types, availability impact, frequency of failures, and cost impact.

As an automotive producer, everyone under its roof understood the notion of demand. They wanted to leverage this term to integrate the mission of maintenance to that of production. In the past, not every work request had been responded to equally or fairly. By establishing a common priority scheme, they felt they could get operational buy-in for their new methods, while managing their customers' expectations.

The EuroCar team also felt that insight into failure types, frequency, and costs would facilitate the involvement of operations and would be an excellent springboard for initiating autonomous maintenance activities. Everyone would be involved in understanding the nature of asset demand and controlling the associated labor costs.

Demand Response Strategies. The EuroCar team heard the repeated message from the other teams in the executive forum. Could it be true that only 50% of preventive maintenance was necessary? If this was true, how could they identify unnecessary preventive maintenance tasks? Cost savings can be targeted by comparing the frequency of specific preventive maintenance tasks to the specific asset's maintenance strategy within each asset classification. The goal is to decrease the frequency of preventive maintenance tasks without decreasing the asset's reliability and availability.

When EuroCar studied the nature of their inspection activities here is what they discovered:

- Less than 1% of failures were detected during planned maintenance activities.
- Fewer than 5% of the work requests originated from asset failures that were specifically addressed on planned maintenance schedules.
- An average of 8.5 planned maintenance events took place before a specific failure was detected.
- 65% of non-planned maintenance failures occurred on the same asset where planned maintenance was performed.

The statistics were somewhat disturbing in that EuroCar thought their planned maintenance was very good. What was suggested by the data was that they were inspecting too frequently and that they were looking for the wrong things. The team also decided to decrease the frequency of existing planned maintenance tasks. They automatically reduced by half the frequency of inspections for non-revenue producing assets. Analysis of failure type and occurrence led to both the reduction and addition of planned maintenance tasks for revenue producing assets. Further, the team discovered that, by using autonomous maintenance strategies, they could handle simple preventive maintenance tasks without a work order or formal schedule, just operator checklists.

Now that a strategy was beginning to form for planned maintenance, the team set its sights on improving predictive maintenance techniques. EuroCar was very experienced with the use of error proofing devices to prevent a potential product quality problem. The same source inspection logic applied to monitoring equipment performance, deterioration, or failure.

In the maintenance world, source inspection was aptly named predictive maintenance. Early attempts at applying sensors to production lines were less than totally successful. Operations felt that the sensors stopped the line prematurely compared to advance warning of line stoppage from maintenance. The result...a number of the sensors were disconnected or taped over.

Maintenance felt like it needed to error proof the error proofing devices. Meetings were held with the body and paint shop operations to define how to apply predictive maintenance techniques to these constraining operations. If predictive maintenance techniques could not be successfully applied, then the cost of redundant systems would have to be revisited. Reengineering systems would be costly, requiring re-qualification of the redundant systems using process performance studies.

Supply Lead Time Reduction. Continuing its lean manufacturing focus, the EuroCar team thoroughly analyzed their supply lead time for corrective maintenance tasks. Mean time to restore (MTTR) versus mean time to repair was the driving metric for reducing costs of all repairs. Using the word "restore" sent the message that it was critical for revenue producing assets to be back in production.

The team used a standard combination worksheet typically used to analyze common operator and maintenance tasks. What was revealed was that the typical maintenance tasks required considerable time to disassemble and reassemble the asset. The proposed solution was modular maintenance. There were numerous recommendations for improving supply responses and reducing cost with modular maintenance being the most novel.

Several maintenance personnel were asked to attend a quick changeover training session put on by the plant's lean institute. During the session, teams identified ways quick changeover could be applied to their jobs. The initial reaction from maintenance was that this stuff did not apply in their world. However, on closer examination, the team soon realized that certain repairs, when performed on-line, rendered equipment and sometimes the entire line inoperable. Quick changeover would call this an internal activity.

The key was to move as many of the internal activities to external so that efforts could be done off-line while the machine or assembly line continued to run. The maintenance team investigated ways they could quickly connect and disconnect motors, quickly remove and replace access panels, and replace entire modules instead of individual components. The list of opportunities continued to grow! The great "Now we understand" moment transformed the team, which led to coining the term modular maintenance instead of quick changeover maintenance. For revenue producing assets, modular maintenance techniques meant improved availability. Improved availability meant improved revenue streams.

Smart Planning and Scheduling. Borrowing from the tenets of lean manufacturing, the maintenance planning team decided it would follow the consumption model for unplanned maintenance. As corrective maintenance was completed, the scheduling engine would then assign the next activity based on the prioritized queue of work, much like a Kanban system. The work order was in essence a manual Kanban. Except, in this case, maintenance activities would be transmitted electronically through PDA (handheld) technology instead of a physical work order. This method would be integrated with planned and predictive maintenance efforts which handled known demand.

The goal was to maximize maintenance labor utilization, again much like the goals of lean manufacturing. This would require that maintenance personnel become multi-skilled or at least willing to perform tasks requiring lesser skills. This was counterintuitive to the skill classifications currently in place. Achieving competencies in mechanical, electrical, hydraulic, pneumatic, and power transmissions would be a near impossibility.

So, one of the goals of the planners was to match the minimum skill required to the work order. If this minimum skill was not available, the next goal was to maximize labor utilization by using a resource with higher level skills. The goal was not to fill the queue with busy work but to continuously target and schedule resources to the highest priority tasks throughout the workday. Preventative maintenance tasks were given a completion window instead of a definitive time to create flexibility in responding to critical asset needs.

Work Type Management. EuroCar had distinguished itself by its disciplined approach to tracking work orders by work type. The Strategic MRO facilitators challenged their thinking regarding how these work types should be structured. They wanted a business perspective on how maintenance activities were being managed. Tracking cost by work type easily allowed them to determine the business impact of the use of internal versus external resources, on revenue versus non-revenue producing assets, using proactive versus reactive maintenance, and asset versus department or person creating demand.

The analysis yielded several startling results. What was most revealing was that 37% of labor costs were being spent on non-revenue producing assets. A small number of individuals created the preponderance of work requests. Only 30% of the work types had an associated priority classification. And, the scheduling process did not establish a queue for sequencing work orders by type or by priority.

Configuration Management. As an ISO 9000:2000 organization, EuroCar was meticulous about record keeping, except for one area... asset configuration. Frequent daily changes were hard to track therefore they were not tracked. Records were kept. They just were not organized and easy to retrieve. The solution involved connecting the document management technology to their enterprise asset management (EAM) system. Surprisingly they had both systems. They just had not connected the two for improved asset management.

The EuroCar team decided that their focus should be on revenue producing assets. Much like what Superior Water had experienced in starting up its GIS (geographic information system), EuroCar expected that their initial set of records would be fraught with errors. However, they felt that the benefits of up-to-date blueprints, specifications, safety information, asset component information, and location of assets were substantial. Near real time tracking of changes would improve the timeliness of future maintenance diagnostics and repair efforts. This data would also improve the resale value of the asset. And, if done right, configuration management would enable the storeroom to purge unnecessary inventory.

MobileTel

The MobileTel team was clearly not pleased with what they thought were excessive maintenance costs. They had invested in an internal technician staff to keep the network up, at all costs...literally. They rightfully believed that poor service leads to customer turnover. The "at all cost" strategy was interpreted in practice to mean that every failure was a high priority. Even though they had a classification scheme for A through C cells, this had little effect on scheduling labor.

The market was tightening its purse strings. Since the telecom sector peak in the spring of 2000 some $1.4 trillion in investor wealth had evaporated. More than 15 companies had filed bankruptcy reorganization in the last year. And many others were teetering. MobileTel had invested heavily and was strategically poised to continue its investments in UMTS technology. MobileTel's mandate was clear...get costs in line with revenues.

MobileTel Compression Strategies

The MobileTel team directed its energies to understanding and improving technician effectiveness and utilization. They planned to increase and modify the network infrastructure, but do so without adding technicians.

Demand Driven Maintenance. The MobileTel team needed both a logical and enforceable method for prioritizing maintenance activities. They had already completed an asset criticality classification based on cell utilization for revenue producing assets. They had not completed this for non-revenue producing assets. Failure types were not standardized and therefore hard to aggregate and evaluate. Steady state availability was definitely critical for Class A cells where down elements meant lost revenues. As mobile telecommunication traffic increased, they ultimately wanted to achieve steady state availability for all cells. The goal was to achieve this future state without exorbitant maintenance and redundant system costs.

The MobileTel team had analyzed work order frequency data:

- Out of a total of 42,000 sites, 34,064 cells required maintenance last year.
- The highest number of visits made to one cell was 425.
- 11,938 cells were visited once.
- 6,663 cells were visited twice.
- 4,179 cells were visited 3 times.
- 2,907 cells were visited 4 times.
- 1,953 cells were visited 5 times.
- 255 cells were visited more than 10 times.
- 28 cells were visited more than 20 times.
- 3 cells were visited 30 times.

What was not clear was the frequency of certain types of failures by component, by asset, or by asset location. This information was essential to improving MobileTel's understanding of what was creating the demand for technicians. They needed to know whether these failures were time and availability sensitive or could be handled through opportunity maintenance practices. MobileTel's technicians and dispatchers knew the important of having this information...so much so they had individually developed in excess of 450 custom databases.

Finally, MobileTel was unable to clearly articulate costs for each maintenance event, by failure type, or by total costs per cell. Demand driven maintenance practices were their first step in achieving the level information acuity they needed to improve their technician practices and utilization.

Demand Response Strategies. MobileTel felt like it was in a constant reactive maintenance mode. Unfortunately it was hard to look at a circuit board and tell if it was going to fail. And, very little had been done in the way of condition based monitoring to predict failure. Man-machine interfaces quickly alerted key resources of the presence of a fault. In some cases redundant systems were available to keep the network running. Then, during planned maintenance activities printed circuit board diagnostic techniques enabled them to quickly narrow in on a hard-ware problem. The demand response strategy was to get the cell back into service as fast as possible. Therefore board level repair activities were rarely performed at the site. Suspect boards were returned to the technician shop for analysis.

Software failures always required a corrective maintenance response. How does one predict software failure? Control room technology helped to analyze software faults and often the problem could be solved with the physical presence of a technician. Sometimes rebooting or resetting the system became the best solution for an unknown problem.

While establishing the demand response strategies it became clear to MobileTel that improved asset reliability was the key to reducing the maintenance needs. These activities had already begun through the deployment of reliability analysis techniques. What the team needed was a clear way to categorize failures at the component and cell level to use to guide their corrective maintenance activities. The demand criticality analysis was ideal for doing just that.

Smart Planning and Scheduling. The MobileTel team's analysis of current work indicated that in excess of 70% of their work could be planned. Most of the fault conditions did not require an emergency response. The team felt that through the use of demand criticality classification, they could easily exceed 90% planned work. The opportunity for improved labor efficiency was evident as the MobileTel team reviewed aggregated labor hour totals for a one-year period.

- The total available labor-hours for the period were 1,555,000.
- Total hours booked to work were 860,490 (55% of available hours).
- Traveling hours were 239,848 (27.8 % of booked hours).
- Execution hours were 618,230 (71% of booked hours).
- Administration hours were 2,818 (.33% of booked hours).
- 69,135 planned work orders were executed.
- Average time to complete a work order was 7.98 hours. Of the 7.98 hours:

    —32% were completed in less than 2 hours.
    —48% less than 4 hours.
    —65% in less than 6 hours.

Although it was instantly clear that labor was not being effectively scheduled, the data did not provide insight on why. Was it a skill mismatch to the task? Was it excessive travel time? Was it lack of material availability or was it different priority systems used by 50 dispatchers?

The MobileTel team recommended that the smart planning techniques be applied to establish a common priority system based on demand criticality classifi-cation. Unavailable Class A cells would be given the highest priority. At all other cells where the revenue stream was not affected work would be organized by skill requirements, and estimated repair time including transit and geographic prox-imity. This new scheduling logic would be integrated into the EAM technology to provide dispatchers with a prioritized queue of work. Mobile technology would be used to communicate job status to and from the field. After all they were a mobile technology firm.

Multi-Skilling. The MobileTel team knew that they had a challenge facing them as they converted to a UMTS from their existing GMS. This was a parallel conversion where GSM and UMTS technology would be operated side by side until such time that G3 (third generation) technology became the standard for Wideband CDMA (code division multiple access) communications.

The term "third generation" was confusing to most of the technicians. Some had experienced "first generation" analog networks and most had experience with "second generation" digital networks. Packet-switching utilizing Internet Protocol (IP) instead of circuit switch technology was now the new language. Skill distinctions between hardware and software specialists were becoming more and more blurred. Most diagnostic efforts began in the software realm and continued until a hardware fault was identified as the culprit. Much of the hardware repair work was strictly pulling boards and replacing them. The future was clear...multi-skilled resources were needed to complete basic functions.

Configuration Management. The MobileTel team knew that whenever a new component was installed the system reconfigured itself, much like a personal computer does. What was needed was the centralization of this data so that any technician could know what components were being used where. MobileTel felt that this improved the technician's ability to perform advanced diagnostics. It also eliminated customized databases just for configuration management.

Another reason for better configuration management was based on a recent recall event. A leading supplier had indicated that it would exchange potentially defective boards for new ones. The supplier provided MobileTel with applicable model and serial numbers. It was up to MobileTel to locate them. The supplier limited the exchange period to the one month only. MobileTel had in excess of 20,000 of these components and did not have a clue where to look. Component installations were not tracked at this level. The only information they had was that work orders were completed that may have required the component in question. In the end the team found nearly 2,000 components to exchange. The rest were left in service because no one knew where they were.

The team quickly realized that if they did not have the information to perform recall change-outs, they could not do a failure analysis based on manufacturer models. How could they compare product performance, reliability, and durability? If improved reliability was their goal, the historical information they needed was lacking. When they approached the technicians with this dilemma, the technicians expressed their frustration with going to a cell with little clue as to what configuration they would find. This, they added, was why their trucks were filled with multiple parts, more often than not, the wrong ones. This all translated into time consuming trips back to stores to retrieve materials.

MilBase Ops

The MilBase Ops team knew that contractor and staff maintenance labor was their largest cost component. The strategic plan called for a renewed effort to correctly size and shape their workforce. MilBase knew that working smarter meant they needed smarter resources who could expertly execute maintenance tasks. MilBase Ops also felt that it needed to focus on resource recruitment and retention of its core staff even though they were being directed to increase the amount of real property managed by contracts, leases, and other business agreements.

At the same time MilBase Ops was challenged to reduce acquisition, renovation, and repair cycle times. The ultimate goal was reducing base lifecycle costs. The message was clear for the MilBase Ops team: they must figure out ways to do more with less. Recent reduction in force efforts made the "work harder" message clear. But what they really needed was to figure out ways to work smarter.

MilBase Ops Compression Strategies

Demand Driven Maintenance. The notion of demand driven maintenance made sense to the MilBase Ops team. What they did not want was another acronym, DDM, to add to a list that makes the index of the Library of Congress look short. They had glossaries to define glossaries.

What they liked about demand driven maintenance was the aligning of their total efforts on demand elimination, demand response, and demand cost management. The types of assets to be supported ranged from bowling alleys, parking lots, airports, hospitals, barracks, roads, training ranges, and child development centers, to sanitary sewer lines. The MilBase team told the executive forum that they had to respond to demands equivalent to that of a city combined with the demands of the entire business and community organizations contained within that city.

Earlier the team had struggled with asset criticality classifications. It seemed that each asset had components of varying importance. They knew that a leaky roof required repair. They also knew that loss of power would dramatically impact operations. They reasoned that they should look at buildings from a structural integrity perspective without regard for the operations that were being performed inside the building.

They surmised that the new asset criticality classification was mission centric and should improve the prioritization of efforts. Standard failure types had been reduced to a manageable few. These, when combined with the asset criticality classification and the impact of asset downtime, would help in clearly setting priorities of effort. The MilBase Ops team also knew that if it was to have any success it had to capture and manage the information about asset demands. This would allow them to better manage their supply response and reduce costs. Soon, the cost of shifting efforts to civilian maintenance and service agencies would culminate in all the savings that could be attained through this mechanism. But, cost decreases in the future were still expected and had to be attained.

The team recommended that the next phase would integrate EAM systems with those of their contractors. This would give the MilBase Ops team realistic insights of failure types by assets and by frequency. Associated cost factors could then be analyzed, along with the contractors and base service providers, to drive efforts to improve asset lifecycles...all per their command directives.

Demand Response Strategies. The team was again challenged to think of how they conducted predictive and corrective maintenance. "Not again," one team member lamented. "There has got to be something more exciting than this." "Okay," the facilitator stated, "get rid of all planned maintenance tasks. What would this do to your staffing levels?" "Drive them up," the team responded in unison. "How so?" "More things would fail and we would be in a total reactive mode."

"You have been trained well," said the facilitator. "I am sure you have never been challenged to reduce maintenance activities. So play along with me. What planned maintenance tasks would you add back in? What would be your rationale for adding these tasks? Remember resources are scarce."

The team struggled with this exercise. It seemed it was easier to accept the status quo and assume that all planned maintenance tasks were necessary. The team reviewed their records to determine what percentage of planned maintenance tasks actually discovered a failure. Much like EuroCar they discovered less than 1% of failures during planned maintenance activities. Only 3% of the work requests originated from asset failures that were specifically addressed by planned maintenance. Unlike EuroCar, MilBase Ops could not calculate the average number of planned maintenance events before a failure was detected. However, 95% of their corrective maintenance tasks were performed on assets that had planned maintenance schedules.

The MilBase Ops team felt that it was time to overhaul their planned maintenance activities. They decided to establish pursuit and primary response maintenance strategies for each core asset. Guidelines would be established for any asset where run to failure (RTF) was the primary strategy. Certainly they had to maintain base appearances...maybe they could find longer lasting paint...maybe ceramic coatings made sense...one coat guaranteed to last forever. The team had a good laugh until they saw how much money they spent on paint and the associated labor every year.

Using the demand criticality classification logic, MilBase Ops decided to put together strategies for driving predictive versus reactive maintenance plans. They would challenge themselves and their contractors to reassess their activities to determine what made "business sense" to continue, expand, or eliminate. MilBase had regulations, detailed case studies, and cost savings calculators. But none of these seemed to consistently improve field practices. They needed a common sense approach to being proactive *and* reactive in their maintenance efforts.

Supply Lead Time Reduction. The MilBase Ops team did not know what current supply lead times were. This lead time, of course, is the time from when a demand is known to when it is satisfied. Determining these lead times seemed like an overwhelming task.

The team selected three key contractors to complete process level flowcharts. The goal was to determine typical lead times for identifying and initiating a maintenance response. The process flowcharts also contained information regarding what systems were being used and where batch and process delays existed. The results were somewhat disappointing, and left the team thinking about all the things they had taken for granted when they awarded outsourced work.

When they were working through the process flowcharts with the contractors everyone seemed on edge. The contractors were eager to please and wanted the MilBase Ops team to know that they "jumped through the proverbial hoops" and with pleasure when they received a call. But was that what MilBase Ops really wanted?

In reality, all contractors had both batch and process delays. Work requests sometimes were keyed and re-keyed onto various systems. Work orders were stacked high waiting dispatch the next morning. Most contractors had a special stamp for high priority tasks. All had paging or mobile telecommunication systems for rerouting crews throughout the day. None of the contractors could provide overall lead time measures from time of request to time of job completion. All could measure the percentage of jobs completed by the requested date of service.

The team reminded the contractors that the MilBase Ops goal was to maximize demand lead time. This would provide the contractors with the longest possible time to plan, gather materials, and schedule resources. What was important from a supply lead time perspective was that they eliminate unnecessary delays in the work order preparation and scheduling processes.

The contractors were then challenged on how they knew what an appropriate length of time was for conducting standard maintenance tasks. The response was "we bill to your standards." This was not the answer MilBase Ops was looking for, but they were not surprised by it. The team knew that they had studied maintenance tasks to arrive at a set of standards. They also knew that new technology, new designs, and new work methods had reduced time to complete basic tasks. They did not know if these improvements resulted in any cost savings for them and for their contractors. There was little or no incentive for the contractor to share these insights with the MilBase Ops team. The feeling of discomfort began creeping back into their discussions. The MilBase Ops team suggested that both entities would benefit if they could continually identify ways to reduce maintenance task cycle time and thus labor costs.

Smart Planning and Scheduling. The MilBase Ops team progressed to the topic of planning and scheduling with the three contractors. Most of the contractor efforts were focused on planned maintenance activities. After all, they were convinced that planned was always better than reactive. This might be true, except that the planned maintenance tasks had become institutionalized and had never been challenged. The team reinforced the notion that optimizing the supply response to a demand requirement through planning was the key. But not every demand requirement was equal, so not every supply response needed to be an emergency.

The contractors suggested that the new performance level agreements disrupted contractor planning by making every work order equal in priority and timing. They literally had contractor crews scrambling day in and day out fighting fires. They asked the MilBase Ops team how many of them dropped everything they were doing to replace the filter in the furnace of their own homes. Yet this is what they expected of their contractors.

The MilBase Ops team introduced the concept of demand criticality classification. They showed how this would be used to help set priorities. The contractors all breathed a sigh of relief. This was a solution that made sense and took the "jumping through hoops" burden off of their shoulders.

Joint discussions then focused on the impact of travel and how this factor added to response time and costs. The contractors agreed to begin aggregating work orders by geographic proximity. They also agreed to perform opportunity maintenance where appropriate in order to reduce travel time. The MilBase Ops team said it would recommend to the base commander that consideration be given to the co-location of contractors inside proposed consolidated repair centers. This recommendation would reduce the overhead costs of the contractor and thus the price of their services to the base.

Multi-Skilling. The MilBase Ops team felt that in keeping with their detail oriented tradition they should carefully review how skills were being applied against work orders. The variety of skills required for base maintenance included almost every conceivable skill set. They knew the benefits of a multi-skilled workforce. Their strategic plan called for extensive certification and professional licensing programs. They would extend these programs to their contractors who, for the most part, did not have the luxury of specialists unless demand called for it. The contractor typically subcontracted to industry specialists when they needed to. This practice was actually what the MilBase Ops team sought.

Maintenance Practice Compliance. Maintenance practice compliance took on new meaning for the MilBase Ops team. Traditionally compliance meant adherence to required work practice and time standards. This was still necessary. Now the team sought compliance to demand driven maintenance requirements and maintenance response strategies. It also meant the routine challenging of the standards if improved practices existed. The military was renowned for their discipline but they were not sure if the civilians could be trusted to be that disciplined. With the cost constraints currently placed on any organization servicing base operations, discipline was essential.

The contractors had to have systems in place that ensured that asset demands were responded to in a consistent and disciplined fashion while improving service levels and reducing costs. The combined effort of smart planning, multi-skilling, ongoing performance evaluations, and technology deployment was necessary to doing right things right.

TL Freight

TL Freight based its supply strategy on the asset demand coming to the source of supply. This was reverse of what was experienced by EuroCar and MobileTel. Considerable investments had been made in strategically located repair centers while hiring the best of the best technicians and service advisors.

TL Freight knew it needed clear direction for its labor resources. Much of the use of these labor resources was predicated on the decision making process of those who checked in the trucks at the gates, technicians who assisted at the pumps, and the service managers.

Demand Driven Maintenance. The TL Freight team was excited about creating a consistent standard for decision making by using the demand criticality classification. Availability, failure types, frequency, and costs were easily calculated and analyzed and used to drive maintenance improvement. The TL Freight team, like many of the other executive forum members, felt that the term demand driven maintenance put the proper focus on the asset. It allowed them to roll up multiple programs under one title and reenergize their maintenance efforts.

Demand Response Strategies. Preventive maintenance was the key to success for TL Freight. They could not afford to have either the trailer or the tractor out of service. But preventive maintenance techniques only needed to be applied to some of the potential failures. Many of the time and cycle based maintenance practices had been standardized. Now it was time to review existing technologies that support condition based monitoring techniques.

If they could get 1,000 to 5,000 more miles out of their oil life, substantial savings would result. New sensors on the market enabled this. With a consistent measurement scheme for oil they could begin to track oil life patterns to determine if it was impacted by load characteristics, engine age, and driver habits. Vehicle operating conditions were monitored constantly through sensor technology. This information could be uploaded to TL Freight centers on demand.

With the push for newer and integrated technologies, TL Freight had to figure out a way to identify and prioritize opportunity maintenance. As trucks came in for tire changes, radio knobs were being replaced. These opportunity maintenance initiatives were usually associated with components that could fail without any safety or performance consequences.

Unplanned maintenance of any type taxed the resources of the service center. Low priority maintenance seems to tax everyone emotionally. What was low priority for the company may have been high priority for the driver and vice versa. The demand criticality classification enabled the service centers and the drivers to work cooperatively to improve total vehicle readiness and driver comfort.

Supply Lead Time Reduction. The first task was to improve demand lead time. This meant having drivers notify the "maintenance system" of any trailer or tractor concerns at the earliest possible time. This contrasted with the customary "roll down the window at the gate and complain loudly" routine. Mobile communication existed in all tractors. Getting drivers to use it was another thing. This required discipline. Given the new expectations of demand driven maintenance, drivers had to learn that better service would come with advance warning.

Supply lead time was analyzed. Clearly trucks sat in queues awaiting repairs. To speed up routine service, oil, fluid, and tire changes were handled through a separate facility. If a trailer needed to move and the tractor was not capable, the TL Freight dispatch system would match a new tractor to the load. The question was "Do we work on the down tractor or complete other repairs on other tractors that needed to be on the road?" These decisions were a function of smart scheduling practices that each of the service centers agreed upon.

Matching the right labor skills to the demand was important to reducing supply lead time. Most specialized technicians liked to work the first shift. However, demand could occur in a 16-hour window. The TL Freight team reviewed the nature of the demands and the timing of their occurrence and decided to shift and balance resources between two shifts.

Often emergency breakdowns occurred nowhere near a TL Freight service center. To speed up time to repair, TL Freight initiated 24-hour control of vehicle maintenance expense including non-scheduled maintenance through preset expenditure limits. TL Freight belonged to an emergency road service system that provided professional technicians on a 24/7/365 basis. The challenge was capturing repair data so that it could be easily fed into the TL Freight smart planning and scheduling system.

Smart Planning and Scheduling. The supply lead time reduction efforts pointed to numerous opportunities to improve scheduling practices. The first to be implemented was a disciplined approach to scheduling based on the demand criticality classification. The second was matching vehicle location to a service center at the time of need without disrupting customer delivery requirements.

Drivers were informed of vehicle maintenance schedules via mobile telecommunication technology that was built into the cab of the tractor. This information included the nearest service center. When a driver neared the location he/she could transmit his/her location and what services were required. The service station would then indicate the repair time frame that the driver could be serviced within.

The third component was capturing emergency or other maintenance activities performed by other service providers. The lack of current knowledge of these events was frustrating to the team. It meant that parts were allocated wrongly and maintenance schedules were inappropriately booked. Further, TL Freight had little control over the type of repairs conducted even though guidelines were clear as to what constituted emergency maintenance. Emergency maintenance also added another layer of complexity to warranty tracking.

The last component of smart planning and scheduling was managing opportunity maintenance activities without impacting other time-sensitive maintenance tasks. Rules were established using the demand criticality classification to indicate what failures could be handled as an opportunity.

Work Type Management. To improve maintenance practices the TL Freight team recommended a review of all services performed by work type. This information would provide insight on what percentage of work orders were generated because of safety, availability, or other performance issues. By capturing work types by vehicle they could begin to build service profiles by vehicle types for future purchasing or early equipment management considerations. They could develop driver profiles regardless of what vehicle was being driven. The same was true for tracking technician repair performance based on the vehicle and the associated work type.

The list of possible reporting combinations was imponderable. Thus the TL Freight team recommended that they start with simply understanding costs by work type, then drilling down to determine what factors impacted these costs. Work type management allowed them to stratify maintenance data to improve the asset's lifecycle and reduce total costs.

Accelerated Diagnostics and Treatment. Technology has advanced so far that, often, diagnostics involve simply plugging a tractor's electronic control module (ECM) into a diagnostics unit. This was not true for all electrical and mechanical failures. Reference and diagnostics manuals were bulky and had been transferred to CD ROM based systems that were available to all service centers. The TL Freight team recommended that this system be web-enabled to support two-way communications. The system they sought would allow technicians and drivers to access online diagnostic information. The system would also record any new or revised diagnostic information as it was generated in the field.

The driver would act much like an educated patient, thus accelerating the diagnostic process at the service center. That funny squeak in the rear of the vehicle could be easily pinpointed and diagnosed well in advance of the repair. Advance diagnostic information could then be used to improve smart scheduling practices.

Define the Management Strategy

The members of the executive forum were glad that the principle of connecting supply to demand was broken into the two components of labor and materials. Until the creation of the ultimate biological system, that is, one that repaired itself, every organization would face labor challenges to keep their assets in service at the lowest total costs.

If all failures and all demands must be connected to the asset, then all supply information must be connected to demand. Together, demand and supply information are a part of the asset profile. This information gives the asset owner the best chance of effectively managing the condition of assets, proactively determining maintenance and supply strategies, and ultimately maximizing return on assets.

The key to connecting supply to demand is to ensure that maintenance activities are driven by an understanding and appreciation of the various types of asset demands. *Demand driven maintenance* connects demand with supply while focusing many disparate, parallel, and confused maintenance efforts. The goal is to eliminate sources of demand where practical and to respond to the remaining sources of demand in an objective manner.

The *demand response strategies* are purposely designed to have both a pursuit and a primary response strategy. A company may pursue a run-to-failure strategy even though their current primary response strategy is planned maintenance. They may pursue autonomous maintenance even though their primary response strategy is run to failure. Why two strategies? To force an asset owner to continuously push resources toward a future perfect…highest performance at the lowest total costs.

Once the response strategies have been developed for assets, the next step is developing *smart planning and scheduling* processes to meet overall asset perfomance and cost goals. Labor either goes to the asset or the asset comes to the labor. In either case the objective is to minimize costly asset downtime and maximize costly labor utilization. Not all asset downtime is costly. However all labor downtime is, by definition, costly. Therefore *opportunity maintenance* should be combined into the smart planning and scheduling activities to maximize labor utilization for necessary work, not just "busy" work.

The demand criticality classifications focus on what to do first, second, and third. *Work type management* enables an organization to clearly measure and manage maintenance activities from an event perspective. How many? How often? By whom? To what? At what cost? These can be answered by asset classification, by failure types, and by other parameters using work type management. Applying Pareto principles to work order frequency and costs, 20% of the factors create 80% of the activities or cost.

To improve labor utilization, more and more organizations are seeking ways to develop *multi-skilled* resources. Multi-skilling requires a concerted effort on the part of the associates as well as leadership. Often, work rules, labor agreements, salary, incentives, professional development, and personal goals must be taken into consideration before making the leap into multi-skilling. The end result is a flexible resource that, in the long run, enjoys increased job security while reducing overall cost of operations for the company.

Maintenance technicians must be thought of as asset doctors. They must be given both the tools and knowledge for *accelerated diagnostics and treatment* activities. Getting the diagnosis right the first time reduces the probability of rework, and ancillary failures, and minimizes asset downtime.

All in all, *maintenance practices compliance* means a disciplined approach to asset demand response. The technician must be provided with clear expectations for work performance and adherence to standards. If every technician is setting their own priorities, using different materials, or applying different remedies to the same problem, then the asset owner suffers.

How does an asset owner ensure that short- and long-term memory exists regarding the inventory and makeup of their critical assets? *Configuration management* is the key. It is not a simple process. It requires defined work processes, supporting systems, and a disciplined approach to keeping records accurate and up to date. Configuration management is the snapshot of all the labor and material solutions that have been applied to the assets. Without this snapshot the organization suffers the pains of excess labor and materials, all at a cost to the bottom line.

Paul's Reflections

Paul's value stream was under pressure. Sales were slumping, cash was tight, and the investors were worried. He knew that his firm's assets supported the company's value stream. These assets were not all equal. These assets created demands. These demands were not all equal. Each demand had an associated source of supply. The supply chain needed to be managed according to the overall needs of the value stream.

At his last count he estimated that he had nearly $4 million invested in excess labor, materials, and outside resources. Paul felt that his current asset management practices did not create customer confidence in order fulfillment, kept his team in a constant reactive mode, and drained his cash flow.

He left this session of the executive forum with the understanding that it took a combination of skilled people, well conceived processes, and integrated asset management technology to achieve the results he knew were possible.

He had several initiatives that he would launch with his staff when he got back to the office. He knew he had loaded their plates when he had asked them to develop a zero-based budget.

Now he needed to provide guidance on supply side labor improvements. The list of tasks was very long. Complete a thorough lead time analysis for both demand and supply. Establish pursuit and primary response strategies for his core assets. Review his current labor planning, scheduling, and dispatch process. Understand the technician skill requirements needed for his operations. And, get a handle on documentation.

As he left the executive forum meeting it was clear to Paul why his operational costs were so high. He wondered if he had the patience and commitment to do something about it. The list of to do's was getting long and they still had to figure out what to do with MRO materials.

Chapter 9

Connect Supply to Demand: Materials

Executive Summary: This chapter is devoted to the materials component of supply and how to design and manage the Strategic MRO supply chain. It starts with breaking apart the supply chain, reforming it, and then focusing it. The next challenge is compressing waste and non-value added activities out of day-to-day activities. The final step is executing tactical MRO supply chain management methods that match the demand driven by an organization's assets. There are a wide variety of alternatives an organization can use, including Web-based e-commerce technology, inventory optimization analysis, smart storerooms, variable pricing models, and system integration, to drive improvement.

This time Paul's team was prepared. He had challenged them to develop a zero-based budget for operations and asset demand for the next year. And they responded! His staff beamed. "We have installed that $1-million EAM software you requested. We got it done in a week. We built an entire asset register in less than one day. We have installed condition-based monitoring technology in our core unit operations and have tied its output to our planning and scheduling module. And, Paul, we completed the detailed reliability analysis for 15 major pieces of equipment. We think we have figured out how to improve availability by 15% and save the company no less than $2 million in labor costs."

"We have also transferred all MRO inventory records into the EAM technology. Its e-enabled purchasing module is connected to no less then 1,000 preferred suppliers. Our ten preferred suppliers have all agreed to buy back our entire inventory at no charge just for the privilege of doing business with us. And they agreed to respond to all material needs within five minutes of a request. We have worked with their financial resources and we do not have to pay anything for materials the first year... and it is interest free."

Just then the alarm went off. Paul woke up and shook his head. What a nice dream to start the day! Reality was different for Paul. His team had some critical decisions on how they would re-architect internal practices and technology deployment. It was not going to be as easy or practical as his dream suggested.

Review DSC Guiding Principle #4: Connect Supply to Demand

The facilitators reminded the executive forum teams that they were continuing their train of thought from the previous session. The center of attention was still the fourth DSC principle: *Connect supply to demand.* They were reminded that the focus of this session was the materials component of supply. The key was to match materials with labor.

Labor can perform maintenance activities without materials, but if materials are involved, labor is needed. The challenge facing most organizations is overcoming the considerable time spent by labor to identify, locate, purchase, and expedite the delivery of materials. The goal of this principle—connecting supply to demand—is to streamline this process to meet asset performance requirements while reducing total cost of ownership.

Supply Defined. The facilitators reminded the teams that supply consists of labor, materials, and the special equipment/tools needed to respond to asset demand. *Labor* consists of all human resources required to maintain asset performance. *Materials* consist of asset components and consumable items necessary to perform maintenance tasks in a safe and efficient manner. *Special equipment/ tools* comprise the working assets of those involved in the maintenance of assets.

Demand Engines. What are direct materials to an asset maker are indirect materials to the asset owner. Two very different demand engines pull direct and indirect materials through the channels, using similar business logic but different scheduling and procurement drivers.

A company procures direct materials (the materials that go into the products they make and sell to their customers) based on production schedules tied to customer orders and, perhaps, forecasts. The need for direct materials is said to be dependent on demand in that it is dependent on scheduled production.

Indirect materials (materials used for maintenance, repair, and operations/overhaul) are procured, in part, based on maintenance schedules composed of work orders for future repairs and maintenance. The balance of procurement for MRO materials is triggered by the day-to-day use of materials causing quantities on hand to fall below preset minimums. These minimums are usually set based on past usage of the material.

So the need for indirect materials is a curious mix between dependent and independent demand. The need that is associated with work orders for future maintenance is dependent on that scheduled maintenance. The rest is said to be independent because it cannot be associated with some driving factor other than failures that seemingly occur in a random fashion. For many companies, the independent need for MRO materials is far larger than the need that is dependent on future scheduled maintenance.

The point here is that there are two very different engines driving demand for direct and indirect materials. Both demand engines can create emergency procurement requirements. But, for the most part, the need for direct materials is fixed when production is scheduled. The future need for indirect materials is almost never known with the same degree of surety as that of direct materials. Past usage of indirect materials is almost universally used to set their reorder points and reorder quantities. These values, sometimes called minimums and maximums, are what ultimately drive the procurement of indirect materials.

The biggest blind spot in industry is the lack of understanding that the asset is the primary demand engine for most industrial supplies. If demand is connected to assets, then future need for MRO materials can be based on the knowledge of what needs those assets created in the past. This may be markedly different from total past usage in that assets used in the past may no longer be in service.

Material Supply Activities. Material supply activities are comprised of stock replenishment and purchase-to-order activities. Stock replenishment can be to central, decentralized, free-issue, and point-of-use stores. By design or because of emergencies, some MRO supplies never make it to the storeroom, barely making it through receiving.

Storerooms can be fixed or mobile. Mobile stores exist within cars, trucks, trailers, rail cars, and even planes. Perhaps the most mobile storeroom is the maintenance technician's toolbox. If one reviews the stocking practices of the MRO supply chain, inventories can be found in wholesale and retail stores, industrial distributor warehouses, in master distributor warehouses, in asset maker finished goods warehouses, in service parts warehouses, and in salvage yards.

The asset makers and service providers must describe MRO materials in such a way that they can be easily sourced, substituted for equivalent parts, upgraded, tracked by revision levels, combined with other parts into kits or subassemblies, and associated with engineered assets. Asset owners can add further confusion to asset and component description by creating their own naming conventions, often unique by department and operational sites. When an asset owner begins to investigate investments in MRO materials, it becomes difficult to take stock of what truly exists. We have seen it all: the same bearing called by many different names—a bearing, a sleeve, a bushing, and so on.

MRO materials flow from their origin through many routes to ultimately end up installed in the asset that created the demand. All four logistic routes of air, land, rail, and water are used to transport MRO materials through various channels of distribution. Often, these materials are bought in bulk and then redistributed by various entities participating in the channel.

Each stocking and transportation and redistribution activity adds time to the supply lead time. This often makes it difficult for supply lead time to be less than demand lead time. Thus, by design or perhaps lack of design, inventory must be held at various points in the channel to meet demand requirements. These inventories exist, in part, because of poor practices and lack of communication among channel members. We have addressed many of these practices and communication issues in Chapter 3, Islands of Pain.

Some suggest that the mosquito will survive a nuclear holocaust. We suggest that excess MRO supplies in the channel will be there to keep the mosquito company.

Review Future Perfect Precept

The connect supply to demand principle guides our thinking as we make progress toward the future perfect objective to achieve zero total cost of ownership (TCO) for all assets. Not only do assets have a total cost of ownership, so do their individual components. For that matter, any purchased MRO item has an associated TCO.

Future Perfect Material TCO. Total cost of ownership (TCO) consists of purchase price, acquisition cost, possession cost, and disposal cost. Future perfect TCO for MRO materials delays the material purchase until the moment just before the asset needing the material fails. The asset owner pays the absolute lowest price for the necessary component(s). The component will perform as required without failure throughout the useful life of the asset. The component is not held in inventory but arrives at the job site exactly when it is needed. As discussed previously in modular maintenance, the component is installed and verified at the absolute minimum labor cost. Finally, that the component enables the estimated disposal value of the asset at the end of its useful life to be zero or equal to the exact replacement cost for a similar asset in new condition.

Future Perfect Material Supply Response. In the future perfect world, MRO materials would be instantaneously produced and delivered to the point of use. No excess inventory, no consolidated material requests, no aggregated spends, no special freight considerations, no consignment...just the exact component(s) arriving when and where they are needed at exactly the time of need.

By its simplicity, future perfect highlights the complexity of the current MRO acquisition and supply chain practices. Sometimes these practices are so complicated that they are left to their own devices. The market knows what to do with an uneducated asset owner. Let the buyer beware.

Determine Organizational Impact

The cost of not having a good MRO material strategy often manifests itself as high prices, excess inventory, unnecessary overtime, extended or unplanned asset downtime, and employee frustration. Here are a few statistics to remind us of our folly:

- Lack of an MRO material strategy conservatively results in a 10–15% price penalty.
- A lack of a consumables, spares, and repair strategy implemented by asset criticality class can easily generate 20% excess MRO spend.
- Inability to quickly source and locate materials adds no less than 5% extra labor cost per day or an average 30 minutes per day per maintenance resource.
- Typically, 80% of the purchasing staff's sourcing activities are allocated to acquiring MRO or indirect materials.
- The average purchase order for MRO materials has a transaction cost of $175 to $250.
- The range of inventory turnover for asset owners is approximately 1 to 2. This means that on average of six months to a year's worth of MRO expenditures exist in inventory. Rare exceptions exist where inventory turns are much higher. It is more common to see turns less than 1. In most cases an industrial distributor needs between 3 to 4 turns just to stay in business.
- An average annual MRO inventory carrying cost of 22%. Thus the asset owner experiences an annual cost of 22 cents for every dollar invested in inventory.
- For every dollar invested in inventory a company with 5% earnings needs to create $20 in revenue just to stay even.

These numbers suggest there is plenty of savings opportunity in MRO materials. Consider a major manufacturer who offered no less than 40 distributors the chance to act as an integrated supplier for 100% of its MRO materials. The conditions were simple. The supplier would have to provide 100% of the plants' MRO material needs priced at 80% of the previous year's expenditures. They would receive this payment in a lump sum amount equal to 1/12th of the 80% dollar figure every month. How many distributors refused to be considered for the deal? None at last count. What does this say about the known waste in MRO material supply chain practices?

Reflect on the Islands of Pain

The islands of pain for MRO materials are profound. Most companies have figured out why *not* to perform certain practices for direct materials, yet continue to perform those same activities for MRO materials.

The three common demand engines are the unit of value produced, the people working in a company, and the assets used by a company. These have different demand patterns. Each requires a different strategy and different procurement processes. Therefore, thinking that buying office products is the same as buying maintenance products is the same as buying direct materials is a costly fallacy.

As each of the executive forum teams reviewed their purchasing and inventory management practices, it was clear that confusion existed between that which was consumed versus what they communicated to the supply chain as demand. The inability to create visibility of consumption data made it impossible to engage the supply chain in meaningful discussions on reducing MRO supply costs.

An awkward laugh emanated from many a leadership team as they began to understand how not connecting the supply engine to the demand engine was driving supply response time up. This decreased maintenance effectiveness and ultimately drove costs ever higher.

After some robust discussions, the executive forum members now understood that the asset is the demand engine, not the maintenance function. Without this understanding, their actions to control costs via better inventory management while ignoring the underlying generation function were definitely misguided and actually caused MRO inventories to grow.

Maverick purchases become standard practice when people think that purchasing controls reduce the maintenance spend. Lack of confidence in the system creates numerous uncontrolled caches of maintenance parts throughout the organization.

Another hiding place for inventory is the accounting system when materials are directly expensed to a job or department as they are acquired. Thus it does not show on the books. But this logic is counterbalanced by a belief by accounting that MRO inventory is an asset and shouldn't be written off even if the inventory will never be used.

How about the notion of buying bulk to save money? If we buy more, our price per piece goes down. So buy more and save. We are not confused about consumption and demand; everything that we bought bulk last year must have been needed. So we should aggregate all of last year's spend by commodity grouping and conduct a reverse auction to drive down total cost.

The executive forum members let out a collective sigh.

Define Value Density Metrics

The following MRO material investment metrics guide the analysis of how much money is invested in MRO inventory:

- *Inventory turnover.* Annual inventory purchases/average inventory value by inventory class. For an asset owner higher is always better. This includes critical spares. Some argue that the best inventory turnover for an asset owner is zero. This means that zero MRO materials are owned. The industrial distributor, on the other hand, must balance on-time delivery (OTD) requirements with inventory turns to ensure that asset owner service levels are met.

- *Inventory carrying costs.* The industry rule of thumb is 25%. What does this mean? Inventory carrying costs can be thought of as money that was invested by an asset owner because they chose to own inventory in advance of an asset demand. This money is not available for other opportunities. Inventory carrying cost consists of capital costs, shrinkage, obsolescence, inventory handling costs, and storage space costs.
- *Inventory investment by inventory item class.* This value density metric measures how much money is invested in various MRO inventory item classes. Item classes are usually formed by grouping items by annual dollar usage. Thus, all items with high annual dollar usage are placed in a class. Likewise, items with medium and low annual dollar usage are placed in their respective classes. This measure can be expressed in percentages. The goal is to reduce the investment in all item classes.
- *MRO materials acquisition and disposal labor costs.* This metric requires an organization use activity based costing methods to estimate the TCO elements of acquisition and disposal. Typical areas studied include procurement, engineering, facilities, maintenance, accounting, administration, and supervision. The goal is to reduce TCO by improving acquisition and disposal processes. This metric can be divided by the total number of transactions to determine transaction costs per purchase order, per purchase request, per work order, etc.

The following MRO material service level obtainment metrics provide insight on how well the asset owner is being serviced by the MRO materials supply chain.

- *On-time delivery (OTD)* tops the MRO materials service level value density metric list. Why? It can do the most to improve or harm the channel depending on how it is used. *OTD* is a measure of the MRO material supplier's ability to meet the asset owners need date. OTD delivery is typically measured at the line item level. For example, 9 out of 10 line items arriving on time represents 90%. Some asset owners measure at the order level; 1 line late means the whole order is late. OTD is an excellent measure for unearthing poor planning, order processing, and inventory management practices. OTD can also help identify unrealistic or artificial need dates.

  These poor practices usually exist in the asset owner's company. Yet, more often than not, the asset service provider is not allowed to address these subjects. They are expected to deliver by the need date established by the asset owner.

  Certainly, supply practices can contribute to poor OTD practices. There are many reasons for late deliveries. However, the threat of OTD penalties often causes stock replenishment orders to be delivered early. This results in excess inventories.

- *Stockouts* is a measure of how many times an MRO inventory item went to zero. To an asset owner a stockout may be perceived as bad. This means that the supply chain did not do its job of keeping the storeroom stocked. Improvement strategies rely on the stockout measure to pinpoint needed changes in replenishment triggers.

  If one never has stockouts, the probability is high that one has excessive inventories. Likewise, excessive stockouts can indicate that inventory levels are too low. Remember that the storeroom shelf is not the creator of the demand. The asset creates demand. Understanding asset demand is a better tool than just managing stockouts. Improving maintenance planning and better management of supply chain activities should both be pursued.

- *Material lead time* measures the average time it takes for the asset owner to procure MRO materials. Material lead time is the time from when a material need is communicated to the time the materials arrive at the designated location, whether that is a storeroom or a worksite.

  Ideally, material lead time is synchronized with labor lead time to ensure that materials arrive when labor is available. Can material lead time be too short? Yes, if this means that excessive inventory sits idle. Can material lead time be too long? Certainly. Often assets are designed to use critical engineered components that have long lead times. Is this a lead time issue or a design issue?

  The largest portion of material lead time usually consists of administrative tasks when compared to the time to manufacture, pick from inventory, pack, ship, and deliver an item.

Inventory Metrics. A collection of metrics can be used to describe inventory management and consumption practices. Inventory turnover as described previously is an example. Other metrics include:

- *Material issues ratios* – Percentage of SKUs (stock keeping units) actually issued as a percentage of all SKUs. This provides insight on how many items are actually moving. Percentages can be calculated by total line items, by average inventory value, or item classes.
- *Issues to work order ratio* – Percentages of items issued against a work order tied to an asset. This enables the asset owner to determine usage by asset. Further refinement of this measure occurs when actual items used are recorded on the work order. Actual items used may vary substantially from items issued.
- *Critical spares ratio* – Percentage of items designated as critical spares. Almost by definition critical spares sit. They are kept just in case not just in time. The next metric shines light on good critical spares designation.
- *Critical spares commodity designation ratio* – Percentage of critical spares that can be obtained with short lead times from the commodity distribution chan-

nel. This metric can be supplemented by the percentage of critical spares that would experience a demand greater than one at any given time. Why stock an item if it can be easily obtained through existing channels?

- *MRO inventory allocation by asset criticality classification* – How much inventory is being carried by the asset criticality class? Using the seven asset criticality classes, an asset owner can estimate the investment in MRO materials that are held to service each class. This metric provides insight on current inventory investment by asset impact on the revenue stream.

Commodity Grouping Metrics. These provide insight on the supply characteristics by the following commodity groupings.

- *Commodity group ratios* – Measure the percentage by SKU and by value of the commodity groups identified by the asset owner. Commodity groups typically follow the product line cards of industrial distributors. Examples include electrical supplies, safety supplies, general industrial supplies, pipe, valves and fittings, and others.
- *Number of suppliers by commodity group* – Measures the number of suppliers that an asset owner has procured from in a predetermined time frame, typically the last two to three years. This metric is used to drive supply consolidation or rationalization.

MRO Cataloging Metrics. These aid in determining the standardization of descriptions necessary to achieve cataloging and inventory sharing goals. They are:

- *Number of different descriptions for the same part* – This metric calculates the number of different descriptions for the same part in all the systems used by the asset owner. This metric can be further analyzed to indicate whether the part description matches the manufacturer or distributor descriptions. The wide variety of ways to describe an item creates excess system and administrative overhead in the channel. The use of common attribute names and standardized attribute nomenclature enables databases to be easily searched.
- *Percentage of parts identified as kitted items* – Identifies the total percentage of items that are identified as a kitted item. Kitting reduces sourcing errors, reduces supply lead time, and ensures that all necessary parts are available for maintenance efforts.
- *Percentage of catalog items with an identifiable source of supply* – This percentage enables the asset owner to determine if sourcing information is contained within the catalog or is linked to another system.
- *Percentage of items with linked pricing* – This metric indicates the percentages of cataloged items that have an associated list or contract price. The goal is to reduce pricing discovery prior to issuing a purchase order. If pricing is obtained as a part of procurement activities, this percentage should indicate how many items have associated pricing from spot buys.

- *Percentage of cataloged items assigned to an asset* – This percentage reveals whether connectivity has been established between the asset and its associated components. This percentage provides the asset owner insight on asset specific components versus general supplies. With this connection the asset owner improves the accounting of asset costs. For instance $7,500 was spent on materials for the distillation column last year and we currently hold stock of $85,000 for the same distillation column.

Contract Metrics. This metric is used to determine contract effectiveness and includes the following:

- *Strategic sourcing compliance* – Percentage of MRO items bought to contract. This metric is used to determine the extent to which off-contract expenditures are occurring. If significant numbers of off-contract buys are occurring the asset owner needs to investigate why this is happening. What an asset owner may find is that there are potential savings opportunities to be gained from reviewing current contract relationships. It may be revealed that the local contract performance is suspect and that local compliance to contracts is not perceived as critical to the success of the operations. From this metric the asset owner can calculate the cost of nonconformance.
- *Ratio of inventory replenishment to spot buy transactions* – This metric compares the number of inventory replenishment transactions to the number of spot buy transactions. This metric considers a release against a purchase order as a transaction. This metric should be carefully analyzed. One can reduce inventory replenishment transactions by increasing the number of bulk buys. One can reduce the number of spot buys through purchase request consolidation. Both of these have cost implications.

In a future perfect world each need for a particular part would generate its own transaction communicated instantly to the supply chain. So, theoretically, the goal is to increase the number of spot buys to inventory replenishment buys. This does not mean every spot buy gets its own shipping container and delivery truck. It means that demand lead time is extended to the asset service provider thus improving its ability to meet demand requirements.

Identify Compression Strategies—Materials

The compression strategies are divided into the areas of strategic design and tactical execution. Strategic design activities establish the direction of the MRO materials supply processes. Tactical activities are executed against these designs.

An asset owner seeks to establish processes to enable strategies, methods to ensure compliance to processes, and feedback to drive long- and short-term continuous improvement efforts. The following supply side compression strategies support both the design and execution of a comprehensive Strategic MRO materials supply chain strategy.

Strategic MRO Supply Chain Design. Designing the Strategic MRO supply chain is often positioned as part of a strategic sourcing initiative. In reality it is much more. Should an asset owner conduct Strategic MRO material procurement activities using internal resources or outsource to others? How should MRO materials be acquired, stored, and replenished at the lowest total cost while maintaining asset performance levels? Should material decisions be separated from labor decisions?

The goal is to devise and execute against a strategic sourcing plan that is integrated into the overall business plan of the asset owner. Today's executives have been inundated with marketing messages suggesting that companies no longer compete against other companies. Rather, companies and their supply chains compete against other companies and their supply chains.

This competitive supply chain concept is suggested as reality. However, there is often one fundamental principle that is overlooked. How a product or service—the unit of value—is designed determines the nature of the supply chain. I only need a rubber gasket supplier if my product is designed for rubber gaskets. Change the design and a company could easily need both a rubber gasket supplier and a cork gasket supplier or no gasket supplier at all! Thus, the need for supply is a fundamental outcome of the design of the unit of value. This is exactly true for assets as well.

How does this competitive supply chain logic apply to Strategic MRO? Contrary to popular belief, it is not simply a company and its supply chain competing against other such combinations. Analysis of most MRO supply chains reveals that competing asset-owning organizations within the same geographic areas tend to buy from the same sources. They own like assets, and like assets have like designs. Like designs require like supplies.

If competition is truly national or global in nature, pricing advantages are at best short-lived. When an asset owner takes the time to study MRO supply chain costs it becomes clear that the management of the demand engine—the use and maintenance of an asset—determines the competitiveness of an organization.

To reemphasize a critical point: the demand engine is the asset. If the asset fails less, is more durable, requires less lubrication, fewer bearings, and less maintenance, then less supply is needed. Negotiating a 5% cost reduction for bearings may not be a cause for celebration. Is your competitor consuming 10% fewer bearings?

What are the business objectives that an asset owning company should strive for, with the aid of its supply chain? These business objectives should sound very familiar by now:

- Only produce exactly what is consumed in the market.
- Only invest in assets that produce what is consumed in the market.
- Only invest in assets that never fail over their useful life.
- Achieve zero total cost of ownership (TCO) for all assets.
- Only invest in resources that enable the first four future perfect objectives.

Strategic MRO materials supply chain objectives must support these future perfect objectives. Existing supply relationships must be broken apart, reformed, and refocused to achieve an absolute advantage in the market. Breaking apart the supply chain requires an evaluation of the internal organizational structure and the MRO materials being acquired.

An asset owner breaks apart its organizational structure by evaluating the cost competitiveness and the performance of its internal core competencies. An asset owner breaks apart materials by analyzing commodity groupings.

Reforming the supply chain is done to align supply practices with asset requirements. A straw model is developed to outline desired practices and required performance levels. From this model supplier capabilities are assessed. Suppliers are selected and the contracting process begins. The result: the supply chain is reformed.

Refocusing requires the asset owner and its newly formed supply chain to work in a collaborative partnership to implement the better and best practices. Detailed plans accompanied by performance metrics drive operational changes to achieve predicted business results.

Thus the elements of designing the Strategic MRO supply chain are:

- Breaking apart the supply chain:
    - —Core competency evaluation.
    - —MRO parts commodity analysis.
- Reforming the MRO supply chain:
    - —Strategic MRO (SMRO) operational model.
    - —Supplier evaluation and selection.
    - —SMRO operational model detail design.
    - —SMRO performance expectations.
    - —SMRO pricing.
    - —Contract negotiations.
- Focusing the MRO supply chain:
    - —SMRO implementation planning.
    - —Supplier relationship and performance management.

The following discussions review each of these elements in more detail.

Breaking Apart the Supply Chain

Breaking apart the supply chain is the literal objective. Asset owners must take an honest look at themselves and their value streams. The philosophy of "See what you see, say what you see, no right or wrong, simply is" drives this type of analysis.

Ultimately, decisions such as whether to continue to perform certain procurement tasks with internal resources and whether to be in the MRO inventory ownership business will have to be made.

Core Competency Analysis. In the same way that there are revenue and non-revenue producing assets, there are revenue and non-revenue producing functions. Revenue producing functions comprise the internal value stream for the production and delivery of products and services. Non-revenue producing functions are considered the cost of doing business. Typical core competency reviews begin to challenge the notion of performing all functions internally. The first target for outsourcing considerations is non-revenue producing functions.

What Strategic MRO functions are typically reviewed?

- Purchasing.
- Information technology and services.
- Plant engineering.
- Maintenance.
- MRO inventory control.
- MRO storeroom.
- Accounting.
- Freight.

What external resources are lining up to perform these internal functions for the asset owners? Review Chapter 2, with a new perspective on core competencies and business motives of asset service providers and asset makers. With internal and external functions broken apart, it is now time to perform a similar analysis of MRO materials.

MRO Parts Commodity Analysis. Commodity groups have traditionally been defined by the structure of the distributor channel. Examples include:

- Electrical.
- Electronics.
- Pipe, valves, and fittings.
- Power transmission.
- Fluid power.
- Safety.
- Industrial supplies.
- Building materials.
- Office supplies.

This is a natural grouping based on market offerings. However, this grouping is not often well aligned with asset demand. Because of this lack of alignment, it is easy to understand why supply has been consistently disconnected from demand and why asset owners perceive MRO supply management to be a procurement function and not an asset management function. But, because of these market groupings, it is easier to outsource inventory management, storeroom management, and procurement to distributors. What is missing is the connectivity to asset demand.

A Strategic MRO compression strategy must first group assets by asset criticality class. Hopefully you have already thought through this. Then analyze commodity group material consumption by asset criticality class. For example, what quantities of materials in each commodity group were consumed by Class 1 assets? The breakdown by asset criticality class is important in that stocking strategies should be based on asset availability requirements. Refer to the availability modeling described in Chapter 6.

Commodity groups are then analyzed by the number of current sources, the number of different manufacturers, current spend, frequency of buys, minimum order quantities, stores issue frequency, and other relevant factors. Patterns usually reveal themselves. Remember that the goal is to reduce demand and thus reduce the need for supply.

Some MRO supplies are consumable by nature and thus need to be made available on a scheduled basis. Some MRO supplies are deemed critical because of their association with a critical asset. These are often called spares and include both repairable and disposable spares. Spares can be further classified as engineered items or commodity items.

So what should an asset owner do with the commodity analysis? Here are some thought starters. This analysis should help determine:

- MRO spend by asset criticality class.
- Unreasonable MRO spends.
- Where standardization could be applied.
- Whether purchasing leverage is being achieved, either through standardization or through single sourcing.
- If excessive consumption of certain MRO items is occurring and whether there are longer life alternatives.
- If excessive money is being spent on certain MRO items.
- Where product equals can be leveraged and acceptable substitutions can be used.
- If there are excessive critical spares by asset class and if these critical spares are market commodities.
- If more than one month's worth of MRO supplies exist on the shelf. (That's right, one month.)
- Where commodity spares can replace engineered items.
- What spares are repairable assets requiring a service plan.
- What needs to be stocked versus non-stocked.
- What items exist in inventory with no expectation of being used.
- If materials can be moved back to the supply channel.

After accomplishing the core competency and MRO commodity grouping analyses, the asset owner can begin to craft a better or best practice based Strategic MRO materials supply chain model.

Reforming the MRO Supply Chain

Strategic MRO Materials Operational Model. Knowledge of the capabilities of asset service providers and asset makers is essential to the development of a future state Strategic MRO materials operational model. Read and understand Chapter 2. Supplement this reading with market research regarding supply capabilities. It is vital that every Strategic MRO model change be tied to a definable business objective.

Figure 9.1 is an example of a core competency study where a distributor integrator is being considered. In this case the distributor integrator assumes responsibility for inventory management and secondary responsibility for purchasing.

MRO Functions	Standard Services			Integrated Services & Supply						
	MRO Manufacturer	Distributor	Customer	Distributor Integrator	Manufacturer Directed Integrator	3rd Party Integrator	Technology Provider Integrator	E&C Integrator	O&M Integrator	3rd Party Logistics Provider
Sales & Marketing				☓						
Sales Order Processing	☓	☓		☓						
Procurement			☓	☓						
Payment		☓	☓							
Inventory Management				☓						
Storeroom Management			☓							
Maintenance Management			☓							
Asset Recovery	☓	☓	☓	☓						

Figure 9.1- Distributor Core Competency Matrix

Compare this to a similar matrix developed for an operations and maintenance (O&M) integrator shown in Figure 9.2. In this case the asset owner desires to shift primary responsibility for procurement, inventory management, storeroom management, and maintenance management to the asset service provider.

MRO Functions	MRO Supply Chain									
	Standard Services			Integrated Services & Supply						
	MRO Manufacturer	Distributor	Customer	Distributor Integrator	Manufacturer Directed Integrator	3rd Party Integrator	Technology Provider Integrator	E&C Integrator	O&M Integrator	3rd Party Logistics Provider
Sales & Marketing									●	
Sales Order Processing	●	●		●					●	●
Procurement			●						●	
Payment		●	●						●	
Inventory Management				●					●	
Storeroom Management									●	●
Maintenance Management			●						●	
Asset Recovery	●	●	●	●					●	

Figure 9.2 - O&M Integrator Core Competency Matrix

In addition to the functional aspects, the Strategic MRO operational model must take into consideration location factors that impact resource and supply availability. Many parts of the world still have disjointed and administrative laden processes for inbound supplies. These cause delays in the MRO material channels that require the asset owner to hold larger than optimal inventories. Labor is another point of contention as individual communication and technical skills must match both the culture and the operational environment. Global organizations often cite "single sourcing" as a goal that is currently unattainable.

What questions should be answered when reforming the MRO supply chain?

- Where can performance increase and cost reduction objectives be achieved through internal process improvement?
- Where can these performance and cost objectives be achieved through external processes and resources?
- Where can technology deployment improve MRO channel functions?
- How do physical locations of asset owners, asset service providers, and asset makers impact the MRO supply chain?
- How will this supply source improve asset demand? This is the most important question when selecting a supplier to replace or integrate with internal core competencies, bar none.

When an asset owner begins to think about how the MRO supply chain can be reformed, experience suggests that flexibility crafting the supply chain operational model is desirable. Take what the supply chain has to offer and then work in a collaborative manner to drive improvements. Too many initiatives have failed to produce results as an asset owner tries to force the MRO supply chain to meet their unique needs.

Supplier Evaluation and Selection. This is a formal process for aligning supply capabilities with the Strategic MRO operational model. The result sought is a smaller, more integrated, more focused supply relationship. This relationship should be one where joint success is recognized and rewarded. If internal resources win out, they need to understand that it is not business as usual…process changes are inevitable and results are expected.

Too often, when searching for outside assistance, the supplier evaluation and selection process becomes an extension of existing relationships and personal preferences. This search should be one guided by an unbiased approach based on a clear set of performance objectives. A team approach to supplier evaluation and selection improves decision-making and organizational buy-in to the final supplier selections. Here is a typical sequence followed to evaluate and select Strategic MRO suppliers:

1. Customer forms Strategic MRO (SMRO) operational team.
2. The SMRO team conducts a current state analysis of existing practices and compares it to industry better and best practices.
3. The SMRO team develops the SMRO operational model based on the assessment results.
4. The SMRO team searches for potential supplier candidates based on the Strategic MRO operational model. Many techniques such as reverse auctions, bid boards, industry research, and request for information (RFI) solicitations are used to identify potential supply candidates. Some of these techniques, such as reverse auctions, can lead to inappropriate short-term decisions. See past discussions entitled "reverse auctions drive down total cost" in the Islands of Pain chapter.
5. Supplier candidates complete SMRO capabilities worksheet. A list of firm candidates is developed based upon response.
6. The SMRO team reevaluates its SMRO operational model based on supplier capabilities. RFP is developed to address the model's attributes. RFPs are sent to supply candidates.
7. Supplier candidates respond to the RFP. Proposal evaluation compares candidates' strengths and weaknesses to SMRO operational model.
8. The SMRO team visits supply candidate(s) for on-site evaluation. The SMRO team completes on-site SMRO evaluation and verification worksheets.
9. The SMRO team scores final candidate worksheets and compares capabilities to SCM model. Be wary of the lowest price as the sole selection method. The goal is the lowest total cost.
10. SMRO supply sources are selected and notified.

All of the above is sound in theory. What does an asset owner do if it has no procurement leverage in the market? Suppliers do not always cooperate with our grand plans. Clearly, an asset owner needs to understand its buying position in the market. The small asset owner must seek out buying groups, consortiums, e-commerce exchanges, and other business alliances that can help increase buying leverage for materials. There are lots of tricks of the trade to look bigger and gain more perceived leverage. Just remember the goal of Strategic MRO is to eliminate demand sources. What is more desirable, more leverage or less demand?

SMRO Operational Model Detail Design. The real work begins as existing and new supply sources work collaboratively with the asset owner to construct detailed work processes, technology infrastructures, and job roles and responsibilities. Work and technology process details are mapped, procedures written, trained, tested, and launched in accordance with the scope of the Strategic MRO operational model. The SMRO operational team stays in place during this phase to ensure that the SMRO operational model objectives are being addressed. This team is augmented with focus teams comprised of both internal and external resources.

Ultimately, new work methods must be built into the day-to-day activities of the company operations. A transition plan to natural leadership and associate roles must be developed. This requires that the SMRO operational team, as the designee of the asset owner, use change management principles and practices to increase organizational acceptance of these new business and operational transformations.

SMRO Performance Expectations. If the SMRO operational model is designed correctly the asset owner will have baseline data regarding current performance levels and a return on investment (ROI) analysis of the costs and expected benefits of the planned improvements. The performance objectives need to be reviewed in a collaborative fashion with both internal and external resources.

For example, suppose the customer wants to reduce inventory investment through inventory consignment by suppliers. The customer's objective is to retain only critical spares. The customer also wants the supplier to maintain high fill rates and superior on-time delivery. These fill rate and OTD expectations are usually greater than any level currently enjoyed by the asset owner. These objectives are initially seen as reasonable until the supplier finds that the customer wants to continue to exercise control over inventory reorder points and reorder quantities. This will result in higher inventory investment and reduced inventory turnover for the supplier. This is not win-win.

It is recommended that the value density metrics discussed previously be used to establish performance expectations. Once these target performance expectations are established and communicated to the supplier, allow the supplier to develop, without outside hindrance, processes that will minimize total cost. Wisdom suggests entering into supply relationships with entities capable of self management and improvement.

SMRO Pricing. Fixed and variable pricing strategies are used in the industrial supply chain to establish fair trade values for product and services provided. Ultimately, SMRO pricing is more than an exchange rate for products and services. SMRO pricing is also used to drive ongoing cost improvement efforts. These cost improvement efforts usually result in future beneficial pricing arrangements between the asset owner, the asset service provider, and the asset maker. The focus of this pricing discussion is MRO materials and outsourced labor—not the asset itself.

Fixed Pricing Strategies are aimed at locking in price for a contract period. Adjustments can be made during the contract period if agreed upon by both the buyer and seller. Included in these methods are:

- *Fixed-price contract:* The negotiated price/cost is firm throughout the life of the contract. This method offers the most predictability for the customer. Projected cost can be determined based on historical product usage.
- *Fixed price with escalation/de-escalation:* Similar to a fixed price contract except that the terms permit product cost changes to be passed along. These price variations are usually due to economic reasons or market changes. Pricing adjustments (up or down) can benefit the customer or supplier.
- *Fixed price with incentive:* This contract should be negotiated to protect the customer from contracting at too high a price to cover all the supplier's unknowns. It requires that four criteria be established:
  1. Maximum contract price—The sum of the most optimistic projected cost plus the most optimistic projected profit.
  2. Target contract price—The most likely cost outcome of the contract expected by the buyer and seller.
  3. Target supplier profit—A negotiated amount that is fair and reasonable for the supplier.
  4. A sharing formula—The ratio of shared cost to profit that determines the slope of the incentive curve.

  These contract elements are both estimated and negotiated and plotted on a cost versus profit chart. This chart establishes the range of probable outcomes for the contract price and supplier incentive. Said another way, the cost-incentive chart visually projects the risk to reward for both contract parties. The advantage of this method is that both the asset owner and asset service provider have price protection for difficult-to-define or unusual products. The sharing formula provides for price adjustments for unknowns where each party participates in the "pain or gain."

- *Discounts and rebates offer real dollar savings for fixed price contracts:* There are several discounts and rebates offered for fixed pricing arrangements. Trade discounts take into account variability in the market, purchasing patterns, and payment terms.

- *Trade discounts*: These are reductions from list price available to asset service providers and sometimes asset owners (when buying direct from the manufacturer) to compensate them for assuming certain product marketing responsibilities. The discounts are often offered as a series of individual discounts (for example, 20%, 15%, 8% . . .) with each percentage applied to the discounted price at the previous level.
- *Quantity discounts:* Price reductions offered for purchasing increasingly larger volumes of product. They normally fall within one of three scenarios:

  1. Buying a specific quantity of items at the same time.
  2. Buying a specific dollar amount of many different items at the same time.
  3. Buying a cumulative dollar total of many different items over a specified time frame.

- *Annual rebates*: These are usually additional negotiated percentages of annual purchase volume based on the buyer exceeding a pre-set level of annual purchases. The rebate is often paid in cash at the end of the year. Asset owners should discuss the potential of sharing in manufacturer-paid rebates with suppliers based on some equitable ratio and cost to serve measure.
- *Cash discounts:* These are one of the most familiar discounts offered to buyers that pay their invoices within a pre-set time period. One common cash discount term is "2/10 net 30," which means the buyer can deduct two percent of his invoice amount if the bill is paid in ten days or he must pay the full amount within thirty days. By taking the two percent discount, the buyer earns an annualized return on that money of approximately 36% (365 days ‚ 20 days early pmt. = 18 payment periods x 2% = 36%). Few investments can earn that kind of return. Even if the asset service provider does not offer cash discount terms, the asset owner should attempt to evaluate whether an early payment could benefit the asset service provider and, if so, by how much. Then the asset owner can use their intelligence as a price negotiating point. This type of education and arrangement can easily produce a win–win situation for all parties.

Variable pricing strategies encompass techniques to change pricing on a more frequent, incremental basis over the life of the contract.

- *Consistent gross margin pricing:* A variation of fixed price with escalation/de-escalation. The premise behind constant gross margin pricing is that the asset owner will receive pricing escalations/de-escalations based on the asset service provider's ability to hold gross margins to an agreed-upon level by commodity group. Pricing reviews and adjustments are made at an agreed-upon interval. Independent auditors are often used to verify adherence to gross margin agreements. The advantage of this method is that the asset owner and asset service provider have a measurable method for controlling cost escalations and de-escalation that can be easily audited.

- *Cost-plus-fee pricing:* In this contract, the asset service provider is paid for all his negotiated costs. In addition, a fee is added to the asset service provider's costs to establish the final price. The method for determining the additional fee varies according to type of purchase, buyer/supplier negotiation skills, and customer requirements. Three types of add-on fees are:

  1. Incentive fee—As explained in the fixed-price with incentive, this variable amount reflects a shared cost versus incentive philosophy between the buyer and seller.
  2. Fixed fee—With this arrangement, a negotiated amount of money is paid above the seller's costs.
  3. Award fee—Usually used in the public sector, this arrangement adds a purchaser-determined bonus award at contract completion.

  The advantages of this method are that the asset service provider is protected if its margins and accounting systems are deficient. Further the asset owner can select only the services wanted and needed.

- *Return on sales (ROS) pricing:* Return on sales pricing strategies attempt to reflect the incremental changes in cost and gross profit due to sales volumes and operational improvements. Thus, the customer and supplier are both rewarded for incremental gains in sales and reductions in costs through price reductions. Conversely, as sales volumes drop, prices increase due to increases in incremental costs. Return on sales pricing is determined based on the following:

  - Collecting identifiable expenses for facilities, sales support, management, warehousing and delivery services, operating supplies, and administrative support. Activity-based costing will aid in the identification and costing of customer-related expenses.
  - Sales volumes are identified.
  - An agreement is reached regarding a ROS percentage.
  - The ROS percentage is applied to the expected sales volumes to yield a net profit after tax figure.

  To determine the gross margins necessary to achieve ROS expectations the following calculations must be performed.

  - Calculate the before-tax figure by dividing the reciprocal of the known tax rate into the after-tax profit.
  - Add the total expenses to the before-tax profit figure for the total transaction margin.
  - Divide the transaction margin by the expected sales volume to determine the gross margin rate for the given ROS percentage.

A sample ROS pricing model is shown in Figure 9.3.

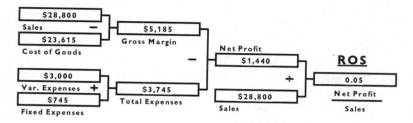

Figure 9.3 - ROS Pricing Model

The advantages of this method are that return on sales (ROS) percentages can be adjusted based on increases/decreases associated with the incremental costs of sales increases/decreases. In addition, disclosure of transactional cost helps identify inefficient activities and opportunities for further cost reduction in the customer's and supplier's operation.

- *Activity-based Costing.* This pricing contract is based upon the supplier's activity costs plus cost of goods sold plus a negotiated profit percentage. Activity-based costing results are used to understand and determine variable expenses that would be used in a ROS pricing model. The advantages of this method are that both the asset service provider and asset owner fully understand the basis for the purchased product cost; therefore there are no surprises. Use of this technique provides more detailed insight regarding inefficient activities and opportunities for further cost reduction in both the asset owner and asset service provider's operation.
- *Return on assets (ROA) pricing.* This pricing contract for products and services is based on a negotiated supplier return on assets. An adjustment is made at regular intervals (usually each year) to reflect changes in the asset service provider's ROA. A sample ROA pricing model is shown in Figure 9.4.

The advantages of this method are that the asset service provider can earn its required return on assets. Further, the asset owner has some assurance the asset service provider has a viable business and is not earning "excessive profits."

Contract Negotiations. Much has been written and written and written into contracts. Most are designed to protect the asset owner and hold the supplier liable for everything including whether the sun rises in the east. Performance penalties are standard; performance incentives are not. Cost savings are typically taken and not shared. There is little incentive built in for the supply resource to reduce labor as this will reduce revenue. Systems are typically not integrated and any move-

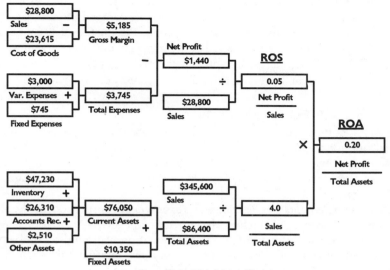

Figure 9.4 - ROA Pricing Model

ments to do so are slowed by fears of becoming too integrated and too open with information.

Contracts should be created based on a desire for long-term business relationships. The relationship must provide the revenue stream and profit levels required by the supplier to invest in the time and resources necessary to achieve agreed-upon performance objectives.

The contract elements must be well defined so that all can know what terms, pricing, products, services, and performance metrics will be imposed and what the impact on costs will be. Allow for contracts to be amended based on changing business conditions. If contracts are designed to harm the supplier it is recommended the supplier walk away from the deal. Likewise, if a supplier is unable to fulfill contract obligations, the asset owner needs a good escape clause.

Hold pricing separate from the main body of the contract due to its volatility. Pricing negotiations may begin with fixed price arrangements and terms for timely payments. What an asset maker seeks is the best price in the market and what the supplier seeks is a fair return on its products and services. Sometimes these two objectives collide even with the best of intentions. Strategic MRO pricing objectives can be advanced by introducing variable pricing models such as constant gross margin pricing, return on sales pricing, inventory turnover based pricing, and return on asset pricing. It should be noted that these latter pricing practices seek to cause hard dollar improvements in business practices.

There are certainly a number of pricing strategies that attempt to leverage volume either with a product standard or with a single source. Industry consortiums and buying exchanges are attempting to consolidate spending patterns through multiple tier levels and use this aggregation to reduce pricing. Sadly, this approach does not take into account the objective of reducing demand and ultimately improving work processes to drive down total costs. Pricing pressures are not new nor are the psychological games played between buyers and sellers to achieve a fair and profitable trade exchange. Just remember best price does not always equate to lowest cost. However, lowest demand almost assuredly does.

Focusing the MRO Supply Chain

The last component of a Strategic MRO sourcing initiative is keeping the participants focused. Focus is, in essence, directed attention. Direction must be continuously reviewed and focused through a formal planning process. The participants' attention is held by ongoing relationship management and performance monitoring.

SMRO Implementation Planning. The basic tenet is, "plan to do, do the plan." Planning categories should include all elements of the SMRO operational model implementation activities. SMRO implementation planning should be positioned inside of a change management process where internal and external communications are given great importance. Plans should be driven by performance objectives, realistic adoption rates, and clear knowledge of plan costs. SMRO implementation usually requires joint facilitation by resources from the asset owner and their chosen suppliers. Last, the SMRO implementation plan should have a budget.

Supplier Relationship and Performance Management. The purpose of this phase of strategic sourcing is to create an ongoing cooperative and collaborative work environment. Open and honest discussions regarding the performance objectives and performance efficiencies must occur. Agreed-upon problem reporting and resolution practices should be standardized, learned, and followed by all participants. Performance achievements should be recognized and rewarded within the operational and cultural standards of participating organizations. Finally, performance results should be communicated to upper level management to ensure business objectives are being met and to continuously evaluate the effectiveness of the Strategic MRO operational model.

Executing Tactical MRO Supply Chain Management

Up to this point the asset owner has broken apart, reformed and focused his MRO supply chain. The next challenge is compressing waste and non-value added activities out of day-to-day activities.

This section will address the following opportunities.

- MRO line of sight procurement.
- E-procurement.
- Consumption driven inventory management.

- Smart storeroom management.
- Smart payment practices.
- MRO supply chain compliance.

MRO "Line of Sight" Procurement. This is defined as the ability of the organization to connect purchasing practices directly to the sources of demand. Other frequently used terms for this ability are supply transparency or supply visibility. However, line of sight procurement emphasizes the ability of the source of demand to see supply without going through an organizational and technological maze. Demand connectivity for "line of sight" procurement begins with condition based monitoring (CBM), man–machine interfaces (MMI), autonomous maintenance, preventive maintenance, and corrective maintenance activities. Remember that reorder quantities for inventory do not constitute asset demand. These are supply transactions and may have little or no relationship to consumption patterns of the asset.

In the optimal system, the asset must be able to communicate its demand requirements in real time to the sources of supply. A number of technologies exist for identifying what is needed and who is the best source of supply in lieu of searching through deep stacks of past material requests, purchase requisitions, purchase orders, and invoices.

EAM asset catalogs are useful in capturing actual purchase and storeroom issuing activities and recording them against an asset. This enables a maintenance resource to look up an asset in an asset registry, quickly review past activities, select components, and initiate search activities. If storeroom information is contained in the EAM technology, the maintenance resource can quickly search for part availability, quantities available, and location. The ultimate connectivity is achieved when the maintenance resource can look beyond internal store inventory and see directly into distributor and manufacturer inventories through the use of electronic cataloguing capabilities.

Illustrated parts catalogs overcome significant but basic barriers to quickly identifying and sourcing MRO materials. What part do I need, what is it called, and what is its part number?

An illustrated parts catalog as depicted in Figure 9.5 does the following:

- Maintains an online asset maintenance library of parts illustrations.
- Provides search capabilities for maintenance documentation.
- Enables quick identification and location of maintenance parts.
- Quickly navigates through volumes of catalogs.
- Associates specific maintenance manuals with pieces of equipment.
- Adds parts information to work orders, job plans, purchase requests, purchase orders, and transfers.
- Provides a visual hierarchy that enables real time drilldown to needed parts.
- Performs contextual parts selections to easily identify all parts needed for a job.

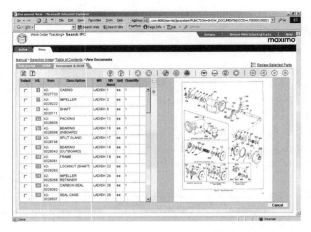

Figure 9.5 - Illustrated Parts Catalog

Electronic catalogs contain a listing of information (text and usually graphics) that describe what a supplier sells. Historically, asset makers and asset service providers have used printed catalogs. Electronic catalogs are different from their printed counterparts in several ways. Truly useful electronic catalogs are not just a spreadsheet or database containing part numbers and product attributes. They are usually not a digitized copy of a printed catalog stored on a CD ROM or website. Last, they are not an ERP (enterprise resource planning) transaction file containing part number, price, and a long description filled with abbreviations and acronyms. If this is what electronic catalogs are not, then what is an electronic catalog?

Of course, an electronic catalog is a collection of information about what a supplier sells or what an asset owner buys. To be considered a Strategic MRO compression method, an electronic catalog must have several important characteristics that improve the business benefits of its use:

- *Rich content.* Rich content includes structured content such as detailed product specifications, transactional content such as part number and price, and multimedia content such as images, hyperlinks, schematics, and data sheets.
- *Classification, granularity, and metadata.* Product information is organized in a hierarchy of categories and subcategories, stored by individual values (as opposed to long descriptions), and enhanced metadata. These characteristics facilitate asset owner searches and exchange of data with internal resources and the MRO supply channel.

Metadata is data about data. An electronic catalog contains descriptive information (metadata) about products (data). Metadata can have metadata. For example, price list expiration dates are metadata to price lists.

218

- *Customization.* The ability to "slice and dice" and modify catalogs to support customer and channel needs for different product mixes, pricing, data structures and file formats.
- *Adaptability.* The ability of the catalog to evolve over time to accommodate new products and features, updates to existing products, catalogs from merged or acquired companies, new customer and channel requirements, and internal project timelines.

MRO line of sight procurement also goes the next step in decentralizing purchasing activities, thus empowering the asset user and maintenance resource to procure. For many organizations this is a scary proposition. Often cited reasons include too much exposure and too little control. These are the same companies who issue their associates procurement cards with little or no traceability to purchased items and what assets they were bought for.

What does it take to make line of sight procurement successful? Basic ingredients include:

- A trustworthy workforce.
- The requirement to identify purchases with assets and their associated accounting codes.
- Directed sourcing to suppliers of choice.
- The ability to create real-time comparisons to budgets.
- The ability to monitor and approve spending limits in real time.
- The ability to create historical buying behavior and exception reports per purchaser.

Recent use of workflow technology has made it possible for some organizations to completely decentralize purchasing. Does this mean that the purchasing department disappears? No. Does this mean every organization should empower its workforce to conduct procurement activities? No. Does this mean that the demand resources need to see the sources of supply, quantities, and availability? Yes. Does this mean that, at the minimum, purchase requests and actual materials purchased are associated with the asset creating the demand? Absolutely.

E-procurement. The next step in the evolution of electronic commerce is Internet technology (HTML, XML) based buy-sell transactions. This is often called e-procurement. The origins of the term e-commerce originated from the advent of electronic data interchange (EDI). EDI is point-to-point ordering relationships with key suppliers. EDI sometimes includes the use of front-end requisitioning, specific database catalogs, and cross-reference tables.

E-procurement has expanded these capabilities to include electronic catalog requisitioning, automated approval routings, electronic ordering, invoicing, receiving, and automated payments. Buyers have the ability to browse and requisition items in real time using a single user interface for most, if not all, goods or services. Corporate reports can be generated by back-office integration of procurement, inventory, and accounting systems. Other E-procurement characteristics include online auctions, collaborative commerce, and integrated logistics processes.

MRO line of sight procurement requires the use of web-enabled e-procurement technology to create visibility to the external supply chain's inventory. The e-procurement world is filled with entities that seek to make considerable money off of these types of transactions either through transaction or subscription fees. The market response suggests that these models will not last long. The Internet has set the standard for unlimited transactions for a simple monthly ISP (internet service provider) access fee. Businesses will soon deploy technology to quickly connect to each other without an expensive third party intermediary.

A perfect example of low transaction costs to move massive dollar quantities of trade is the New York Stock Exchange (NYSE). In 2000, the NYSE trading volume, expressed in dollar terms, was $11.1 trillion. It doubled its trading capacity from 1,000 mps (messages per second) to 2,000 mps and invested heavily in real-time connections to improve information flow between itself and other agencies.

The NYSE completes about 28.8 million transactions per day. Based on 255 trading days, this is 7.34 billion transactions per year. If this seems unrealistic, then consider that the NYSE averaged in excess of a billion shares traded per day. On average this is 34.7 shares per transaction. The NYSE revenue from operations in that year was $765.7 million. This means revenue per transaction was approximately $0.10 or 0.00690% of total dollar trading volume. Compare this to $0.25 to $1.25 per line item in current MRO exchange fees or credit cards charges of 2% to 3% of purchase amount.

Exchanges do have value, just like the NYSE has value. They serve a vital role in aggregating demand information within industry sectors and geographic regions. They clearly focus the industry's attention on the cost of doing business and promote doing business efficiently. Unfortunately, transaction technology is not the answer to basic industry problems. Aggregating expenditures and leveraging purchasing power is always good, but managing asset demands is always better.

This is why most e-commerce exchanges now include value added services in their offering much like stockbrokers provide many services above and beyond executing buy/sell transactions. The exchange service providers are there to help the channel implement best practices. Regrettably, many service providers lack the depth of knowledge it takes to improve the asset management space.

When will industry realize that real people, using real assets, create real products and services for real money? When will the industry recognize that asset management is a complex problem requiring specialized skills and technology to comprehend its intricacies? When will the industry see that common sense asset management solutions based on sound business principles win the day? Reducing the cost per purchase order can be illusionary. Reducing costs per asset is real.

Consumption Driven Inventory Management. The discussion of consumption versus demand is not a well-trodden path. Strategic MRO focuses its energy on asset consumption versus inventory replenishment generated demand. Three fundamental questions must be answered in order for an asset owner to utilize consumption driven inventory management. These questions are:

1. What is the forecasted consumption of an asset?
2. What is the actual consumption by the asset?
3. What is the most likely period of time before failure occurs again?

For example, suppose the yearly forecast for a Class 1 (revenue generating) mixer is that it will need one set of blades and lubrication. During the year the mixer did not require blades but it did consume approximately 8 ounces of lubricant. However the mixer also needed a motor replaced. What should the asset owner keep in stock? One set of blades, lubricant, and another motor? What is the most likely scenario for need? This was the first motor failure in five years. The lubricant is a consumable. The blade wear is based on production usage, which can be tracked and estimated for the future.

Typically, inventory shelves are full of items that have no real forecast, expected use, or next use information associated with it. The forecast should be based on best estimates and analysis of actual failure patterns—mean time between failure (MTBF) statistics. This failure frequency information is based on averages so is subject to timing error. However, past MTBF data is probably the best starting point available.

Actual consumption data should come from what was reported as used on the work order not from what was issued or bought. Clearly, what gets issued or bought does not always get used.

The next fundamental question to be addressed is whether an item should be stocked. This question has been abused in both theory and in practice. Common sense would suggest that asset owners should own assets and not MRO inventory. This logic drives the asset owner to only purchasing MRO supplies at the time of need. Why do people buy MRO supplies in advance of a need? The answer is straightforward. The demand lead time is less than the supply lead time. Thus the need to hold inventory in the channel.

So what drives up inventory levels beyond reasonable amounts? Part of the answer is that asset owners tend to treat every asset and failure the same. The result is that every demand lead time is short and a high priority. Consequently asset owners stock excessively, require excessive consignments from suppliers, and negotiate unreasonable fill rates and on-time delivery requirements. This means that supply must provide thousands of SKUs in two-hour or same day delivery windows. The reality is that only a few SKUs need a delivery window this short

So what does one do to combat excessive inventory levels? Here are a few suggested approaches.

- Asset based inventory purging.
- Consumable, spare, and repairable designations.
- MRO inventory optimization.
- MRO component standardization.
- Inventory buybacks.
- Inventory consignment.
- Inventory sharing networks.
- Monitor and adjust inventory replenishment strategies.

Asset based inventory purging is a first step that probably has been performed many times. Nevertheless, an asset maker confronted with large MRO inventory investments needs to conduct a structured purge. This purging process follows the steps associated with the lean manufacturing 5S process.

Strategic MRO adds a sixth "S." These steps are:

1. Sort.
2. Shine.
3. Smart storeroom.
4. Set in order.
5. Standardize.
6. Sustain.

Sort all inventory according to its relationship to an asset. If no identifiable relationship exists then set inventory aside in a red tag area. The remaining inventory is compared to annual demand. Inventory in excess of a year's supply is set aside either physically or in record.

Shine is just that: clean up the storeroom, free bins, tool boxes, parts lockers and other inventory storage areas. Take note of where the inventory is really stored.

Smart Storeroom requires inventory and storeroom personnel to think before they put things back. Smart storeroom practices are identified later in this chapter.

Set in order is done both physically in stocking locations and in information technology. From a data cleansing perspective, this is when organizations apply asset description standards to known good parts.

Standardize requires that asset owners standardize stocking practices, inventory replenishment practices, and part description practices. In addition, the asset owning company or outsourced service provider promotes ongoing system audits and performance reviews to ensure standard practices are being complied with.

Sustain means to develop procedures that will make it unnecessary to perform the first 5 steps again.

Consumable, spare, and repairable designations are made during the purging of physical inventory and associated records. This designation is essential to the filtering process for inventory stocking practices.

Consumables should be reviewed to reduce unnecessary usage. Spares and repairable assets should be reviewed for their status as an engineered item or as a commodity. Commodity spares should be stocked based on asset availability (refer to asset availability analysis in Chapter 6) requirements and their associated supply lead time. Engineered items should be reviewed for potential commodity substitutions. Repairable assets should have an associated strategy, such as modular maintenance, for mitigating asset downtime during repair cycles. A structured approach to consumables, spares, and repairable assets can easily decrease inventory investments by 10% or more.

MRO inventory optimization is an inventory strategy that uses past consumption and issue size analysis to set inventory levels and establish replenishment strategies. Asset owner inventory managers set target inventory turnover rates as well as service levels. The optimization recommends stocking status, reorder points, and reorder quantities for each item such that turnover and service level targets are met.

As can be seen in Figure 9.6, inventory optimization software allows parameters to be set that control how inventory replenishment trigger points and inventory levels are calculated. These parameters include stock status, service level, and turnover targets.

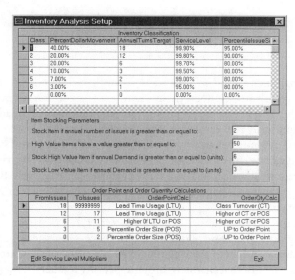

Figure 9.6 - Inventory Optimization Parameters

As can be seen Figure 9.7, application of the inventory optimization process results in replenishment and stocking procedures that will increase inventory turnover and significantly reduce inventory investment while preserving service levels for critical items.

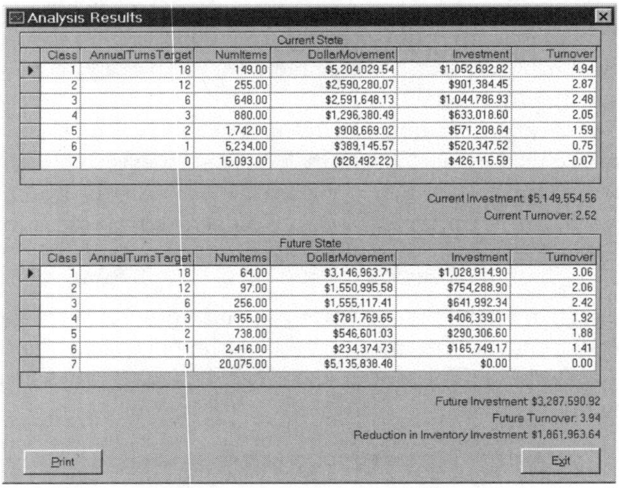

Analysis Results

Current State

Class	AnnualTurnsTarget	NumItems	DollarMovement	Investment	Turnover
1	18	149.00	$5,204,029.54	$1,052,692.82	4.94
2	12	255.00	$2,590,280.07	$901,384.45	2.87
3	6	648.00	$2,591,648.13	$1,044,786.93	2.48
4	3	880.00	$1,296,380.49	$633,018.60	2.05
5	2	1,742.00	$908,669.02	$571,208.64	1.59
6	1	5,234.00	$389,145.57	$520,347.52	0.75
7	0	15,093.00	($28,492.22)	$426,115.59	-0.07

Current Investment: $5,149,554.56
Current Turnover: 2.52

Future State

Class	AnnualTurnsTarget	NumItems	DollarMovement	Investment	Turnover
1	18	64.00	$3,146,963.71	$1,028,914.90	3.06
2	12	97.00	$1,550,995.58	$754,288.90	2.06
3	6	256.00	$1,555,117.41	$641,992.34	2.42
4	3	355.00	$781,769.65	$406,339.01	1.92
5	2	738.00	$546,601.03	$290,306.60	1.88
6	1	2,416.00	$234,374.73	$165,749.17	1.41
7	0	20,075.00	$5,135,838.48	$0.00	0.00

Future Investment: $3,287,590.92
Future Turnover: 3.94
Reduction in Inventory Investment: $1,861,963.64

Print   Exit

Figure 9.7 - Inventory Optimization Analysis Projected Results

MRO component standardization significantly reduces the number of alternatives from which an engineer, maintenance, construction, or purchasing resource may choose. This streamlines sourcing and purchase order administration while simultaneously reducing inventory investments. The logic is simple. For every stocked part number an investment is required. Therefore stocking multiple parts that can be substituted for each other will drive inventory investments up. Component standardization is a necessary step in controlling MRO inventory expenditures. Refer to Chapter 7 for more details on asset and component standardization practices.

Inventory buybacks are good for the asset owner, but there are no established rules covering how to dispose of dead stock and excess inventory quantities. The supplier can assist with determining the resale potential of these items as well as providing alternate disposal channels through specialty resellers, salvage companies, or buying networks. At the asset owner's request, suppliers will often negotiate a buyback arrangement for certain inventory items. It is important to draw a distinction between two types of excess inventories. These are no–usage stock (dead) and low–usage stock (slow moving).

- No–usage stock—This category is defined as dead stock that has had no usage for more than two years.
- Low–usage stock—This category is defined as excess inventory above the target stock level and having some amount of usage.

Based on practical experience, general considerations for negotiating a supplier buyback of excess items are:

- The items must be in saleable condition.
- The buyback will occur over a negotiated time period (typically 12–24 months).
- The negotiated buyback price will be less than the customer's original or average purchase price (customer's cost less a restocking fee).
- The total amount of stock buyback will not exceed 10%–20% of customer's current annual purchases with the supplier.

Inventory buybacks may seem unfair to the supply channel and are often the deciding factor on whether one supplier is selected over another. The reality is that inefficient buy–sell practices have created excess inventory.

With *inventory consignment*, the supplier places inventory at the asset owner's location but does not transfer ownership. Transfer of ownership occurs at time of use at which time the supplier is compensated based upon agreed –upon pricing and payment terms.

Why is consignment a viable practice? Consignment allows the supplier to sell more by becoming a single source for a selected commodity group. Consignments allow the customer to avoid an investment in inventory yet have the material on-site when needed. Consignments allow both parties to avoid the administrative costs associated with many small orders for inexpensive items.

Consignment arrangements go awry when the customer dictates stocking levels instead of service levels. Even worse is when the service levels dictated are based on the notion that all assets and all failures are equal and require equal supply response. Additional problems occur when the consignor is not allowed to move excess or slow moving items back into the general market.

A consignment process can create excess cost when critical spares and highly engineered items are involved. The supplier places the items in the customer's plant to "lock in the business." But the supplier still owns the investment. This has the effect of moving the investment from a lower cost of capital entity (the industrial customer) to a higher cost of capital company (the supplier). Thus, inventory carrying costs in the channel increase.

Inventory sharing networks are used in some industrial and retail distribution sectors. Entities have electronic visibility to each other's inventory. Given common product descriptions, items can be easily sourced, transferred, and sold out of multiple shipping points.

Inventory sharing between storerooms and plants should be a goal for asset owners. However, storerooms are not normally able to conduct such a straightforward function. Different storerooms have different part descriptions. Different plants have different part descriptions. Each new acquisition has different part descriptions.

Each existing and new operation has multiple asset standards with little or no incentive to standardize descriptions at the component level. Business rules have not been established to allow for asset transfers to flow easily from one operating unit to another and back again. But if they could, think of the opportunities to drive inventory levels down through internal consumption.

The inventory sharing financial model is simple. Multiple min/max stocking locations will always carry more inventory than one centralized stocking location for any given item. Think of an inventory sharing network as a single virtual stocking location.

When using inventory sharing as a source of supply, a company must be willing to tolerate slower delivery of the transferred item than they would expect from an outside supplier. Why does this slower delivery occur? It is because the transferring entity does not feel compelled to supply the item quickly to the degree that an outside company would.

Why would a company tolerate this slower delivery? Because they know that, usually, the work order needing the transferred item could be put off until the next day or even the day after next. Because of these slower deliveries, use of an inventory sharing policy creates the need for better work planning. So, legislating an internal inventory transfer when the item is available often results in improved planning. And such a policy uses inventory investments more efficiently.

In the industrial distribution world differing opinions abound regarding inventory sharing. Some say that buying the needed item (even from a local source) is always better than an internal transfer. They suggest that internal transfers reward poor planners, allowing them to achieve higher inventory turn rates than those attained by the sites where inventory is available to be transferred. Others suggest that good inventory sharing allows inventory to move toward the true sources of demand and indeed improves inventory stocking practices.

Inventory sharing is sometimes implemented among multiple companies. Often these companies are situated in close geographic proximity. Common inventories tend to be electrical, safety, general industrial, office, and facility supplies. Perhaps the biggest challenge is establishing common item descriptions and implementing integrated systems. This is why most inventory sharing networks implemented among different companies never enjoy high utilization. An alternative solution is to achieve the same leverage by establishing an integrated supply using consigned inventory that is shared by all. In this case, the integrator acts as the designer, host, and administrator for inventory sharing activities.

Monitor and adjust inventory replenishment strategies can break all the rules. Some level of stockout is good. On-time delivery is not necessarily the coveted metric it is made out to be. Indeed, seeking perfection in both of these measures at the asset owner's expense may be too costly and may be unnecessary.

The message is simple: connect supply to demand. Extend demand lead time and plan supply lead time to match demand timing requirements.

Class 1 assets tend to have the highest availability requirements. Thus, inventory should be adjusted based upon its availability during acceptable downtime intervals. For example, if Asset X can be down for 8 hours with no impact on production or service levels, then do not stock those items available in the market for delivery in 8 hours. Here is a case where a stockout is okay but on-time delivery (OTD) is absolutely essential.

In the above example, one could argue that if you had the item in stock you could keep your maintenance resources busy. Repeat this logic aloud three times. Then ask the question: Is your goal to keep maintenance resources busy or to minimize total cost of ownership? For all asset portfolios, Class 1 through 7, inventory stocking strategies should be reviewed and restructured to meet TCO objectives.

Local stockouts should begin to increase as progress is made in bleeding down inventory levels. Adjust as necessary. Remember that too much inventory allows for sloppy processes, inadequate data collection, and mediocre resource utilization. This is exactly what lean manufacturing, synchronous production, continuous flow manufacturing, quick response manufacturing, time-based competition, and every other philosophy have been preaching and practicing for years.

Monitor and adjust requires that inventory safety stocks be systematically lowered. This lowers reorder quantities. When system performance begins to show signs of suffering, then adjust safety stock quantities accordingly. Most companies never lower safety stock for material already on the shelf. These safety stocks tend to rise over time in response to a stockout caused by an extraordinarily large demand. This causes inventory investments to increase.

Do we want to stock inventory in the quantities necessary to cover even extraordinary demands? Probably not. This implies that stockouts caused by extraordinary demands are to be expected. Thus, a policy to decrease all stockouts across the board makes little sense.

Monitor and adjust strategies are used to fine-tune inventory replenishment trigger points and stocking levels after performing the inventory optimization discussed previously. Inventory optimization, which uses statistical procedures to set inventory reorder points and stock levels, quickly adjusts inventory replenishment triggers and stocking levels to theoretically correct values. Monitor and adjust fine-tunes those values to match the reality of a particular operating environment. Monitor and adjust, used without the inventory optimization, often proves unsatisfactory due to inventory adjustments happening too slowly. This is because of the sheer number of items that need to be adjusted. Many of these items will have replenishment trigger points and stocking levels set higher than what is actually needed. Often, these high values were the result of past adjustments that were a knee-jerk reaction to extraordinary demands.

Why the overwhelming industry emphasis on on-time delivery? And why is on-time delivery often associated with short delivery windows such as next day or less? These are good questions that need to be debated in all circles and at all levels of the MRO demand-supply chain. Quick delivery to replenish inventory that will not move for 3 to 6 months or even a year should not be rewarded. This only creates higher inventory investments and high inventory carrying costs.

OTD is important. So are short delivery windows. But OTD should be to schedule, not just quick. Labor and materials need to be available at the time demand needs to be satisfied.

So, the final question: Why do we have considerable investments in inventory that can be easily obtained from local suppliers in less than a day's time? Explain that one to the new CFO.

Smart Storeroom Management. The smart storeroom creates an environment where MRO items can be quickly received, stored, pulled, issued, and accounted for. A smart storeroom is designed to provide visual cues to material locations, order statuses, handling instructions, safety precautions, and other operational requirements. A smart storeroom takes advantage of technology to automate and error proof work processes.

Consider the smart storeroom design for an automotive assembly operation in Figure 9.8.

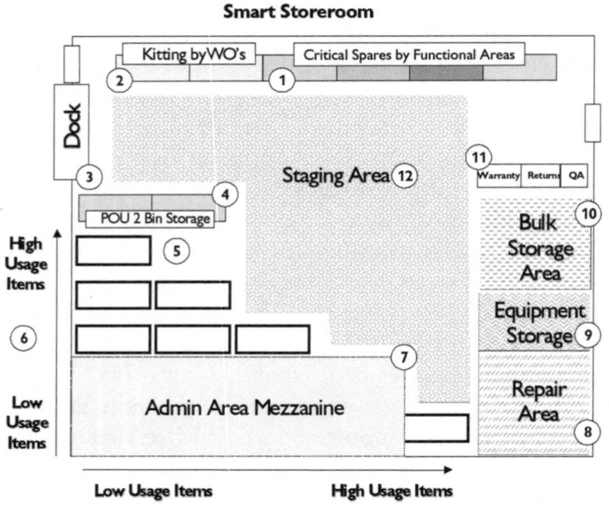

Figure 9.8 - Smart Storeroom Layout

Key design points, as numbered above, include the following:

1. Critical spares by functional areas – Critical spares can be separated by functional areas within the plant. Examples include tire, chassis, trim, paint, and final assembly. Storage can be color coded to functional plant areas.

2. Kitting by work order – Using EAM technology capabilities, materials can be pre-staged for both preventive maintenance and repair work orders.
3. Dock – The dock is designed to support receiving and shipping activities.
4. POU two bin storage – This area is designated for free bin storage referred to by the customer as point of use (POU) storage. Inventory contained in these racks is destined for the plant. Empty bins are awaiting transport to the distributor for order fulfillment.
5. Storage bins and racks – Bins and racks are designed to hold multiple size and weight products. Racks and bins are laid out to provide line of sight (visual management) indicators for stock locations. Rows, aisles, racks, and bins can be colored coded by material or product type.
6. High/low usage storage scheme – High usage items should be placed nearest to the staging area and low-usage items further away.
7. Administrative area mezzanine – The administrative area should contain meeting/training rooms, office spaces, restrooms, employee break rooms and, potentially, inventory held under lock and key. A mezzanine area is used to maximize utilization of floor space.
8. Repair area – This area will be used if O&M assumes repair responsibility or subcontracts this service.
9. Equipment storage – This area is required for fork trucks and other material handling equipment.
10. Bulk storage area – This is an area designed to hold material that cannot easily be stored on racks or in bins, such as tubing and conduit. Outside bulk storage should be considered as well.
11. Warranty, returns, QA – This special storage area is provided for warranty, returns, and defective products.
12. Staging area – This area is used to cross-dock orders being fulfilled from multiple sources. It is also used to support pull, pack, and ship activities for orders pulled from inventory.

Other important aspects of smart storeroom management include the incorporation of point of use (POU) stores, bar-coding technology, and warranty management.

POU stores located in or outside the plant typically support the smart storeroom. Figure 9.9 depicts POU operations for an automotive assembly operation.

In Figure 9.9 a two-bin system is used to manage inventory flow to and from POU locations. POU stores are often used to maintain critical spares near the "owning" asset. Also, frequently used consumables are located within departmental areas to support autonomous maintenance activities, personal protective equipment requirements, and other operational needs where going back and forth to a central store would be time consuming.

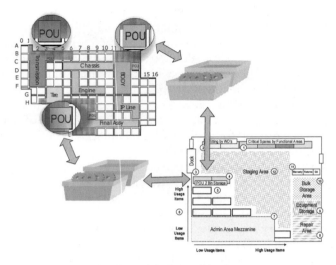

Figure 9.9 - Point of Use Stores

Bar coding is another core practice used in a smart storeroom. This technology is used to eliminate manual data entry wherever repetitive computer data entry takes place. Examples include receiving, and storeroom issue as well as tool and tooling issue and return.

Bar coding can be quite helpful in managing items with a limited shelf life. Perishable materials can be bar coded to reflect the dates by which the product must be used or consumed. Bar coding permits the item manager to dispose of those items not used or consumed by the bar code date.

E-commerce used along with bar codes enables high levels of automation in the procurement, material receipt, payment, material issue, and use cycle. Exceptionally rapid receiving is accomplished by scanning bar codes. Computerized links between receiving and accounting reduce the use of paper documents and increase inventory accuracy. Automation can also allow the electronic transmittal of invoices, the electronic comparison of invoices, and payment of invoices. In addition, the supplier's use of bar codes to generate advance shipping notices leads to the implementation of planned receipts and shipments to drop zones.

Warranty management is defined as the process of tracking items currently carried under manufacturer warranty and correctly applying agreed-upon warranty practices. Warranty management does not imply that product abuse and misuse should be hidden and passed back as a defective product. This simply adds cost to the channel and covers up poor operator and maintenance practices that the asset owner is responsible for.

Warranties typically begin at the time of the purchase instead of the time of installation. This is a critical distinction for those asset owners who own excess inventory. Managing warranties is an essential maintenance cost management activity.

Records of warranty items are entered at the time of purchase in one of several applicable systems: the purchasing system, EAM system, storeroom system, or customized warranty databases. What is essential is the proper identification of the asset or component in question as a warranty item. Procurement, engineering, operations, and maintenance personnel can hold warranty terms and conditions in document management or EAM systems for ease of access.

Today's EAM systems can provide a comprehensive warranty management process that can flag warranty items, track warranty periods, provide templates for problem reporting, link vital warranty documents, and return material handling instructions.

Smart Payment. Increasingly, the terms of payment are becoming critical to the overall financial viability of the asset owners, asset service providers, and asset makers. The flow of monies between trading entities is as important as the flow of goods. Smart payment suggests that the quicker the flow of monies between trading entities the better. Some would argue that the industrial procurement process would be better served if it followed retail practices of payment at the time of product possession. Payment at the time of material acquisition might lead to wondering if the material is actually needed now. This would place emphasis on better demand management and prevention of demand.

Organizations see the postponement of payments to suppliers as a way to allow others to fund their capital needs. Payment delays often exceed 60 days. The logic is simple: operate off the credit of your suppliers. Virtually all industrial suppliers are willing to play this game with their customers, necessitating a similar arrangement with their suppliers as well. Much jockeying takes place as players seek to collect funds quicker than they have to pay them.

Now we see procurement cards being used to pay for MRO supplies. When a procurement card is used, the supplier receives payment within one to two days of the sale and the customer has up to 45 days (theoretically) to pay for the purchase. For quicker payment, the supplier pays a sponsoring bank 2% to 3% of the transaction amount. The customer, even the most "hardened" of price negotiators, has got to believe they are ultimately paying for this 2% to 3% fee through product pricing. The bank underwriting the procurement card is living off of the unwillingness of financially sound companies to streamline procurement and payment practices.

Procurement cards have a definite and positive role for most asset owners. For example, enabling emergency purchases to occur at off-hours is one distinct advantage. But, for routine purchases between known and reputable trading entities, the procurement card premium has a real channel cost that must be recognized.

Another smart payment process is electronic receipt settlement (ERS). Using ERS the buyer can receive and pay based on the shipping documentation attached to shipments instead of waiting for the traditional invoicing process to occur. The traditional invoicing process usually is a three-way match that begins with a physical count of goods received, which is verified against the packing list. Then the receiving count, the purchase order quantity, and invoice are matched. None of these matches are needed when conducting business with suppliers who routinely ship what is ordered.

ERS reduces both buyer and supplier costs associated with the receiving and payment process. Electronic receipt settlement is a practice that takes advantage of the Internet-enabled collaboration and integration of inter-company processes. This practice allows hands-off, automated processing of the entire payment process and can eliminate entire subprocesses from the existing payment process of an organization.

MRO Supply Chain Compliance. Conventional wisdom suggests that the secret to success is discipline. But, if this wisdom is so conventional, why do so few organizations possess exemplary discipline? Why do so many expertly crafted, common sense solutions, began to fail after the first six months of implementation? People lose focus, the original solution intent is lost, and it is easier, yet more costly, to return to the familiarity of past practices.

There are three components always found in companies that have achieved sustainable competitive advantage. The first is a focus on continuous business process improvement. Processes are always documented. This process documentation is the second component and serves as training content. Most organizations cite the need for training and retraining. But, where does training content come from? Training content comes from process documentation. The last component is compliance. An organization can have the best processes known but if they are not complied with...well you get the picture.

The steps seem too simple:

1. Develop good processes and continuously improve them.
2. Document the processes and update the documentation with the changes from continuous improvement efforts.
3. Use the process documentation as training content. Train and retrain.
4. Require compliance with process steps. If the process steps can be improved go back to Step 1.

The compression strategy used to achieve supply chain compliance requires that every process from demand recognition to supply fulfillment be reviewed for critical tasks that must be complied with to meet performance or contractual obligations. Endeavors are undertaken to build in error proofing. Document, then train and require compliance. If we have designed the best, most error proof processes, why would we not require compliance to those process steps?

While all business processes are important, compliance in the following areas is absolutely essential:

- Associating all labor, material, and special equipment costs with the asset creating the demand.
- Use of asset and component standards.
- Use of preferred sources of materials.
- Use of approved product substitutes.
- Configuration management.

In connecting supply to demand we have articulated the final business system components of the Strategic MRO process. Compliance is essential for the business success of the asset owner, the asset service provider, and the asset maker.

Develop Case Study Examples

If the light bulbs came on during the last session, they now glowed brightly! The executive forum teams knew that total costs of ownership could be divided neatly into four components: purchase price, acquisition costs, possession costs, and disposal costs. Poor initial asset design and specifications drive up possession costs. These costs can be reduced but only through tactical redesign of the asset or the supply chain or both. Strategic use of early equipment management and maintenance prevention practices means that subsequent acquisitions will not repeat the same mistakes. Given their current reality, the executive forum teams focused on the here and now. What should and could they do to improve Strategic MRO supply practices?

Superior Water

The Superior Water executive forum team members paused, mumbled, and ultimately confessed to already having executed quite an abrupt strategy in reducing supply costs: outsource everything having to do with the call center and line maintenance, replacement, and extensions. The goal was to quickly reduce labor costs. In hindsight they now recognized that they had disconnected demand from supply in organizations, in workflows, and in systems. The results were counter to their business objective of improved customer response time while reducing operational costs. To help other executive forum members understand their basic supply process, the diagram shown in Figure 9.10 was presented.

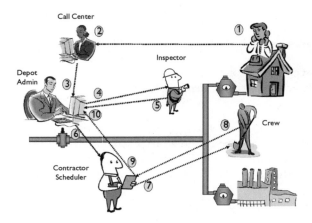

Figure 9.10 - Superior Water Connects Supply to Demand

The sequence of the supply response to demand is:

1. Customer observes leak at the meter.
2. Customer notifies the call center of the leak. Information is keyed into the call center database.
3. Call center notifies the appropriate regional depot of the leak.
4. Depot administrator keys information into the depot work order system.
5. Inspector conducts inspection of the customer location and verifies existence of the leak.
6. Depot creates a work order directing the outside contractor to repair the leak.
7. Work order is given to the crew team leader during the morning scheduling meeting.
8. Repair crew fixes the leak and completes the necessary work order paperwork.
9. Contract scheduler reviews the accuracy of the work order and submits monthly with a summary tracking sheet for billing.
10. Depot administrator logs the work as complete.

The process seems quite straightforward but contains many disconnects potentially resulting in delays. The team briefly explained:

- That the call center was not on the same information system as the depot.
- When the customer inquired as to the status of the repair, the call center was unable to answer. This meant that the calls had to be routed to a central dispatch that had access to the work order system.

- Because the depot used a different system than the call center customer information had to be re-keyed into the depot system. To save time information was e-mailed to the depot. A split screen was used to allow the depot clerks to view two data tables at once. Every depot clerk was provided with a new 21" monitor to improve the readability of the information.
- A work order was generated for the inspector and placed in an in-basket for the inspector to pick up the next day. If the problem was reported after 5:00 P.M. a trouble crew was dispatched and simply conducted the inspection and if possible repaired the item. If unable to perform the repair, the trouble crew turned off the water until the contractor crews could perform the repair the following day.
- Crews would visit the site prepared to conduct routine repairs, but upon further inspection, they often needed additional or different parts. Because they had no information access to the MRO storeroom inventory, they usually dispatched one crew member to retrieve parts while the rest of the crew completed paperwork from previous jobs.
- Because crews did not report their whereabouts or the status of work orders, it was hard to locate crews for emergency or high priority work that came up during the day. Crews were really hard to reach after 3:30 P.M. because this usually meant overtime work was imminent and most crews wanted to avoid overtime.

The list of disconnects, delays, and misalignments became so long that the executive forum team resorted to presenting statistics that indicated:

- Response time had jumped from 2 days to 4 days on average.
- 95% of inspector activities resulted in verification of a problem and a subsequent work order for the contractor.
- Nearly 45% of complaints originated after 3:30 P.M. when residential customers returned home. This increased the number of personnel required for the after-hours trouble department.
- Long delays in completion of work order administration by the contractor resulted in poor job status tracking and inaccurate billings. Some of these inaccuracies resulted in overcharges as high as 35%.

Superior Water pays nearly $90 million annually for contractor services. It spends nearly $15 million for MRO supplies each year. It maintains $10 million in average MRO inventory value. Superior maintains a fleet of nearly 150 service trucks used primarily by inspectors. The move to outsource the call center and network maintenance looked great to the accountants and horrible to operations. The customers were left shaking their collective heads over the drop in service. This is the information age. How could so many people be this disconnected?

Superior Water Compression Strategies

Superior Water felt the time was right to optimize and streamline integrated work practices. They focused on compression strategies that would lead them to improved response time and reduced costs.

Strategic MRO Supply Chain Design. Superior Water had just completed an entire review of its internal core competencies. This analysis indicated they should outsource call center and water network maintenance functions. Superior would retain network inspection, depot administration, and work order dispatch as internal core competencies.

The MRO parts commodity analysis was fairly straightforward in that Superior Water maintained contracts with approximately 20 suppliers. Nearly 70% of their contract purchases were from five major "stock" distributors. These key commodity groups included meter boxes and fittings, meters, ductile pipe and fittings, plastic pipe and couplings, and flange adapters.

Strategic MRO Operational Model. Superior Water felt that they were well on their way to finalizing their Strategic MRO operational model. The other executive forum teams agreed. However the team felt that there were some definite performance barriers that needed to be overcome. Somehow procurement and inventory practices needed to be overhauled to support the new outsourced labor structure.

Consumption Driven Inventory Management. The next step taken to improve the new work processes was to transfer inventory to the operations and maintenance (O&M) contractor. Superior Water no longer wanted to be in the MRO inventory ownership business. The contractor agreed in principle, but first wanted to understand what was being bought for inventory and directly for jobs. They wanted to know current inventory turns for every item in the storerooms.

The analysis was painful for both parties because of the lack of information relating inventory used to work orders. At the end of the day, Superior Water and the O&M contractor agreed to an inventory bleed-down strategy for all fast moving parts. This meant that that Superior Water would own all current inventory until it was depleted. The O&M contractor would own all new inventory. Critical spares would be owned by Superior Water but would be stored by the contractor. Superior would pay the O&M contractor a fee for this storage service.

Asset Based Inventory Purging. The O&M contractor began working with Superior Water storeroom and maintenance resources to positively identify every item in stock and indicate what part of the network it was intended for. If the item was a component, the asset in the network it supported was indicated.

When the inventory analysis was completed, the O&M contractor segregated slow moving or unidentifiable inventory items. The O&M contractor compared all inventory levels against past usage to determine where excess stock existed. In the spirit of cooperation the O&M contractor requested that the procurement leadership at Superior participate in inventory consignment and buyback negotiations with the five key distributors. Superior Water agreed.

Supply Chain Compliance. The burden of managing inventory requirements for work orders now fell squarely on the shoulders of the O&M contractor. Each work order submitted for payment contained exactly the labor and materials used. This meant that the need to control sourcing, expenditures, material usage, and warranty practices was an absolute must. Because of these actions alone Superior Water estimated savings exceeding $1 million in the first year.

One company's relief quickly became another company's burden. The O&M contractor leadership asked if they could participate in the executive forum. They said they needed to understand methods for optimizing labor and material scheduling now that they were responsible. The Superior Water team invited them to the next session.

EuroCar

The first dilemma for the EuroCar team was that maintenance and procurement were, for all practical purposes, in different hemispheres. It was the role of maintenance to keep machines running. It was procurement's role to make sure the parts were available. The line of demarcation was so well established that even EuroCar leadership dared not cross it.

The disconnect between demand and supply was clear to every member of the executive forum. Yet all of them understood the historical precedence of giving procurement control of the storerooms. They all had done it. Thinking that procurement somehow controlled expenditures was now seen as the mistake that it is. The knowledge that it is the asset that determines what needs to be spent revealed past erroneous thinking.

Aggregating corporate spends had netted better prices. But inventory levels remained the same or grew slightly. This corporate strategy did nothing to reduce emergency or one-off spot buys.

Maverick purchases became the new topic of debate because off-contract purchases and blatant circumvention of normal procurement steps was becoming commonplace. Something had to be done. The rift between maintenance and procurement was growing and the prognosis for an all-out war was no longer something to laugh about.

EuroCar Compression Strategies

The process had to be broken apart in order for it to be fixed. The EuroCar team opted to follow the Strategic MRO supply chain design strategies presented during their workshop. It was not easy…but neither was adopting a new lean production system.

Strategic MRO Supply Chain Design. The EuroCar team gathered its supporters and formed a focus group for the sole purpose of reviewing its current Strategic MRO supply chain design. A review of internal core competencies was invigorating, polite, and at times followed by an awkward silence. The results were clear: EuroCar would continue to perform all Strategic MRO functions with internal resources.

They all agreed that EuroCar had done an excellent job of creating and maintaining MRO commodity groups. What was missing was the relationship between these commodity groups and their associated assets. The team believed a breakthrough might occur if they could align inventories with the asset criticality classes established by maintenance. A focus team was established for just this purpose.

The results from this focus team revealed that, in almost all categories, excess inventory was being held. This was inventory that could be supplied within two hours of issuing a request to their preferred suppliers. A closer look at critical spares indicated a very liberal policy for their designation. Many items designated as critical spares were readily available in the market.

It was also found that a large number of new stock items were being added to the storeroom. It was as if procurement did not want to rock the maintenance boat and maintenance wanted to prove they were the only ones who knew what was needed. This "tit for tat" game, waged at the operations level, had ballooned inventory, to the good of no one.

One more point the team felt was important to mention was the fact that everyone believed that EuroCar should be in the inventory ownership business. Certainly their processes had to be superior to those of an industrial distributor. Or were they?

Strategic MRO Operational Model. The EuroCar team agreed that reviewing current industrial distribution and storeroom practices was a worthy pursuit. At the minimum they could prove their superiority. At a maximum they could drive out unnecessary costs. Every team member felt the pressure of the 5% cost reduction targets that had been mandated by management.

What the team found as a result of their review amazed them. Integrated supply concepts had grown by leaps and bounds. Sourcing technology had improved dramatically. Inventory replenishment strategies were focused on asset velocity rather than simply filling the shelves of customers. Quality assurance practices rivaled their own internal ISO standards. Handheld storeroom technology allowed for accurate and efficient daily cycle counts. Modification of reorder quantities based on changing consumption was routine. Yearly maintenance and changeover schedules could be reviewed for MRO material needs giving the industrial supply chain the best opportunity to fill orders directly from the factory. The list of possibilities was long and proof positive that sometimes it is worth taking that small peek outside of one's own company.

Ultimately, EuroCar wanted out of the inventory ownership business. But they knew that outsourcing the entire storeroom and its inventory management practices all at once was too big a change for their culture. Go slow, get it right, win by making no mistakes was the prevailing thought.

The first move, then, was to establish integrated supply contracts with distributors by major commodity groups. Each distributor integrator would be responsible for moving its inventory to consignment, establishing restocking practices, and ensuring that service levels were being achieved. All purchase requests would be routed through EuroCar procurement for approval prior to restocking. This policy would be revisited based on performance.

MRO Line of Sight Procurement. Each distributor integrator was required to develop electronic catalogs. These catalogs would cover items retained on site and all other approved items that met EuroCar standards within their respective commodity groups. These catalogs would be connected to EuroCar's procurement and accounting system. The electronic catalogs would act as the conduit for automating inquiries, quotes, purchase orders, and invoices.

EuroCar's procurement system would be upgraded to support e-procurement and integrated with their recently upgraded "Web architected" EAM technology. Some suggested that the EAM technology perform the purchasing functions. "Too big a change" was the response. However, purchase requests could originate from the EAM technology. This connectivity enabled the maintenance technician to see distributor inventory availability in real time. With the addition of workflow technology, the maintenance technician would be able to execute timely one-off spot buys within certain monetary limits. The EuroCar team stressed that, in all cases, work order related purchases must be assigned to an asset. EuroCar understood discipline.

EAM Asset Catalogs. To leverage their EAM investment, EuroCar began developing detailed asset catalogs based on work order activities. They had already spent several months developing asset and location hierarchies. Now their goal was to attach materials and sourcing data to these structures. Because they now had EAM asset catalogs, maintenance technicians no longer needed to shuffle through old work orders or purchase requests to find sourcing and other information for parts they needed.

Illustrated Parts Catalogs. The EuroCar team felt that, for certain critical equipment like that used in constraining operations, it was worth the investment to build illustrated parts catalogs. These catalogs would expedite part identification and sourcing activities. In addition, the illustrated parts catalogs would streamline configuration management efforts by systematically identifying asset changes and communicating these to engineering via Intranet messaging.

Consumption Driven Inventory Management. A huge challenge related to inventory management was changing the paradigm of both EuroCar and their distributor integrators to only stock the shelves with items with known consumption patterns. Consignment contracts rapidly opened the eyes of the distributor integrators to the wisdom of only stocking what has reasonable probability of being consumed.

EuroCar initially wanted to retain established min/max stocking levels, reorder points, and reorder quantities. The distributor integrators were finally able to convince EuroCar to focus on service levels. Using service level performance as the primary goal, the distributor would first apply inventory optimization statistical procedures to set replenishment triggers and stocking levels to theoretically correct values given past consumption. Then the monitor and adjust inventory strategies would be used to fine-tune the replenishment system.

The monitor and adjust practice was the same one used by EuroCar with the direct materials kanban replenishment system. EuroCar knew that this was a good practice and that the limits had to be tested in order to get close to optimal inventory levels.

Given the nature of monitor and adjust, EuroCar was willing to sacrifice 100% service levels which typically drive stock levels through the roof. Maintenance would have to do better planning and communicate more effectively with the distributor integrators for this process to work. The cost savings were anticipated to be substantial for both parties.

Asset Based Inventory Purging. All parties agreed to an old-fashioned inventory purging. This would be a prelude to deciding what should be stocked on-site. It would also be the mechanism that would identify inventory that should be moved back through the channel. Finally, the purging would identify inventory that must be disposed of.

The EuroCar team understood the power of a Visual Factory 5S process. The 5S was a component of their EuroCar Production System. They liked the idea of adding the sixth S of smart storeroom. The distributor integrators were unfamiliar with the 6S terminology but understood it immediately upon explanation.

EuroCar set up an official red-tag area to hold unidentifiable and excess inventories. Excess inventories were determined through the use of an *MRO inventory optimization* algorithm, which developed recommended minimums and maximums. The distributor integrators would review the contents of the red tag area to recommend a market disposition for each item. Ultimately accounting would have to review these disposition recommendations for their impact on EuroCar's books.

Consumable, Spare, and Repairable Designation. The next phase of improvement began when it became clear that not all stock in the storeroom was equal. The distributor integrators wanted guidance on what parts were considered consumables, spares, and repairable assets. This knowledge, combined with the criticality of the asset the item supported, helped establish initial replenishment strategies for each item.

Smart Storeroom. The improvements were coming fast and furious and all of them significant. Perhaps the most visible sign of EuroCar's improvement was their storeroom. It was now half the size from whence they started. The storeroom attendants were open to rearranging materials by their commodity groupings, making it easier for the distributor integrators to locate their materials and conduct inventory activities. Additionally the EuroCar team wanted to make sure that it kept track of critical spares by the by asset and department they were held for. Making the critical spares visible and keeping the costs of these spares separate by asset and department spread the organizational pressure to "mind the store." In addition to the central stores, EuroCar reorganized their "free issue" POU stocking locations using a two-bin system. They already had free issue bins. A separate

240

POU center was set up within the central stores to enable the distributor integrators to systematically replenish them on an as-needed basis. Much like a kanban system, each department would either return empty bins to the storeroom, or the storeroom attendant would make the rounds gathering up empty bins. The goal was not to have the distributor integrators roaming through the plant.

MobileTel

The MobileTel team knew that the inventory was a costly proposition for them and their supply chain. Electronic components required special handling and storage. Because MobileTel had 55 stocking locations, they intuitively knew that they had excess inventories. Contributing factors were many.

The competitive environment of the electronics, computer, and software industry caused new products to be offered yearly. This meant that MobileTel's storeroom was full of different slightly different versions of the same parts. Often these differences were minor upgrades to existing components. Did this mean they should throw away the older versions?

Another factor was the recent emphasis on reducing travel time to and from sites. The natural consequence was to build local inventories to decrease dependence on the central store. Was it better to centralize or decentralize stocking locations? The team felt that taking a step back and looking at the whole picture would benefit them greatly.

MobileTel Compression Strategies

As a geographically dispersed asset owner, MobileTel wanted compression strategies that would enable them to respond to failures in a manner that would minimize impact on customer service and cost of operations. They had already begun designing more detailed demand criticality classifications. The MobileTel team felt they could use this demand logic to architect a better material supply solution.

Strategic MRO Supply Chain Design. The team reviewed MobileTel's core competencies and decided that the best option was to conduct all maintenance activities using internal resources. However, they wanted to investigate outsourcing storeroom management functions. MobileTel also wanted to streamline all processes through the use of EAM technology to reduce labor content. The MRO parts commodity analysis revealed nearly $6 million in inventories spread across multiple commodity groups including electronic and electrical, computers, cables and fittings, test equipment, and office supplies.

Strategic MRO Operational Model. After much debate and study of capabilities, the MobileTel team decided to outsource storeroom management to a single MRO logistics integrator. The integrator was a logistics specialist who would coordinate inventory replenishment strategies with national distributors and OEMs. The MRO logistics integrator would be required to use MobileTel's EAM technology to ensure visibility of inventory by technicians and other operational resources. The integrator would not take possession of inventories but would begin systematic negotiations with distributors and OEM to achieve 50% or better inventory consignment. MobileTel agreed to work with the MRO logistics integrator to achieve e-enablement of all order fulfillment processes in order to reduce transaction costs.

All inventory receipts would be captured in the EAM system. The EAM system was linked to MobileTel's enterprise system. All one-off purchase orders would continue to go through MobileTel's procurement department. All stock replenishment orders would be releases against master purchase orders and would be executed without procurement involvement.

EAM Asset Catalog. The MobileTel team knew that there was more to maintenance than just testing and replacing circuit boards. Facilities and structures had their own maintenance needs as well. They began systematically converting existing legacy data regarding asset and location hierarchies to their new EAM system. Then they would purge any obsolete information and update new asset data in real time. This was much like what Superior Water was doing with its GIS system.

MobileTel's goal was the same as others in the executive forum...build an asset catalog that provided online asset parent–child drill–down capabilities and captured service history. The goal also included integrating the asset catalog with storeroom inventories and using the asset catalog information, where practical, when issuing purchase requests.

E-Procurement. MobileTel agreed to support the MRO logistics integrator's objective to use e-procurement technology for stock replenishment activities. MobileTel understood that these capacities would improve their ability to do one-off or emergency buys. The electronics industry had jointly participated in the founding and development of an industrial exchange, ElectroConnect.com. Startup costs were significant, but the market was there, as this exchange supported both retail and industrial sales efforts. It was through this exchange that the MRO logistics integrator would connect key suppliers via Web–based technology.

Consumption Driven Inventory Management. The MRO logistics integrator was well aware of the challenges it faced in understanding the consumption patterns of MobileTel's assets. It was critical to their success that MobileTel technicians record actual usage against work orders and return goods that were issued but not consumed.

When MobileTel began negotiating consignment contracts with major distributors and manufacturers, they were overwhelmed with complaints about suspect warranty claims. Infant mortality was one thing; rough handling was another. Nearly 25% of all items sold by a supplier to MobileTel had warranty claims submitted against them. This caused the suppliers to be concerned about maintenance practices.

Excessive warranty claims eventually raised the prices of components. The MRO logistics integrator saw firsthand the nonchalant way in which boards were tossed around, left exposed to the environment, and handled in a manner that sometimes caused static electricity damage. The MRO logistics integrator facilitated a meeting between MobileTel and its key suppliers to resolve the warranty issue. This needs to be resolved before any supplier would agree to consignment.

Using the new EAM technology, MobileTel and the MRO logistics integrator could easily track the who, what, and where of warranty failures. This increased accountability dramatically reduced the number of warranty claims.

Asset Based Inventory Purging. Like so many others, the MRO logistics integrator felt that a good inventory purging was in order. The MobileTel team shared with them the 6S process they had learned at the executive forum sessions. This methodology would be initiated within the first quarter of the contract after all had settled into their new roles. Both MobileTel and the MRO logistics integrator would marshal resources to complete the task as expeditiously as possible. Participation from key MRO suppliers was expected, as inventories would ultimately move to a consigned status.

Slowly but surely they would conduct 6S activities at all 55 stocking locations. The objective was disposition of slow moving or dead stock items by returning them to the distribution channel for credit or auctioning them off through ElectroConnect.com. As a last resort, truly unusable inventory would be scrapped.

The cost of the purging inventory was going to be substantial. It had taken years for the inventory to evolve into the current woeful state. With the conversion to UMTS technology and the planned network expansion activities, MRO inventories had to be in top-notch shape. Now was the time to take back physical control of the inventory.

MRO Inventory Optimization. The MRO logistics integrator used MobilTel's own in-house tool to analyze inventory movement and to determine inventory turnover targets by standard inventory classes. The first cut was an analysis using the highest possible service levels with the lowest acceptable inventory turn rates. Choosing high service level targets and lower turn rate parameters for the analysis would result in the highest theoretically correct inventory levels. Still the analysis indicated that inventory could be reduced by 25% to 30%.

Past inventory turnover statistics had been artificially inflated due to the high levels of warranty based replacements and repairs. With real inventory turns at 4, their stretch goal was 8. They felt this was doable if they worked diligently to track true consumption based on actual materials used reported through the work order system instead of materials issued from the storeroom. Discrepancies between what was used and issued would be addressed through ongoing improvement meetings.

The MobileTel team had no history for the materials required for the new UMTS network. They were given manufacturer recommended spare parts lists. They knew these lists were inflated. Using consumption rates of like components, the MRO logistics integrator developed a forecasting algorithm to predict inventory needs. The consumption rates were adjusted for planned network growth with declining failure rates. From this they established their initial stocking levels.

SMRO Pricing. The MRO logistics integrator had plans to tie inventory turnover results into price negotiation leverage with the distributors. This would be accomplished through a return on assets (ROA) variable pricing model. The incentive for all was to reduce expenditures, reduce costs, and to increase inventory velocity. This provided a mutual incentive for MobileTel to improve its handling of electronic products in the field.

Inventory Sharing Networks. The issue of centralized versus decentralized inventory stocking practices was next on the table for resolution. The MRO logistics integrator recognized the inconvenience associated with maintenance technicians having to return all unused materials to a central warehouse. They also understood the need to keep certain parts at regional locations and in their service truck. MobileTel and the MRO logistics integrators agreed that their 55 stocking locations would have centralized inventory item master data.

All stocking location inventories would be viewable through the Web architected EAM technology, allowing for complete visibility of parts in all locations. This would enable the movement of parts between the central store and the stocking locations and between stocking locations. To the MRO logistics integrator this was normal practice; to MobileTel this was a breakthrough. Their new EAM technology gave them the ability to act as their own internal distributor. The MRO logistics integrator would be responsible for setting up and operating the inventory sharing network.

Smart Storeroom. MobileTel and the MRO logistics integrator developed smart storeroom practices to ensure separation of UMTS and GSM components. They introduced a color coding scheme: yellow for GSM and blue for UMTS. The goal was to continue to purge GSM inventory as these cells were replaced. Keeping items separated both in the system and in the storeroom rooms was a practical solution. They also set up two separate work areas for testing components. Again these were yellow for GSM and blue for UMTS. The same logic was applied to receiving, return materials staging areas, and quality control hold areas. Even packaging was color coded to reduce shipping mistakes.

MilBase Ops

The MilBase Ops team took a timeout to attend a speech by the Secretary of Defense given at the DoD Acquisition and Logistics Excellence program. They shared part of what they heard with the members of the executive forum. The following are excerpted quotes from the Secretary of Defense:

"Just as we must transform America's military capability to meet changing threats, we must transform the way the department works and what it works on....

A new idea ignored may be the next threat overlooked. A person employed in a redundant task is one who could be countering terrorism or nuclear proliferation. Every dollar squandered on waste is one denied to the warfighter. That is why we are here today challenging us all to wage an all-out campaign to shift Pentagon resources from bureaucracy to the battlefield, from tail to the tooth....

The men and women of this department, civilian and military, are our allies, not our enemies. They too are fed up with bureaucracy. They too live with frustrations. I hear it every day. And I will bet a dollar to a dime that they too want to fix it. In fact, I bet they even know how to fix it, and if asked, will get about the task of fixing it. And I'm asking.

They know the taxpayers deserve better. Every dollar we spend was entrusted to us by a taxpayer who earned it by creating something of value with sweat and skill—a cashier in Chicago, a waitress in San Francisco. An average American family works an entire year to generate $6,000 in income taxes. Here, we waste many times that amount every hour by duplication and by inattention.

That is wrong. It is wrong because national defense depends on public trust, and trust, in turn, hinges on respect for the hardworking people of America and the tax dollars they earn. We need to protect them and their efforts.

Waste drains resources from training and tanks, from infrastructure and intelligence, from helicopters and housing. Outdated systems crush ideas that could save a life. Redundant processes prevent us from adapting to evolving threats with the speed and agility that today's world demands.

Above all, the shift from bureaucracy to the battlefield is a matter of national security. In this period of limited funds, we need every nickel, every good idea, every innovation, and every effort to help modernize and transform the U.S. military...

We maintain 20 to 25 percent more base infrastructure than we need to support our forces, at an annual waste to taxpayers of some $3 to $4 billion. Fully half of our resources go to infrastructure and overhead, and in addition to draining resources from warfighting, these costly and outdated systems, procedures and programs stifle innovation as well....

But we have the ability and, therefore, the responsibility—to reduce waste and improve operational efficiency on our own. Already we have made some progress. We've eliminated some 31 of the 72 acquisition-related advisory boards. We now budget based on realistic estimates. We're improving the acquisition process. We're investing $400 million in public-private partnerships for military housing. Many utility services to military installations will be privatized.

When an entire industry exists to run warehouses efficiently, why do we own and operate so many of our own? At bases around the world, why do we pick up our own garbage and mop our own floors, rather than contracting services out, as many businesses do? And surely we can outsource more computer systems support.

Maybe we need agencies for some of those functions. Indeed, I know we do. Perhaps a public-private partnership would make sense for others, and I do not doubt that at least a few could be outsourced altogether....

To transform the department, we must take advantage of the private sector's expertise. I've asked the members of the Senior Executive Council to streamline the acquisition process and spur innovation in our traditional supplier base."

The MilBase Ops team was motivated but they knew tackling the complexities of MRO materials was going to be a real challenge. Like the private sector firm's of the executive forum, they could choose to be or not to be in the MRO inventory ownership business.

The MilBase Ops asset base varied dramatically in type and location. Their current maintenance planning, work order, storeroom management, inventory management, and purchasing systems were relatively old and difficult to maintain and integrate with other systems. As one team member commented, "Do I need to remind you how hard it was just to get a special report out on what we had bought and from whom? It took me 3 people and 40 hours to generate the report."

We still cannot associate all materials bought with a work order. Our system cannot report cost per asset because of lack of integration. If understanding the demand profile of an asset is critical to reducing it, then we have a long way to go with our system." The team knew that the collection of information systems required permanent administrative staff positions to fill the information voids.

After their review of asset standardization or the lack thereof, MilBase Ops decided to review the contracts in place for MRO materials. These contracts were supposed to assure the lowest possible MRO supply cost. They found that many different parts were being bought, not with asset life or service requirements in mind, but simply low acquisition costs. Assets on the shelf were not tied to asset criticality. Many parts were sitting on the shelf that would have been better positioned on the shelves of distributors or retailers. The MilBase Ops team members decided that they no longer wanted to be in the inventory ownership business.

MilBase Ops Compression Strategies

Strategic MRO Supply Chain Design. After the Secretary of Defense speech, the MilBase Ops team decided to review the possibility of outsourcing warehouses and MRO materials management. Their base was already part of a wider program to study warehouse operations. They wanted to be the pilot site for using private sector resources. They recalled the Secretary of Defense statement, "A new idea ignored may be the next threat overlooked...." The team was given the go-ahead for their pilot project.

The MilBase Ops team had already conducted a thorough analysis of their MRO material stock. In their request for information sent to potential outsourced MRO materials management candidates they inquired as to how the supplier would both manage inventory and reduce it.

With their new insight on connecting demand to the asset the team wanted to know how an outsourced service provider would approach demand reduction. Would it be the standard response of finding inventory through better information systems, thus reducing unnecessary purchases? Would the response be reducing reorder quantities to challenge past spending patterns? Would the candidates have the insight to capture asset information, maintenance technician information, user information, and component failure information to help analyze what is causing the demand? Would the candidates work with MilBase Ops resources to identify more reliable and durable materials? Would they know how to calculate total cost of ownership (TCO)? Would they know what to do to reduce TCO? The team knew these questions would separate supply specialists from demand specialists. They needed both.

Strategic MRO Operational Model. The MilBase Ops team reviewed, and then rejected, the traditional industry integrated supply models offered by industrial distribution. They felt these models were inappropriate for their endeavors. Instead they chose an operations and maintenance integrator to assume warehouse and inventory responsibilities.

The O&M integrator proposed the addition of engineering resources to conduct demand and reliability analyses. The O&M integrator agreed to integrate their warehouse management system with the MilBase Ops EAM technology to improve traceability of information to the asset. System integration would provide real time visibility into inventory availability and order status. The O&M integrator also planned to pursue consigned inventory as a strategy to reduce inventory carrying costs. The MilBase Ops team supported the consigned inventory strategy.

E-procurement. As part of the agreement the O&M integrator would have to connect into the DoD Web-enabled exchange for its primary sourcing tool. The O&M integrator resisted the notion of using the exchange for inventory replenishment purchases. Its argument was that the exchange appeared to be designed for spot buys. It also felt that the current list of exchange suppliers could not supply all of the needed materials. The MilBase Ops team agreed but still required the O&M integrator to use the DoD web exchange to purchase materials within the commodity groups where adequate suppliers existed.

The MilBase Ops team negotiated a cost-plus fixed fee contract for the procurement of items. The O&M integrator would pass through all product prices and include a fixed fee administrative charge for handling these transactions.

The MilBase Ops team decided to outsource the labor to run their warehouses. However, existing material and service provider contracts were retained. The O&M integrator would have to find ways to negotiate pricing with the approved group of suppliers. If the O&M integrator had alternate supply resources that met the needs of the military base these sources would have to go through the normal application and approval process. In the back of their minds the MilBase Ops team wondered if they had just hamstrung the O&M integrator by imposing these restrictions.

Consumption Driven Inventory Management. It was not much of a challenge to get the maintenance and contractor resources to record what materials were actually used. It was a bigger challenge to verify that the work order existed before material was issued. The EAM software required maintenance and contract resources had to have an approved work order before material was issued. Material had to be issued against a valid work order. This included emergency work as well. The O&M contractor was reminded of the need to ensure that the work order identified the asset that the materials were intended for. Because of these new procedures the average amount of material issued dropped a full 25% the first month.

The O&M integrator performed a thorough analysis of material consumption patterns. It then performed an inventory optimization analysis based on these new consumption patterns. The analysis indicated that inventory levels could be reduced without affecting service levels. Item categories where large reductions could be attained included paint, lubrication, duct tape, sandpaper, and general industrial supplies. The final result was an across-the-board inventory reduction of 35%.

Supply Chain Compliance. The O&M integrator was excited about being awarded the pilot project for outsourcing warehouse management. The good news was that it was selected. The bad news was that it was selected. In its excitement it failed to carefully read the fine print of the contract.

The first uncomfortable encounter was the requirement to use the DoD exchange. The second was that the priority purchases must be given to ENAC (Environmental Attribute Code) products that have a lesser or reduced effect on human health and the environment when compared with competing products. The MilBase Ops team and the O&M integrator had to work through several reliability issues with certain products. A significant number of the ENAC identified products were proven not to last as long as a competitive product. For example a wax-based lubricant had to be reapplied nearly 10 times more often than a similar petroleum-based product. Each reliability issue had to be studied carefully. These and other difficult decisions continued to challenge the MilBase Ops team.

The O&M integrator was required to alert all base and contractor resources of hazardous materials prior to their issue. The DoD maintained an exhaustive database in its Hazardous Material Information System (HMIS). The military base EAM system could link to this system to ensure that the maintenance resources had access to pertinent information. All items purchased through the DoD exchange had an NSN (National Stock Number). NSNs classified as hazardous were so identified in the system. The O&M integrator was required to identify all hazardous materials whether purchased through the DoD exchange or elsewhere. Linkages between the EAM system and the HMIS system were made so that required documents would be available upon request.

What about CAGE codes and CCR records, and ... no wonder the private sector stays as far away as they can from these so-called lucrative government contracts. More acronyms, more regulations, more policies, more hidden and buried requirements, more absolutes, more, more, more…bureaucracy.

The words of the Secretary of Defense echoed in the minds of the MilBase Ops team as they worked through these and many more issues with the O&M integrator:

> *"The adversarys closer to home. It's the Pentagon bureaucracy. Not the people, but the processes. Not the civilians, but the systems. Not the men and women in uniform, but the uniformity of thought and action that we too often impose on them."*

TL Freight

TL Freight's mobile assets required that their supply strategy be based on the asset going to the source of supply. The trucking industry in general had the same problem. Tractors and trailers could fail virtually anytime and anywhere. The nation's highways were dotted with service and repair centers. If the tractor could not make it to a repair center then repair personnel were sent to the vehicle. If needed the disabled tractor-trailer was towed to a repair center. Considerable investments had been made by all industry players to keep their assets operational...the shipments had to keep rolling.

TL Freight Compression Strategies

Strategic MRO Supply Chain Design. TL Freight was challenged to manage materials expenditures efficiently as overall margins were low. Most freight companies simply used the existing repair infrastructure and paid the going market rates for service. TL Freight believed it could reduce cost of operations by operating their own service and repair centers. This meant that they were in the inventory ownership business. Lately TL Freight executive leadership wondered about the sanity of this decision. If they were going to stay in the service center business they needed to find a way to lower their costs.

TL Freight had skilled technicians. Some would say the best in the industry. They made the decision to continue operating their service centers. In addition they decided to turn them into profit centers by offering their services first to their contract carriers and then to competing carriers. Most of TL Freight's tractors were bought from the same manufacturer. The same was true for their contract carriers. The MRO parts commodity analysis for those items used on their own trucks was well understood. What would be a challenge was to develop similar profiles for the other five dominant manufacturers of tractors.

Illustrated Parts Catalogs. The TL Freight team decided to investigate systems, methods, and improvement strategies that would facilitate turning their service centers into profit centers. They knew that unfamiliarity with other truck brands could be overcome with illustrated parts catalog technology. They had been impressed with the software investments made by their vehicle manufacturer. What they did not know was whether other manufacturers were equally advanced.

What they found disappointed them. Some of the oldest, most prestigious names in the industry still operated from CD ROM versions of hardcover catalogs. This was not what they needed to reduce the costs of their new service offering. They wondered how other service centers made money with these systems. They reasoned that the market rates charged for service by these entities must be elevated to overcome extended searches for diagnostic and part information. TL Freight knew they had their work cut out for them. However, if they could apply some of their internal best practices to the contemplated for-profit service center venture they should be very competitive in this space.

Consumption Driven Inventory Management. TL Freight knew there was plenty of room for improvement in their inventory management practices. Their tractors were on the road an average of seven years. During that period many interchangeable and superceded parts were used during maintenance and repair procedures. Each of these represented individual events and part numbers not easily aggregated to get a clear profile of asset consumption patterns.

One seventh of their fleet turned over every year and parts unique to those vehicles were not pulled from stock. Bulk buys, conservative safety stock levels, planned obsolescence, and technician preferences also left them with significant overstock and dead inventory. The TL Freight team decided to perform an inventory optimization analysis to determine what their usage patterns were. The analysis included inventory held at their 9 warehouses and 15 service centers. The results enabled them to reduce safety stock across the board by 20% and reduce reorder quantities by 25%. Expected savings in annual purchases and inventory carrying costs exceeded $1.3 million annually.

Inventory Sharing Networks. The TL Freight team noted during the inventory optimization analysis that they had three different inventory management systems. Their options were to connect these systems or replace them with a single system. They recommended that a single solution be found. The benefits included managing only one inventory item master, the ability to link this single system to multiple manufacturer and distributor catalogs in the future, improved warranty management, and inventory sharing between all 24 locations. The benefit of inventory sharing alone could help reduce inventory by another 20%.

Define the Management Strategy

Nearly exhausted, the executive forum teams paused to review their efforts since they began tackling the seemingly mundane topic of Strategic MRO. It was now apparent that the variety, quantity, and ultimately the cost of MRO materials was a direct result of their inability to understand and apply Strategic MRO future perfect objectives, guiding principles, compression strategies, and value density metrics.

Connecting supply to demand was more involved than many had thought. They heartily recommended that companies begin by redesigning their Strategic MRO supply chain based on achieving the lowest total cost of ownership. Breaking apart, reforming, and focusing the MRO supply chain was a logical approach that should be performed at least every five years. All the team members agreed that reviewing core competencies and commodity groups made sense in establishing the Strategic MRO operational model. Selecting suppliers was not as simple as finding out who sells what at the lowest price. All the teams agreed that this strategy did not guarantee the lowest total costs.

The discussions became quite lively as teams discussed how they executed tactical MRO supply chain management methods. There were an unbelievable number of alternatives that an organization could use. Unfortunately, there was no one-size-fits-all model.

E-commerce had looked like it would totally transform the work of business until many of the dot-coms turned into dot-bombs. The forum members realized that creating asset catalogs, e-catalogs, and illustrated parts catalogs and connecting these to EAM and ERP systems was no small task. The members did not think e-commerce was going to go away. It made too much sense. It was just going to take time for supply chains to adopt and integrate Web-based e-commerce technology.

All teams elected to purge their inventories and conduct some form of inventory optimization analysis. This time the focus was on not owning inventory and stocking only what gets consumed. Every team also considered the practicality of consigned inventory and outsourcing warehouse activities. The goal was not simply cost shifting but to look for ways to truly streamline operations, improve cash flow, and remove costs from the channel.

The teams realized that, as asset owners, they did not view their warehouses as moneymakers like an industrial distributor would. Organizing smart storerooms that worked for and not against organizational goals made sense. Connecting storerooms through technology so that inventory could be shared made even more sense.

With all these new practices in place, the executive forum teams began to see how they could move to variable pricing models. They could use these pricing models to motivate improvement throughout the supply chain. Using system integration they hoped to improve supply chain compliance. The forum members noted that compliance means adherence to the procedures currently in place. They agreed, however, that all should be open to change so as not to stifle new ideas for improvements.

Paul's Reflections

Like others in the executive forum, Paul had had no idea of the scope and magnitude of Strategic MRO efforts. One thing he knew for sure: no organization was exempt.

Paul's company began its Strategic MRO supply chain redesign just like the others in the forum. His team reluctantly admitted that their business mission was to produce and distribute its chemical products, not perform maintenance and storeroom tasks. Based on these discussions and intense market research on available solutions, his company decided to outsource them "whole hog," as his operations director affectionately referred to it.

Much like others they chose an operations and maintenance (O&M) integrator to optimize both maintenance and supply practices. The O&M integrator had a strong track record at several chemical companies throughout the world. In all cases savings were substantial. Using approaches like those discussed in this and previous chapters, the O&M integrator worked very closely with suppliers to reduce the supply base, improve stocking practices, and reduce pricing.

Paul was amazed at how much of his inventory just sat there and how willing the supply chain was to help him with his dilemma. As fortune would have it, their O&M integrator also used the same EAM technology that Paul's company had already invested in. But the integrator used it better and with more discipline. This meant that, together, they could transfer legacy data more quickly and begin working on ways to extend asset life, improve maintenance response time, and began to drive down material costs almost immediately.

Paul wondered why he had not taken the steps just described right from the beginning. The answer was simple. He did not know what he wanted, what could be done, and what success looked like. He needed support from his leadership team and a clear and understandable vision that all would support. Stumbling across the Demand Supply Compression (DSC) principles that powered Strategic MRO was a stroke of good fortune. The first time he heard these principles he had wondered whether the discussion would be too simple, with no substance to address his issues. He had been wrong about that. These principles made plenty of sense to him now:

1. Define the value stream.
2. Connect the asset to the value stream.
3. Connect demand to the asset.
4. Connect supply to demand.
5. Compress demand supply connections.

These guiding principles were designed to address the complexities of enterprise asset management and MRO supply chain management using a practical, common sense approach. Paul now realized that common sense only belonged to them that have it. His leadership now understood that also.

The next chapter reflects Paul's journey into understanding the specific roles of technology in Strategic MRO and how he would systematically transform his organization into a Strategic MRO leader.

Chapter 10

Information Technology Connectivity

Executive Summary: Strategic MRO technology options include maintenance modules bolted onto enterprise resource planning systems, enterprise asset management versions of computerized maintenance management systems, e-commerce platforms, and e-asset management strategies. Information systems streamline the flow of activities, manage the flow of information, and capture data that ultimately will be converted into information for driving performance improvement initiatives. By compressing out waste and non-value added activities, information technology enables work processes, assures compliance to established work practices, and provides information needed to improve work processes.

Paul knew information technology was needed to achieve business objectives. His company had invested significantly in an ERP system to manage production and accounting. It scheduled labor, materials, and equipment to ensure that production schedules aligned with customer requirements. The ERP software provider was eager to sell him a maintenance module to ensure that asset information was included in the big picture. It used all the right words: "Our technology has helped leading companies achieve asset lifecycle management objectives." "Our integrated system means your resources have to use and learn only one system." Good stuff, Paul rightfully thought.

Paul's company currently used a standalone computerized maintenance management system (CMMS) to manage maintenance activities through work orders and planned PM. He was not sure how an ERP maintenance module was going to change or enhance this. Meanwhile, competing software providers had evolved the CMMS term into enterprise asset management. Their message was equally powerful and compelling. "Asset management is not the same as managing production." "Our resources and technology are focused on the asset." "We specialize in maximizing your return on assets." Paul thought this made intuitive sense.

E-commerce vendors also clamored for attention. They offered desktop requisitioning processes designed to improve MRO material procurement processes. Their solutions could connect into either ERP or EAM technology or could stand alone. They promised to reduce maverick purchases, accelerate strategic sourcing, improve buying leverage, and reduce inventory levels through improved visibility in the MRO channel. This, on the surface, seemed like a great concept. Yet, some of the e-commerce vendors he had talked to as recently as a year ago no longer existed. Nevertheless, what they promised Paul needed.

Just when he thought he had heard it all, he was approached by a leading electronic controls manufacturer offering e-asset management strategies that enabled his company to apply real time condition-based monitoring techniques, conduct asset performance monitoring capabilities, and integrate maintenance and production schedules. "We integrate into both ERP and EAM technology. Monitoring the heartbeat of the asset." This was just what Paul was looking for as well. What to do? Certainly there was not a lack of information system technology. The challenge was connecting the right dots for his company.

Paul was no longer alone in his Strategic MRO journey. He had held the attention of his executive forum counterparts throughout several weeks of discussions. From their previous interactions he realized that there was no "one size fits all" solution. Yet there were some basic success factors that he and others consistently recognized.

Paul went back to the DSC guiding principles to see if they could stimulate his thinking regarding these success factors as they related to information systems.

"Define the value stream" clearly implied that information technology had to provide insight on forecasted and actual demand for the units of value his company produced. This knowledge of demand would allow Paul's company to deploy its assets to meet market needs.

Connecting the asset to the value stream required that information technology identify required resources; allocate capacity; and schedule labor, equipment, and material requirements to produce the unit of value. He recalled from his discussion on asset criticality that all assets are not equal, that they are not all directly connected to the value stream. Thus his information technology needed to provide both breadth and depth of focus. Breadth of focus meant that the technology should support all of his asset and people requirements. Depth of focus is the ability to filter out and focus on specific asset and people demand requirements. Paul knew that lack of asset and people availability stopped the show.

Connecting demand to the asset required information technology to help with decisions that would drive the extension of demand lead time and provide data for forecasting asset demands. Ultimately, of course, information technology must help in reducing asset demands. This logic applied to people as well as assets. Indeed, people create demand for office supplies, personal protective equipment, and other items needed to perform their tasks.

Connecting supply to demand required information technology to identify required resources; allocate capacity; and schedule labor, special equipment, and material requirements to perform the maintenance task. And connecting supply to demand provided the supplies people needed to successfully complete work. But now Paul was keenly aware of the three very different demand engines within his company: product, assets, and people.

Paul's focus was on assets. Therefore, compressing demand supply connections implied that his information technology had to enable better or best practices associated with Strategic MRO. Further, the information technology had to enable compliance with these better or best practices. Finally, the information technology had to provide timely information for improving asset performance, reducing costs, and making better practices the best.

Paul summarized his insights related to the Strategic MRO guiding principles in Table 10.1.

Strategic MRO Guiding Principles	Information System Inputs and Outputs
Define the Value Stream	Product and Service Demand
Connect the Asset to the Value Stream	Production & Delivery Schedules
Connect Demand to the Asset	Asset & People Demand
Connect Supply to Demand	Maintenance Schedules & Work Schedules
Compress Demand Supply Connections	Enablement, Compliance, and Improvement

Table 10.1 – Strategic MRO Guiding Principles - Insights

After reviewing the information system inputs and outputs it was easy to understand why everyone's solution was appealing. Every solution dealt with demands and schedules. But Paul now knew that the nature of demand varied due to the differences in the three demand engines at work in his company: product, people, and assets. Paul needed an information system that was built around an understanding of these differences.

Paul knew that the asset was a major focus in the Strategic MRO world and the technology had to support his asset based business objectives. He wanted to ensure that, whatever the solution, it supported the guiding principles and compression strategies of Strategic MRO. Paul sought advice from his peers.

Out of the Box?

The goal is not to reinvent or create a separate set of principles for information technology. As very wise person in the EAM space once said, "Technology is an excellent slave but a bad master." Thus the system should be tailored to desired business and operational practices. Another opinion regarding technology is reflected in the statements from a very senior executive at a large organization, "Do not change the software; use it out of the box. Change your processes to match its capabilities. The cost of modifications and managing these during subsequent upgrades is prohibitive."

Who is right? It is hard to say. Neither is wrong. Information technology providers, through their interaction with the market, must evolve and sometimes revolutionize their offerings to stay in business. This evolution happens in response to customer demands and to leverage technology advances such as the World Wide Web. It is critical to an asset owner to discern which information technology companies listen best, act first, fail fast (meaning learn from their mistakes), and recover stronger than ever.

Commercial off-the-shelf (COTS) providers will continue to dominate the market as the cost of developing, maintaining, and redesigning information technology is too high for most companies to bear alone. Internally developed technology is justified when no reasonable COTS information technology offerings exist in the market.

Fortunately, or maybe unfortunately, information technology providers shy away from telling their customers how to operate their business. These providers focus on guiding the technical deployment of information technology. COTS providers address multiple business approaches by building nearly unlimited flexibility into their applications. This flexibility allows the software to be tailored to the specific processes of a company. This tailoring process can be quite grueling, but well worth it. Customization, on the other hand, can be quite expensive and, as our senior executive stated, converting and reconnecting custom applications during upgrades can be quite costly.

One executive describes his experience saying, "We must not lose our tribal knowledge. However, we must enrich this tribal knowledge with knowledge of best business practices supported by information technology advancements." From his perspective best of breed technology, built around best practices, is the only real path to getting it right.

Before going too deep into the information system discussion a fundamental question needs to be addressed. What information system makes sense to be the core technology for asset lifecycle management: an ERP or an EAM system? In practice, the answer is often politically or fiscally motivated. "We have already spent this money on ERP or EAM technology," or "We need to get a return on our current investment." Our discussion will attempt to remove politics from the decision process by outlining how an asset owner's information system could and should address Strategic MRO objectives.

It behooves the asset owner to know the strengths of each information system offering. Two prevailing market strategies exist: a fully integrated system such as ERP or a best of breed technology such as EAM. Today's technology enables most best in breed technology offerings to communicate with integrated systems and vice versa.

Perhaps the most distinguishing difference between integrated systems and best of breed technology is how accounting practices are handled. ERP technology tends to connect all business activities back to a centralized accounting system. Best of breed technology tends to focus on specific applications and then output information to an integrated system or another best of breed technology. ERP technology tends to focus on the production and management of primary products. EAM technology tends to focus on assets and their maintenance. As discussed earlier, these are three distinct demand engines.

Both systems must be more than an activity manager if they are to help an asset owner reduce costs. For example, an ERP system must provide product contribution margin analysis. Likewise, an EAM technology must provide asset contribution margin analysis.

The following discussions will review other information system technology needs of Strategic MRO. Ultimately it will be up to the asset owner to determine what solution works best for needs and budget.

Where to Start

Paul knew his leadership team wanted to go right to the tactical level of deploying information technology. Work order management, inventory management, scheduling resources, issuing purchase orders and materials are all tactical activities. Executive leadership was tasked with setting the vision for the organization and determining its market and operational strategies. Tactical initiatives are deployed to achieve these strategies. Paul felt his team had to first demonstrate their understanding of Strategic MRO and how technology would fit at this level. Then they would review technology at the tactical levels. Using the guiding principles as a backdrop Paul began exploring the information technology connectivity required to enable Strategic MRO.

Defining the Value Stream

Chapter 5 defined the value stream as the activities, supporting labor, materials, assets, and information required to produce the desired unit of value. Thus the value stream is closely linked to the product lifecycle (PLC) as shown in Figure 10.1.

During the product lifecycle planning, companies use information technology to assess market needs and predict demand. During prototype and pilot activities, design and modeling technologies, such as CAE (Computer Aided Engineering), CAD (Computer Aided Design), and DOE (Design of Experiments) are

Figure 10.1 - Product Lifecycle

combined with value engineering principles to enable companies to architect products that meet projected market needs at a target price.

Once product and service concept designs have been approved the company decides whether to be an asset owner, a brand owner, or an assembler. Does the company want to be a totally vertically structured company or will it rely on a network of suppliers to meet its product and service objectives? A number of existing modeling technologies enable a company to analyze performance and cost factors that drive product and supply chain decisions.

Time to take a mental break. Why review product design and supply chain technology in a Strategic MRO discussion? Because product and service design ultimately determine what assets will be needed to fulfill market demands. If a product designer specifies a metal casting for the valve body...metal casting equipment please. If the decision is for a plastic valve body...plastic injection molding equipment please. If a facility designer decides wood floors are in...time to buy saws, sanders, and buffers. Often such product decisions are made without regard to their impact on current and future asset investments.

Connect the Asset to the Value Stream

Chapter 6 introduced the second DSC principle: connect the asset to the value stream. This principle focuses an organization's enterprise asset management strategies and operational priorities. At its core the principle classifies asset criticality by gauging its impact on revenue creation in the value stream. Clearly, no product has gone to market without assets being deployed. Once the supply chain has been designed, the goal is simple...produce only what the market consumes. This means the assets have to be planned, designed, built, acquired, and installed to meet this objective.

By the time a company reaches the pilot phase of the product lifecycle, preliminary decisions have been made regarding the nature of assets required. The asset is a product that must be planned for, designed, built, acquired, and installed for use by the asset owner as indicated in Figure 10.2.

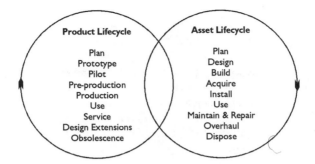

Figure 10.2 - Product Lifecycle and the Asset Lifecycle

Asset Designs. CAE and CAD technology are typically used to design assets. Product standards may be captured in inventory item masters that feed CAD data files to ensure that only approved parts are used. CAE programs may utilize CAD files to lay out assets and conduct throughput or other performance analyses required.

Figure 10.3 shows an example of process simulation analysis software. Ultimately this information technology is used to answer critical asset questions related to capacity, operating rates, reliability estimates, availability requirements, and operating costs (direct and indirect).

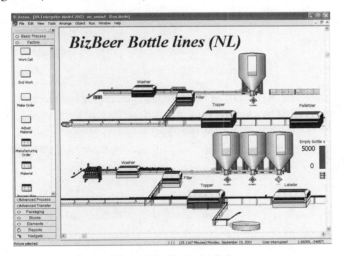

Figure 10.3 - Simulation Software

Asset design and operating parameters set the baseline for all future performance expectations, fault detection, failure analysis, and subsequent maintenance supply behavior. Asset design and operating parameters must be captured and communicated via information technology. The best place to start capturing this information is through the use of an installed asset profile.

Installed Asset Profiles. When an asset owner acquires an asset the fundamental design, operating, and maintenance parameters should be profiled as a condition of purchase. Engineered assets typically have associated blueprints, part numbers, bills of material (BOM), user manuals, safety requirements, critical spares lists, recommended maintenance frequencies, and supply sources. This information should be migrated to the assets owner's enterprise asset management system. This process accelerates the capturing and understanding of asset needs. The EAM system can be a best of breed technology or part of an integrated system.

Figure 10.4 shows an illustrated parts catalog generated through conversion of blueprints and associated bills of materials.

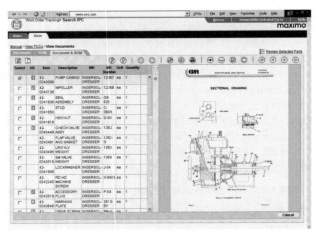

Figure 10.4 - Illustrated Parts Catalog

Recommended spares can be quickly selected either by selection of the part from the drawing or by clicking on the part description. Figure 10.5 drills down one more level to show the source of supply for this part.

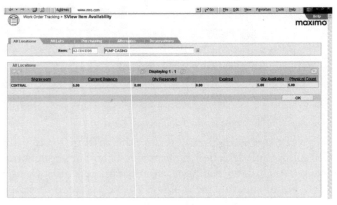

Figure 10.5 - Selected Part Source of Supply

To reemphasize a previous point, the asset owner should be migrating data from source files where practical, instead of creating the initial asset profile manually. The installed asset profile is the foundation for future configuration management activities. Associated asset-specific operational documentation should be electronically captured in a document management system linked to the asset in the EAM technology.

Asset Location Hierarchy. The asset design and installed profile address the physical characteristics of the asset. The location hierarchy physically locates the asset in the value stream. Is the asset in plant 1 or plant 2? Is it located on the first floor or the third floor? Is it in the drying room or the paint booth? Ultimately, location is going to affect the positioning of labor and materials that must respond to asset demands. Virtually all EAM technologies allow for the use of location hierarchies. Figure 10.6 is an example of a location hierarchy where assets are shown in their parent-child relationship within the plant site.

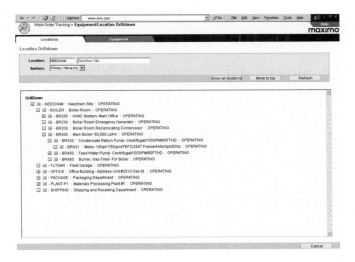

Figure 10.6 - Asset Location Hierarchy

Companies that have significant geographical dispersion of assets often use GIS (geographic iInformation systems) technology to drive their location hierarchies. GIS information technology is capable of assembling, storing, manipulating, and displaying geographically referenced (location) information. Often companies struggle with where to keep primary asset data. Should it be in the GIS system or the EAM technology? Middleware information technology that enables the free flow of data between both GIS and EAM technology can be used where this is an issue.

In connecting the asset to the value stream, technology was used to:

- Establish the baseline design and performance requirements of the asset.
- Capture and transfer information from asset makers.
- Physically locate assets in the value stream.

If asset owners do not manage information from the time of asset acquisition they may spend the rest of their time wishing they had. Money spent to capture information right the first time is well worth the investment. Dealing with inadequate and hard-to-find information accounts for no less than 20% of the maintenance resources.

Connect Demand to the Asset

Chapter 7 covered the DSC principle of connecting the demand to the asset. Remember that this principle focuses an organization's efforts on preventing, detecting, and correcting asset failures that create demand. At the center of this guiding principle is the asset. Asset performance clearly impacts the effectiveness of the value stream.

Information systems play a primary role in documenting an asset's performance. Additional information system roles include the preventing and detecting of asset failures and understanding the nature of asset demands.

Overall Equipment Effectiveness (OEE) Monitoring. Recall from Chapter 6 that asset criticality classifications are based on the proximity of the asset to the revenue creating activities. Overall equipment effectiveness monitoring measures the availability, first time through quality, and performance efficiency of an asset.

Classes 1, 2, and 3 revenue producing assets are typically prime candidates for electronic OEE tracking. Class 2 and 3 assets tend to have steady state availability requirements. A number of sensor and data collection technologies can be used to transmit OEE data to performance monitoring systems and statistical analysis packages. Refer to Chapter 7 for a discussion of the OEE value density metric. As performance degradation is detected, information systems alert workflow and work order systems to manage supply response. See Figure 10.7 for online OEE measurements.

Condition Based Monitoring (CBM). CBM technology monitors asset and component characteristics to determine the potential for or the existence of failure conditions. For example, intelligent instruments and valves continuously run internal diagnostics to check the health of their electronics and the sensors they are attached to. These diagnostics can be used to create preventive or emergency work orders. To take advantage of smart instruments they must be connected to an instrument management application. These solutions allow for easy online configuration changes such as changing the units and re-ranging the instrument. They

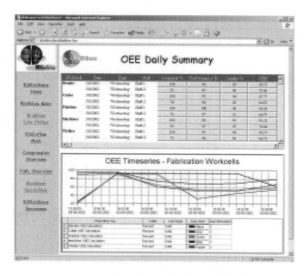

Figure 10.7 - OEE Value Density Metric

also manage calibration, document all changes, and most important of all, monitor the devices for alerts.

Figure 10.8 shows leading edge instrument and valve management technology that allows an asset owner to configure, streamline calibration, and perform diagnostics on field devices from a single software platform. This platform is easily integrated into EAM technology where workflow and work order technology can be triggered.

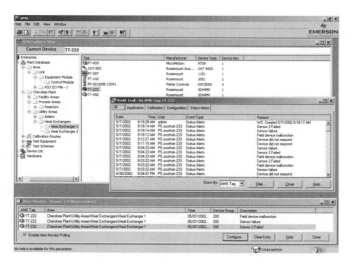

Figure 10.8 - Instrument and Valve Management Technology

Figure 10.9 shows the link between leading edge instrument and valve management technology and EAM technology. Workflow can be streamlined by automatically generating work orders when equipment needs service. Prioritized field device generated alerts can be used to create emergency and preventive work orders.

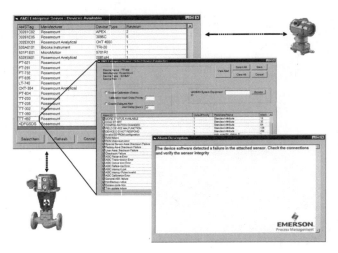

Figure 10.9 - Automated Condition-Based Monitoring

Figure 10.10 indicates upper and lower warning and action limits used to monitor flow rates for a pump impeller. Statistical analysis software can further refine and help interpret CBM trend data.

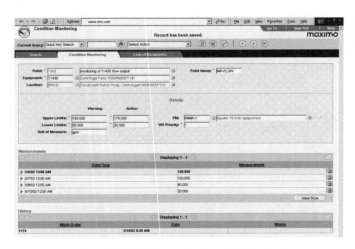

Figure 10.10 - CBM connectivity to EAM Technology

Asset Condition Assessment. Information technology should ultimately provide the asset owner with a system-based synopsis of asset conditions. Typically multiple databases exist within safety, engineering, purchasing, operations, accounting, and maintenance containing the necessary information to create an asset condition assessment.

The databases that might be integrated to develop preliminary asset condition assessment include:

- Safety and environmental risks (safety database).
- Structural integrity for buildings and other structures (engineering database).
- Current performance issues such as operating rates and output quality for equipment (OEE monitoring).
- Current cost profile including direct costs of operation such as energy and operators as well as indirect costs to maintain assets (accounting and work order databases).
- Historical maintenance and repair activities by asset and component and their actual costs (work order database).
- Planned maintenance and estimated cost of labor, materials, and special equipment (planned maintenance schedules, job plans, and resource and inventory databases).
- Planned capital expenditures such as overhaul, major modifications, or replacement and the projected costs (project management, budgets).
- Certification activities and their associated costs as required by industry regulations, applicable laws, or contractual obligations (document management, compliance software).
- Asset valuation to include depreciation, replacement value, market or salvage value, and future earnings (accounting, valuation software).

At the heart of the data collection and report generation process is a common asset identification scheme. Asset condition assessment information is used to direct physical inspection activities that ultimately determine whether maintenance, overhaul or replacement of assets is appropriate.

Asset Failure Tracking. Asset information technology must track failures, their associated root causes, and corrective actions taken. This information drives early equipment management, maintenance prevention activities, standardization decisions, and redundant system design strategies. As shown in Figure 10.11, failure tracking can be accomplished at the asset level and includes the most recent failure occurrence, frequency of failures, mean time between failures (MTBF), and average downtime.

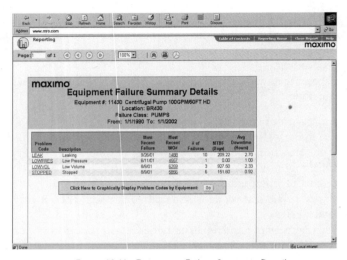

Figure 10.11 - Equipment Failure Summary Details

This information can be filtered through the demand criticality classification to drive the appropriate supply responses and smart scheduling practices.

Connect Supply to Demand—Labor

Chapter 8 introduces the fourth DSC principle of connecting supply to demand. The goal is to focus an organization's efforts on achieving asset management objectives through improving supply capabilities and performance. The operating premise is that for every asset demand there is an appropriate source of supply.

This source of supply must be fully known, understood, and managed to achieve business objectives and the lowest total cost of ownership for existing assets. Supply consists of labor, materials, and the special equipment/tools needed to respond to asset demand. The following discussion focuses on labor required to maintain asset performance.

Information systems play a vital role in identifying, allocating, and scheduling appropriate labor resources to meet demand requirements. Information system connectivity should assist the asset owner first in reducing demand and then in maximizing labor utilization to satisfy these demands.

Work Management Technology. This can signal the presence of a potential or existing failure. The demand queue is then filled with multiple demands coming from multiple sources and, perhaps, multiple locations. What to do? Workflow technology enables an asset owner or asset service provider to develop multiple scenarios for taking action in response to demands.

Proper workflow management results in labor resources performing certain tasks in a desired order. Workflow management ensures that the demand criticality classification is applied to all demands. In additional, workflow management eliminates costly administrative and operational delays and reduces administrative burden. Figure 10.12 is a typical workflow diagram indicating the desired approval process for a work order.

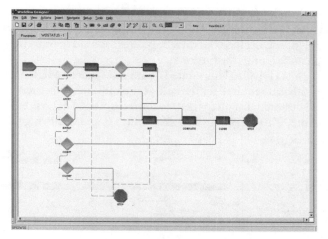

Figure 10.12 - Workflow Application

Matching skill requirements to the task is a normal first step in assigning labor. Information technology populated with maintenance technician skills, certifications, and other special job capabilities can assign labor accordingly. Another part of integration is the connection of records contained in a human resource (HR) database with the work order system. This ensures that classifications and associated wage rates are correct.

When the work order request is issued it begins its journey through the workflow process. The first stop as shown in Figure 10-12 is for request approval. Figure 10.13 shows an approved work order.

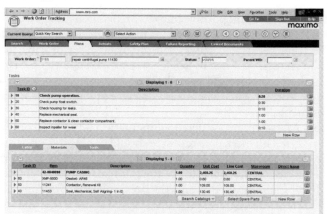

Figure 10-13 - Approved Work Order

Work orders define the basic unit of work performed on an asset. It is the unit of work associated with the work order that is planned, scheduled, dispatched, coordinated, and tracked. For repetitive work orders, job plans are typically generated and stored. They define the tasks, labor requirements, materials, and tools or special equipment needed to satisfy an asset demand.

Job plans can also be developed after the fact to record specific tasks, materials used, and tools needed. These can then be used as a job aid or proofing tool should the asset demand occur in the future.

In Figure 10.14 a job plan is illustrated. It indicates that an ME1, Mechanic First Class, is the lead craft required for the task. It also indicates estimated time for each task. It should be noted that often these estimated times do not represent the entire supply lead time. This is because tasks like sourcing and retrieving materials may not be included.

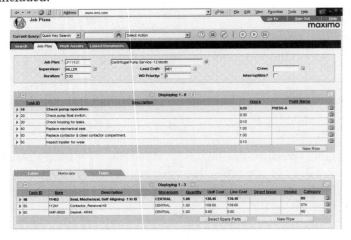

Figure 10.14 - Job Plan

Job plans have significant positive impacts on maintenance practices. But, just like all plans, they need to be monitored for appropriate detail, proper sequence of tasks, standard time versus actual time, standard material versus actual material, and other relevant factors. At a macro level, job plans, like work orders, should be reviewed for their necessity and overall effectiveness. Information system technology should assist an asset owner or asset service provider in completing effectiveness assessments.

Document Management. When documentation is required or requested to complete a task, the maintenance resource should be able to retrieve it via EAM connectivity with document files, document management systems, and e-catalogs. The benefit of connectivity to document management technology is that these systems typically ensure that only the latest versions of documents are used, they control modifications, and provide access to archive files that contain the original source documents.

Connecting EAM workflow to document management systems ensures that users request permission to make changes to assets. Subsequent documentation of asset modifications can occur based on the completion of the work order. Ultimately these changes can be promulgated to blueprints, bills of materials, inventory item masters, and job plans. All of these information connections enable an effective configuration management system. Figure 10.15 shows attached drawings available for use by maintenance resources.

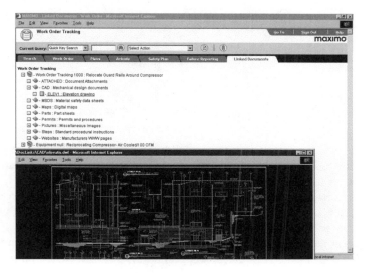

Figure 10.15 - Documentation

Smart Planning and Scheduling. Smart planning and scheduling should manage the entire set of tasks to be performed by maintenance resources. Using a demand criticality classification, tasks should be assigned to the best resource based on capability, availability, and time factors.

Most EAM offerings provide users with either electronic or hard copy work order lists. These work orders can be sorted by location, failure type, work type, and labor resources needed. Few EAM technologies actually complete a demand criticality analysis to prioritize event schedules. Add-on technologies or in-house developed scripts exist that provide these smart scheduling capabilities. Figure 10.16 shows a traditional scheduling input screen for preventative maintenance tasks.

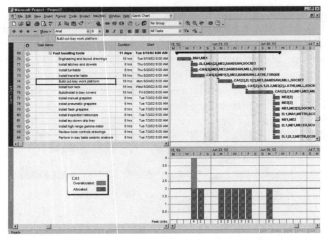

Figure 10.16 - Preventive Maintenance Schedule

Multiple work orders can be managed through traditional project management information technology. Events such as start-ups, outages, planned expansions, and overhauls are handled well by project management scheduling.

Project management techniques can also be used to schedule maintenance events on a monthly, quarterly, or yearly basis. Figure 10.17 shows the use of project management technology applied to work order planning and scheduling. Project management technologies enable a planner to schedule resources to maximize their utilization based on resource loading, and allow for smart scheduling of tasks based on precedence.

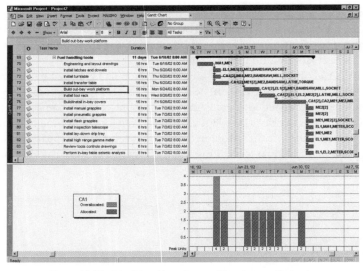

Figure 10.17 - Scheduling Using Project Management Technology

Smart scheduling can be extended to the integrated coordination of production scheduling with maintenance scheduling. This is done through finite capacity scheduling technology as shown in Figure 10.18.

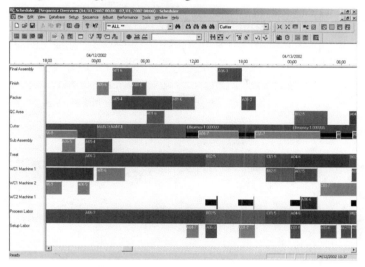

Figure 10.18 - Integrated Scheduling Technology

Contractor Management. Technology helps manage outside contractors. Systems exist that allow contractors to enter data into approval systems directly. Through technology integration, forecasted and actual use of labor, materials, and special equipment, these systems can directly update work orders, thereby eliminating data entry redundancies. Contractor management technology can also integrate into accounting systems for efficient invoice processing. Figure 10.19 is an example of a contractor management technology offering.

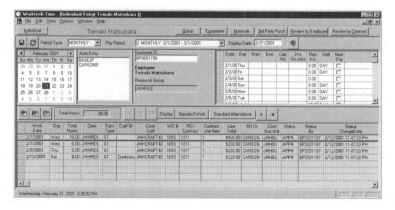

Figure 10.19 - Contractor Management Technology

Labor Time and Attendance Reporting. Two sets of data that rarely reconcile with each other are the labor time charged against work orders and labor hours tracked in a time and attendance system. Technology exists to reduce these discrepancies. Real time connectivity into EAM, HR, and ERP systems increases labor reporting accuracy, eliminates redundant data entry, and improves payroll processing. Figure 10.20 is an example of individual reporting time and attendance reporting.

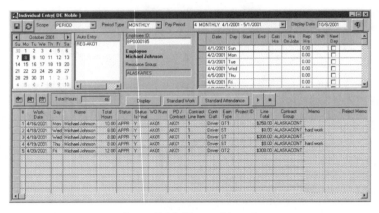

Figure 10.20 - Time and Attendance

Connect Supply to Demand—Materials

Chapter 9 discusses the DSC principle of connecting supply to demand with an emphasis on MRO materials. Information systems play a vital role in identifying and allocating appropriate materials to meet demand requirements.

Part Description Standardization Technology. Asset owners traditionally do not maintain tight control over MRO part descriptions. This would be the kiss of death for a distributor who must manage and sell from multiple locations. Multiple descriptions make it difficult for a company to aggregate MRO spends by commodity groups, share inventory among internal stocking location and multi-site operations, and automate sourcing and procurement functions with the supply chain.

Information system technology exists that helps users achieve standardization of product data. Typically, standard modifier dictionaries (SMD) are used to accomplish this. The technology can manipulate and ultimately repopulate product data to fit the new standard.

A part of this process is illustrated in Figure 10.21. During the standardization process, missing and incomplete information is highlighted and brought to the attention of a user. Without this technology most asset owners have a difficult time achieving the level of MRO product information standardization necessary for wide-scale system connectivity.

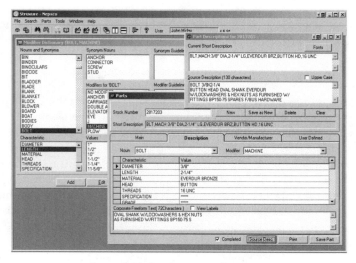

Figure 10.21 - Part Description Standardization

Electronic Catalogs. Electronic catalogs (e-catalogs) enable asset owners, service providers, and makers to improve transparency of product information in the channel as well as streamline the process of procuring the desired products. Figure 10.22 is an example of an electronic catalog. By drilling down through the catalog, part images, specifications, pricing, and availability information can be accessed.

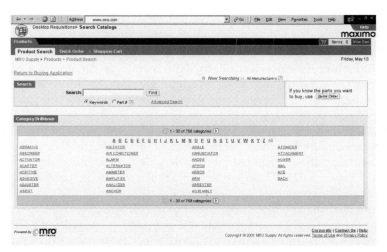

Figure 10.22 - Electronic Catalog

If based on the manufacturer's part number, e-catalogs reduce the need for multiple cross-reference files throughout the supply chain. Using manufacturer numbers also expedites the comparison of competitive or substitute products.

E-catalogs enable operations level users to conduct searches. This reduces the potential bottlenecks created by routing all sourcing activities through purchasing.

Electronic catalogs can be tailored so that only agreed-upon MRO products are shown. In addition, electronic catalog information can be tied directly to invoicing and electronic payment activities such as procurement cards and automated clearing houses.

The integration possibilities for e-catalogs continue to grow as the industry finds new ways to use Internet technology. Without the electronic catalog, real-time, flexible, up-to-date MRO product information system connectivity is difficult at best.

Some companies have achieved MRO product information standardization and synchronization connectivity through the use of in-house technology, dedicated networks, and EDI. The cost of this type of solution when applied to all customers and suppliers is usually prohibitive. Thus, this is usually implemented only for accounts that purchase significant volumes of materials.

Inventory Connectivity. After having built standardized MRO part descriptions and connected to e-catalogs, the asset owner is able to connect inventory procurement functions to the supply community. Spot buys and inventory replenishment represent the two most common inventory transactions where information system connectivity plays an important role.

As work orders are initiated in an EAM system, inventory can be checked to determine if necessary materials exists. The source for the material requirements typically resides in a job plan. For work orders without a job plan, users can search existing inventory records within the EAM application. Often the first disconnect in systems occurs here. The user is unable to see inventory stocking information from within the same system that initiated the work order.

Once the necessary MRO part has been identified it can be reserved against a work order for future use. If the desired internal storeroom does not have the MRO part in question, information technology connectivity enables users to search multiple storerooms and even external distributor and manufacturer inventory.

MRO parts can then be requisitioned through EAM technology or through integration with ERP or other purchasing technology using workflow processes. MRO parts can also be acquired through desktop requisitioning applications as shown in Figure 10.23. Workflow technology can and should be used to control purchase authorizations.

Remember the key to success is to associate all purchases back to the asset creating the demand. Disconnected inventory, purchasing, and work order systems make associating MRO materials with a specific asset cumbersome. This often leaves the asset owner not knowing what was used for what. This, in turn, causes attempts to track material costs by asset to become an administrative headache. Thus it is not done.

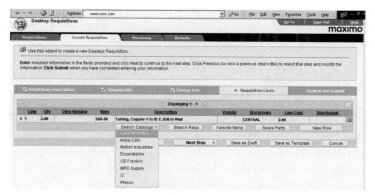

Figure 10.23 - Desktop Requisition

Inventory replenishment activities take a somewhat different information connectivity route than do spot buys. The first question that technology should help answer is whether to stock an item or not. If the product can be obtained with reasonable availability and delivery the MRO product should not be carried in inventory. With the advent of e-catalogs this decision-support feature will ultimately be enabled. Currently such decisions require off-line analysis.

The next technology connectivity that needs to occur is the constant review of inventory usage to drive reorder points and reorder quantities. This typically requires a statistically based system such as the inventory optimizer shown in Figure 10.24.

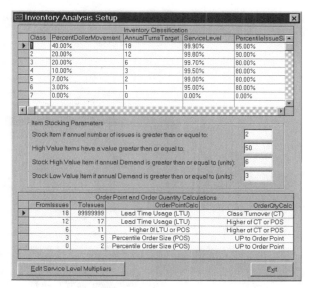

Figure 10.24 - Inventory Optimization Technology

As inventory minimums are reached purchase requests are initiated. At this point workflow enforces organizational policies and controls. Examples of such policies are:

- All buys going to the same source should be aggregated twice per day.
- A department manager must approve all orders in excess of $2,000.

In some cases, lights–out replenishment, wherein an inventory replenishment order works through the system to the supplier without human intervention, is appropriate. But for some, lights–out replenishment is a scary proposition because of lack of confidence in order quantities, pricing, and the source of supply.

All materials must be received. Some firms use a more formal receiving process than do others. A few companies have suggested that the receiving process be bypassed altogether. They point out that the purchasing process captures all the pertinent information. The idea is to do business with reputable suppliers who can be trusted to deliver the ordered materials correctly every time.

Where a more formal approach to receiving is desirable, information connectivity should enable the real time receipt of materials and the associated matching activities. Then real time payments can occur if desired.

Inventory connectivity should provide real time information on what inventory is turning over and what sits patiently awaiting its 15 minutes of fame. Ultimately information technology should assist asset owners and service providers in developing disposal channels either through auction or buyback scenarios.

Mobile and Wireless Technology. All of this connectivity is nice if the user is near a computer. What if the user is mobile? The answer is simple: provide mobile and wireless technology as shown in Figure 10.25. This is the hardware needed to implement real time connectivity. Virtually everything you can do at a computer

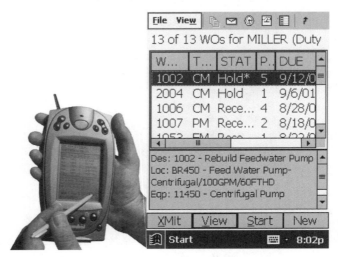

Figure 10.25 - Mobile and Wireless Technology

terminal can be accomplished on mobile computing technologies such as laptops, PDAs (personal digital assistants), or other handheld devices.

Reverse Auctions. Information technology exists to speed bid-buy processes. These packages enable multiple bidders to compete in a real time and secure fashion. Buyers can compare detailed bid packages and assess multiple buy scenarios. Reverse auctions often result in substantial price savings to the asset owner. There is one caveat: price is only one component of the total cost of ownership. Refer to Chapter 9 for additional discussions of this issue.

Budget. Many information system modules contain budgeting information. Project management technology with information derived from planned maintenance schedules and planned outages can be useful in constructing budgets. When based on realistic resource loading, materials, and special equipment associated with job plans, a baseline budget can be derived. This baseline is then augmented with historical consumable and spare parts consumption derived from past expenditures. This approach, however, usually falls well short of actual staffing and materials purchases.

Reporting. Reports are essential to driving Strategic MRO practices and improvement initiatives. Data mining technology continues to advance through web-architected technology. Technology providers typically provide a set of standard reports like those shown in Figure 10.26.

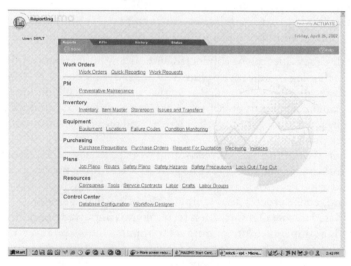

Figure 10-26 - EAM Reporting

Specialized reports can be designed as needed using standard reports as a starting point. The goal is to eliminate the dependency on IT staffs for report development and processing. Because reporting can consume considerable CPU resources, care should be taken in architecting online or off-line data mining and report generation applications.

Compress Demand Supply Connections

In chapters 5 through 9 compression strategies were introduced to improve asset performance and reduce supply costs. Information systems play a vital role in streamlining the flow of activities, managing the flow of information, and capturing data that ultimately will be converted into information for driving performance improvement initiatives.

As discussed previously in this chapter technology exists today to:

- Identify potential failures.
- Check storeroom inventory for parts availability.
- If the part is not in the storeroom, check availability at the local distributor.
- Issue an electronic purchase order.
- Verify the shipment of the part with the third-party carrier.
- Verify the availability of the maintenance labor by skill requirements.
- Verify the need and availability of special equipment.
- Establish work priority based on demand criticality.
- Schedule and coordinate the work order with the production schedule, and availability of resources and equipment.
- Track machine downtime.
- Report failure causes.
- Calculate overall equipment effectiveness (OEE).
- Provide detailed asset condition assessment reports.
- Report all the associated costs.

All of these activities can be conducted without any human intervention. What does this technology connectivity ultimately do for the asset owner? By compressing out waste and non-value added activities, information technology supports three fundamental business objectives. These are enabling work processes, assuring compliance to established work practices, and providing information to improve work processes.

Enabling Work Processes. Agreed-upon work practices can be accomplished through information technology. The goal is to streamline processes, eliminate double and triple keystroking of data, eliminate batch delays through system integration, and reduce process delays through workflow management.

The desired impact of information technology is improved productivity. Productivity is a simple measure of outputs to inputs. Thus, the intended consequence of information technology is to achieve more output with same input. If output stays the same, technology should enable the required inputs to decrease. If output is expected to grow, technology should enable the use of resources to stay the same or go up in smaller proportions. The best case scenario is for outputs to go up and inputs to go down.

Compliance with Work Processes. Agreed-upon work practices result in the desired business benefits. Failure to comply with documented and approved work practices often has disastrous results. At the very least lack of compliance increases costs.

Asset and component standards, procedural standards, configuration management, strategic sourcing, and connecting all activities to an asset require discipline. Technology properly designed and implemented improves the chances of achieving needed discipline. Just having procedures does not mean they will be followed.

Technology requires that certain data be input during an activity. An example might be an asset tag number's being required on a requisition for a consumable from stores. Technology can also limit the selection of data. For example, the selection of suppliers on a purchase order can be limited to those who are approved for the item being purchased. These kinds of requirements and limitations improve compliance.

Improving Work Processes. Information derived from data capture should be used to determine if a process performs as expected and whether work standards are being complied with. Our only caution is that often information systems overload company resources with too much data. This is affectionately referred to as a DRIP, or "data rich information poor" environment.

Most information systems indicate current work order backlog and current completion percentage. How many indicate what work orders and associated costs were attributed to revenue generating assets? What percentage of work orders required the skills of the person assigned to do the tasks?

The value density metrics presented in Chapters 5 through 9 were designed specifically to focus on Strategic MRO practices. Monitor these vital metrics carefully. All data collection activities should have a business purpose that can be directly tied to costs. Information system technology enables asset owners to take charge of their assets and begin operating this important component of their corporate investments based on business logic instead of simply activity management.

Many books are written that blame technology for an organization's failure to achieve improvement objectives. We boldly disagree with such conjecture. The fundamental flaw in this thinking is that technology is to blame for anything. Poor thinking is to blame.

We prefer thinking based on guiding principles and best practices, an understanding of technology as it relates to achieving best practices, and the meshing of practices and technology during implementation. This kind of thinking will drive improvements and attain organizational objectives.

Chapter 11

Program Management

Executive Summary: Strategic MRO is a business process, not an activity management scheme. A lack of focus on common sense principles quickly drives up operating costs. This chapter outlines how a Strategic MRO focus team establishes the framework for successful change and continuous improvement in an organization. The SMRO focus team facilitates the company's clear and deliberate path toward future perfect by adopting the five DSC guiding principles, implementing compression strategies, and monitoring progress through the use of value density metrics. This chapter defines a four-phase approach to achieving Strategic MRO objectives. The phases are stable, smart, quick, and agile.

Paul had insight. He felt as though his journey into understanding the concepts of Strategic MRO made him more aware as a CEO. He was now aware as he walked through his plant, that the assets had a life of their own, their own support network of skilled labor, their own set of spares, a work order system, and something else he couldn't quite identify.

Each asset has a purpose, he pondered. Does the asset's purpose align with the purpose of the organization? He knew all assets were not equal. The asset criticality classification allowed him to clarify the priority of assets. He knew all failures were not equal. The demand criticality classification gave him an easy way to understand that. And he knew that all supply responses did not need to be the same. In his mind he saw these responses ranging from proactive to reactive maintenance, using internal and/or external resources and owning MRO inventory and/or buying materials only when needed. He knew without a shadow of a doubt that information technology existed to help his company elevate its Strategic MRO game, enhance performance, and drive down cost. All the ingredients for success were there.

His challenge was to get his company to dig deeper into its operations and really understand if they were indeed applying the DSC guiding principles to move them toward a future perfect. The Strategic MRO initiative was complex. Certainly the discussions and efforts of the executive forum teams reaffirmed the breadth and depth of the challenges. And this initiative was one that could not be easily handed off to one of his staff. Paul knew he would have to drive this one forward himself.

Paul knew his company needed to change. If he could add another future perfect objective, it would be *change without needing change management*. Unfortunately this future perfect was nowhere near realizable. Paul listed the basic change management principles in his mind:

- Define the current state.
- Determine the future state objectives.
- Analyze gaps between current state and future state objectives.
- Develop a prioritized list of efforts to begin closing the gaps.

Paul knew he somehow had to define realistic goals that would stretch but not paralyze the organization. Paul thought of the principle of enlightened self-interest, which suggests that a company does something because it is the right thing to do and because the company is aware of the negative consequences of not doing it. Strategic MRO is the right thing to do. If we do not and our competitors do… Paul did not even want to contemplate the consequences of inaction.

Paul knew he had to permanently change day-to-day behaviors within his company. He knew behavioral change involved three phases:

- Unfreeze the current mindset.
- Define new behaviors.
- Refreeze the mindset around the new behaviors.

Paul had already begun the behavioral change process of unfreezing by pointing out ineffective actions (islands of pain) that currently existed in the company. He had introduced his leadership team to a new way of approaching enterprise asset management and MRO supply chain management through the DSC guiding principles and compression strategies. This was the "define new behaviors" stage. Paul understood the importance of communicating to people what was to be done, showing them how to do it, and reminding them again how it was done. Now he needed to focus his organization, give his people the skills, and help them refreeze their collective mindset around the new behaviors that would allow the company to achieve Strategic MRO success.

Selecting a Strategic MRO Program Manager

Paul knew that the transition to Strategic MRO requires the completion of a seemingly overwhelming number of tasks. He wanted this process carefully managed. It was clear that the Strategic MRO program would require the full attention of a qualified resource and the assistance of all that person's associates. The fifth future perfect objective was in the minds of the leadership team: *only invest in resources that enable the first four future perfect objectives.* Paul knew that whatever resources he applied would have to get bottom line results. This meant Paul's first task of identifying a resource to assume the role of the Strategic MRO program manager was critical to the success his company sought.

First and foremost the Strategic MRO program manager had to have Strategic MRO skills. He or she needed *political skills* to facilitate change amid various personal and professional agendas. This person had to have *analytical skills* as well. Strategic MRO requires a fact-based approach with rational and well-argued analysis. The two analytical skills required were systems (workflow) analysis and financial analysis.

This person had to have *people skills* with a strong emphasis on communication and interpersonal skills. This individual had to be an effective listener, able to see issues from the eyes of others. This would be critical, as Paul knew his team and the employees of his company challenged each other daily. This process was going to create conflict, and the person he selected must be able to reconcile and resolve the conflict as it occurred.

The Strategic MRO program manager must also have *information system skills,* as technology is an essential ingredient in achieving Strategic MRO success. Finally, this person had to have *business skills.* Simply put, the SMRO program manager needed to understand how a business works.

Quickly Paul checked off the qualifications. The Strategic MRO program manager must have the following skills:

- Understanding of Strategic MRO.
- Political.
- Analytical.
- People.
- Information Systems.
- Business.

Where would Paul find such a person? Usually someone with these skills would be indispensable. He had just a handful of candidates. After lengthy counsel with his leadership team, he approached Denise, the director of their process engineering group, to assume this role. Paul explained to Denise that she would report directly to him, and he would be the executive sponsor of the effort. A Strategic MRO task force would be formed under Denise's leadership and report their progress regularly to the leadership team. She would act as the lead facilitator and coordinator of team-based improvement initiatives.

At Paul's suggestion, Denise met with each member of the leadership team. The team members assured her of their full cooperation. Denise was impressed by the overwhelming support and clear vision expressed by the leadership team. She quickly realized they were serious about improving the bottom line through Strategic MRO.

After long discussions and review of the DSC principles and what the expectations were for the position, Denise accepted the role. She knew full well that her plate definitely would be overloaded and that she needed to devise a plan that met the expectations of the leadership team.

Preparing to Be a Strategic MRO Program Manager

Both Paul and Denise knew she would require specific training in the DSC guiding principles, compression strategies, value density metrics, and management approaches before she could assemble the right team. She attended a five-day Strategic MRO leaders course where she became indoctrinated in the new thinking.

At first Denise felt like she was going through a standard industrial engineering course. But within the first hour she knew something was different. She was not used to discussing assets relative to their value proposition. She learned that Strategic MRO was a business process not an activity management scheme. She quickly realized that a lack of focus on common sense principles quickly drives up operating costs and that asset demand dictates supply response. Her head was swimming, a sensation much like that experienced by Paul and the other members of the executive forum when they had been introduced to Strategic MRO.

Assembling the Strategic MRO Focus Team

Denise's first task upon returning to work was to form a Strategic MRO focus team. Denise was glad she waited until after the training before interviewing and selecting team members. Her old paradigm was to pick people who could get along with each other, had good problem-solving skills and, most important, had the time to participate. In addition to these vital attributes, Denise now knew she needed team members who wanted to make a difference, challenged the edges of thought and practice, had a good grasp of technology, and were open to new ideas.

Denise was such a strong leader that she sometimes dominated weaker team members, moving forward with her ideas even when consensus was not achieved. She needed to temper this urge because the Strategic MRO initiative was bigger than any one person. Denise assembled her Strategic MRO (SMRO) focus team with resources from the following areas:

- Engineering.
- Operations.
- Maintenance.
- Supply chain management.
- Information systems.

- Quality.
- Safety.

The first step in the team's preparation was attending certification training and receiving personal coaching from the Strategic MRO training leaders. The team's next step was to establish a charter to guide its efforts. Their preliminary mission was given to them by the leadership team. They could wordsmith it if they desired, but they were not to stray too far from the intent of the leadership team.

The mission of the Strategic MRO focus team is to identify, implement, and monitor the effectiveness of better and best practices for enterprise asset management and MRO supply chain practices with the expectation of improving overall business performance.

The SMRO focus team had to facilitate the company's clear and deliberate path toward future perfect by adopting the five DSC guiding principles, implementing compression strategies, and monitoring their progress through the use of value density metrics.

Together with the Strategic MRO coaches Denise and the SMRO focus team outlined a four-phase approach to achieving Strategic MRO objectives. The phases of stable, smart, quick, and agile were presented to the leadership team for approval.

- The stable phase is an evaluation of Strategic MRO and enterprise asset management, as they currently exist within the company today. This process is called a current state analysis.
- The smart phase is the process of designing or redesigning the business activities to use industry better and best practices so that Strategic MRO and enterprise asset management objectives can be achieved. This phase is accomplished using tools like future state mapping and ROI analysis.
- The quick phase is where the company implements newly designed practices to achieve performance goals through implementation of people, process, and technology changes.
- Agile phase activities are twofold. First, the company continues to apply Strategic MRO principles across all operational areas. Second, the company adjusts its Strategic MRO activities in response to emerging market trends.

Phase 1—Stable
During the Stable phase, an organization takes stock of its current Strategic MRO practices. The organization defines the scope and timing of its efforts to document current practices, technology, and skills. Then the company launches all current state documentation activities including organizational change manage-

ment efforts. These activities include explanations as to why we are doing a Strategic MRO intervention, expected benefits, participation requirements, expected duration, and how information will be communicated.

Where to begin? The SMRO team was quick to surmise that the leadership was looking for both short- and long-term gains in both performance and cost. The team knew they needed to improve their equipment planning, design, build, and installation processes. But they also knew these were long-term initiatives. They also needed to improve their current asset use, maintenance, and repair activities. Finally they knew they needed to improve the process for overhaul and disposal of assets. Again, the team saw these as long-term initiatives.

The SMRO team established an initial priority of effort as shown in Table 11.1.

Asset Lifecycle	Strategic MRO Priority of Actions
Plan	
Design	
Build	3rd Priority
Acquire	
Install	
Use	1st Priority
Maintain and Repair	
Overhaul	2nd Priority
Dispose	

Table 11.1 - Priority of Actions

The team agreed to use a systematic assessment process patterned after the DSC guiding principles. The team worked with their DSC coaches to devise the following plan of action:

Define the Value Stream – Identify exactly how their company generates revenue. Capture market pressures, competitive pressures, and other factors that create the need for improved Strategic MRO practices. This information will be used for making the case for change that would be communicated to all associates.

Connect the Asset to Value Stream – Calculate asset turnover and return on asset statistics. Complete an inventory of assets by their criticality. Capture data such as asset investment, expenditures, availability, first time through quality, and performance efficiency. The team decided that they would use value stream analysis techniques to identify the current state of revenue producing assets.

Connect Supply to Demand – Identify the labor, material, and special equipment investments made to support maintenance and MRO supply chain efforts. The team would use process-mapping techniques to describe their current maintenance, storeroom, and procurement practices.

Compress Demand Supply Connections – Throughout the assessment team members would identify and record existing performance issues and metrics. They would also identify any improvement initiatives, techniques, and technology changes that should be made.

The Stable Phase Plan –The SMRO team decided it would perform the assessments related to the first three guiding principles as one team. Thus the team would be guided by the principles of *define the value stream, connect the assets to the value stream, and connect demand to the asset.* Another team would devote its efforts to *connect supply to demand for labor.* A third team would *connect supply to demand for materials.* All teams would consider the *compress demand supply connections* principle where appropriate in their respective areas.

Stable Phase Plan

Guiding Principle	Objectives	Deliverables	Involvement
Define the Value Stream	– Determine how revenue is created – Identify industry and market challenges – Develop revenue per hour, per unit of production statistics	– Report on Value Stream challenges and results currently being experienced by the company	– Senior Executive – SMRO Team – DSC Coach
Connect the Asset to the Value Stream	– Determine Asset Turnover and ROA statistics – Complete Value Stream Analysis – Develop statistics by asset criticality classification	– Report on asset financial and operational performance – Value Stream Analysis – Asset Critical Classification analysis	– Senior Executives – SMRO Team – DSC Coach
Connect Demand to the Asset	– Gather current asset performance statistics, i.e., uptime, first time through quality, performance efficiency – Determine average cost per one hour of asset downtime for revenue producing assets and non-revenue producing assets – Determine current level of Early Equipment Management practices employed – Determine current methods use for predicting, preventing, and detecting asset failures – Determine information and hardware technology employed to assess, capture, and communicate asset demands	– Updated Value Stream Analysis with asset performance statistics – Report on Early Equipment Management Practices currently employed – Report on Demand Criticality Classification System and Demand Response System currently employed – Report on current Asset Demand Management technology employed	– SMRO Team – DSC Coach
Connect Supply to Demand Labor	– Determine labor requirements for conducting Strategic MRO activities (engineering, procurement, maintenance, storeroom, contractors, etc.) – Determine current labor utilization and cost statistics – Determine current methods and technology employed for labor planning, scheduling, dispatch, and tracking	– Report on Strategic MRO Labor requirements, utilization, and costs – Report on Labor Management methods and technology	– SMRO Labor Team – DSC Coach
Connect Supply to Demand Materials	– Determine current MRO material requirements, investments, and usage by commodity groups. – Determine current MRO Materials Procurement practices. – Determine current MRO Supply chain configuration and associated financial information. – Determine current MRO Materials inventory management and stocking practices. – Determine current special equipment/tooling requirements. – Determine current materials management technology employed.	– Report on Strategic MRO material utilization – Report on MRO procurement practices – Report on MRO supply chain configuration – Report on MRO inventory management and stocking practices – Report on MRO special equipment/tooling requirements – Report on current MRO materials management technology	– SMRO Materials Team – DSC Coach
Compress Demand Supply Connections	– Refer to SMART Phase – Study current business and industry better and best practices.	– Refer to SMART Phase	– Senior Executives – SMRO Team – DSC Coach

Table 11.2 - Stable Phase Plan

What would the teams do with the stable phase assessment information? Quite simply, they would compare it to what they *could* be doing. This comparison would be performed during the DSC smart phase.

The teams began collecting information through observation of practices, documentation review, and personnel interviews. They tapped into their existing information system to gather performance data as best they could.

The SMRO teams were amazed by how much data they actually had. They were equally amazed when they realized how little of what they had was needed to improve their processes. For example, they were able to determine how many work orders were performed, but not by asset class. They were able to gather total MRO material expenditures, but they were not able to associate the expenditures with specific assets. They knew what had been spent on maintenance labor, but they could not easily determine which specific assets had consumed this labor.

The team quickly found many disconnects in their workflows and information systems. They found multiple systems, standards, approval paths, and methods. At the conclusion of the stable phase, the SMRO teams were ready for a healthy dose of smart.

Phase 2—Smart

During the smart phase, the company identifies better and best practices it can practically apply to existing operations internally and externally. Paul had given strict guidance to Denise that he wanted a return on investment (ROI) study performed if significant investments were required.

Denise held up the completed current state analysis before the SMRO teams. She congratulated the teams on their efforts. Now, she said, we must begin our journey forward. This is what she said:

> Our DSC coaches have exposed us to many industry best practices, but it is up to us to decide which ones work for us. We need to identify what additional initiatives we feel we need to take. With the help of the DSC coaches, I have compiled a list of Strategic MRO best practices by DSC guiding principle. I have also noted where they fit in our priorities. (See Tables 11.3 through 11.7.)

Denise continued addressing the SMRO teams. *I know we have all been through the Strategic MRO powered by Demand Supply Compression leader's course. Now we need to understand fully how these compression strategies will work for us. Knowing full well that our leadership team expects results, let's put forward our best plan of action. Before we begin this phase let me emphasize the following. You will be working diligently to discover and apply new ways of doing things. As such, your personal ownership of the proposed solutions will never be higher. However, we are only looking for a realistic straw model at the end of this phase.*

Our leadership team will be the ultimate decision-makers for most of our proposals. They may find that certain solutions we think are good are cost-prohibitive or are not technologically feasible given our current systems. We may face the emotional challenges of whether to do it ourselves or outsource functions or whole departments. The stable phase was thoroughly challenging. However, the smart phase is where we set the path forward.

Smart Compression Strategy Review

DSC Guiding Principle	Compression Strategy	Asset Lifecycle	Priority
Define the Value Stream	Value Engineering (VE)	Plan	3rd
	Target Pricing	Plan	3rd
	Quality Function Deployment (QFD)	Plan, Design	3rd
	Time Based Strategies	Plan	3rd
	Supply Chain Optimization	Plan	3rd

Table 11.3 - Define the Value Stream

DSC Guiding Principle	Compression Strategy	Asset Lifecycle	Priority
Connect the Asset to the Value Stream	Target Costing	Plan, Design, Acquire, Use	1st
	Value Stream Analysis	Plan, Use	1st
	Right-sizing assets	Plan, Design	3rd
	Contract manufacturing	Plan	3rd
	Leased facilities and other outsourced functions	Plan	3rd
	Asset Criticality Classification	Plan, Use	1st
	Availability Modeling	Plan, Use	1st

Table 11.4 - Connect the Asset to the Value Stream

DSC Guiding Principle	Compression Strategy	Asset Lifecycle	Priority
Connect Demand to the Asset	Total Productive Maintenance (TPM)	Plan, Design, Install, Use, Maintain, and Repair	1st
	Reliability Centered Maintenance (RCM)	Design, Maintain, and Repair, Overhaul	1st
	Zero Breakdown Maintenance	Design, Maintain, and Repair	1st
	Demand Lead Time Analysis	Use, Maintain, and Repair	1st
	Design Reliability Analyses	Design, Use, Maintain, and Repair	3rd
	Asset Condition Assessment	Maintain, and Repair, Overhaul, Dispose	2nd
	Early Equipment Management	Plan, Design, Build, Acquire, Install	3rd
	Maintenance Prevention	Design, Maintain, and Repair	1st
	Accelerated Deterioration Elimination	Design, Install, Use, Maintain and Repair	1st
	Infrastructure, Equipment, and Component Standardization	Planning, Design, Acquire, Install, Use, Maintain, and Repair	1st
	Commodity Configuration Management	Plan, Design	3rd
	Design for Serviceability	Design	3rd
	Demand Criticality Classification	Use, Maintain, and Repair	1st
	Location Failure Analysis	Design, Maintain, and Repair	1st
	Standardized Failure Codes	Design, Maintain, and Repair	1st

Table 11.5 - Connect the Demand to the Asset

DSC Guiding Principle	Compression Strategy	Asset Lifecycle	Priority
Connect Supply to Demand – Labor	Demand Driven Maintenance	Plan, Design, Install, Use, Maintain, Repair, and Overhaul	1st
	Demand Response Strategies	Use, Maintain, and Repair	1st
	Supply Lead Time Reduction	Use, Maintain, Repair, and Overhaul	1st
	Smart Planning and Scheduling	Use, Maintain, Repair, and Overhaul	1st
	Opportunity Maintenance	Use, Maintain, Repair, and Overhaul	1st
	Work Type Management	Use, Maintain, Repair, and Overhaul	1st
	Multi-Skilling	Use, Maintain, Repair, and Overhaul	1st
	Accelerated Diagnostics	Use, Maintain, Repair, and Overhaul	1st
	Maintenance Practices Compliance	Use, Maintain, Repair, and Overhaul	1st
	Configuration Management	Use, Maintain, Repair, and Overhaul	2nd

Table 11.6 - Connect Supply to Demand - Labor

DSC Guiding Principle	Compression Strategy	Asset Lifecycle	Priority
Connect Supply to Demand – Materials	Core Competency Evaluation	Planning, Use	1st
	MRO Parts Commodity Analysis	Design, Build, Acquire, Use, Maintain, Repair, and Disposal	1st
	Strategic MRO (SMRO) Operational Model	Design, Build, Use, Maintain, and Repair	1st
	Supplier Evaluation and Selection	Design, Build, Use, Maintain, and Repair	1st
	SMRO Operational Model Detail Design	Design, Build, Use, Maintain, and Repair	1st
	SMRO Performance Expectations	Design, Build, Use, Maintain, and Repair	1st
	SMRO Pricing	Design, Build, Use, Maintain, and Repair	1st
	Contract Negotiations	Design, Build, Use, Maintain, and Repair	1st
	SMRO Implementation Planning	Acquire, Use, Maintain, and Repair	1st
	Supplier Relationship and Performance Management	Use, Maintain, and Repair	1st
	MRO Line of Sight Procurement	Use, Maintain, Repair, and Overhaul	1st
	E-procurement	Use, Maintain, Repair, and Overhaul	1st
	Consumption Driven Inventory Management	Use, Maintain, Repair, and Overhaul	1st
	Smart Storeroom Management	Use, Maintain, Repair, and Overhaul	1st
	Smart Payment Practices	Use, Maintain, Repair, and Overhaul	1st
	MRO Supply Chain Compliance	Use, Maintain, Repair, and Overhaul	1st

Table 11.7 - Connect Supply to Demand - Materials

The SMRO team members knew they had their work cut out for them. They also knew the seriousness of their mission. The team continued to follow the DSC guiding principles as they reviewed compression strategies. They called in numerous vendors and technology providers. They sent out requests for information (RFI), requests for proposals (RFP) and requests for quotes (RFQ). They had multiple team meetings. Three weeks later they had completed their high-level review of the compression strategies, associated cost savings, and expected performance improvements.

Smart Recommendations. The SMRO teams presented a list of smart recommendations to Paul and the leadership team. The recommendations included:

- Outsource both facility and operations maintenance functions to a third-party operations and maintenance (O&M) integrator.
- Upgrade the current computerized maintenance management system (CMMS) to an EAM best of breed technology to be provided by the O&M integrator.
- Develop asset criticality classifications, demand criticality classifications, and demand response strategies to be agreed upon with plant leadership and the O&M integrator.
- Begin demand driven maintenance training of operators to coincide with O&M integrator activities.
- Develop a strategic sourcing team to begin the redesign process with the intent of moving all inventories with the exception of critical spares to consignment.
- Establish an early equipment management team to begin asset and component standardization efforts.
- Establish a condition assessment team to set standards for asset overhaul and disposal.

The team recommendations were based on achieving the following estimated results:

- 5% to 10% improvement in asset availability.
- 25% reduction in maintenance labor costs over a three-year period.
- 65% reduction in inventory investment over a two-year period.
- 12% purchase price reduction within the first year.
- 20% reduction in MRO inventory purchases.
- 8% reduction in annual capital expenditures.
- 15% reduction in planned outage activities.

The team presented the estimated budget for implementing each of the recommendations and completed the initial return on investment (ROI) calculation. The ROI was calculated using the following approach.

- Compare current state and future state practices. Identify improved labor efficiencies, eliminate non-value adding activities, and reduce material, space, and equipment requirements.
- Identify incremental earnings, displaced cost, avoided cost, and intangibles created by expected improvements. Incremental earnings are earnings before interest and tax created by solutions. Displaced cost is defined as reduction in actual costs created by the solutions. Avoided cost is defined as reduction in potential (future) costs and investments in people, equipment, technology, and facilities created by the solutions. Intangibles are defined as any other benefit or risk avoidance created by the solutions.

- Use hard cost savings only for the actual ROI calculation. Hard cost savings have bottom-line impact. Soft cost savings improvements are those that free up time or a portion of a resource but no to the extent that the resource is not longer required or funded.
- Savings would be estimated over a three-year period based on planned adoption rates for each initiative. Savings would be applied at the end of each planning year.
- Costs would be estimated based on quotes provided by service providers and internal budget estimates. Costs would be broken into the two categories— onetime and recurring. Onetime cost savings would be applied at the beginning of the planning year and recurring cost savings would be applied quarterly.
- The SMRO team would use an internal rate of return of 15%, a cost of capital of 15%, and inventory carrying cost of 22%. All labor estimates would be based on salary plus benefits, plus any tangible associated operating expenses.
- Efficiency estimates would be based on percentage of time allocated to tasks instead of using detailed time and motion studies.

Based on ROI estimates, the SMRO teams were given approval to begin detailed planning and contracting activities to outsource the maintenance function while at the same time beginning MRO Strategic sourcing activities. These activities would be carried out in the quick Phase.

Phase 3—Quick

The quick phase serves as a transition period between project efforts and a complete operational implementation. As such, team membership begins taking on more of an operational feel. The SMRO teams had established the performance targets, the basic operational structures, and the better and best practices to be pursued. These would be passed on to implementation teams. The goal: quickly focus attention on the details of implementation and make it happen.

The SMRO labor team completed several rounds of negotiations before inking the final agreement with the selected O&M integrator. While these negotiations were underway, Paul and his leadership team held companywide meetings to explain the company's Strategic MRO vision and goals. Specific departmental meetings were held with affected personnel. Paul's direction was to transfer his existing workforce to the O&M integrator but there were no assurances that all resources would make the switch.

A detailed transition plan was developed that included elements such as:

- Transition the current workforce to the O&M integrator's company.
- Integrate the O&M integrator's EAM technology to the company's ERP system.

- Develop detailed workflows for demand driven maintenance.
- Develop detailed workflows for MRO material requisition, acquisition, and replenishment.

Figure 11.1 shows the use of project management technology to orchestrate O&M integrator activities.

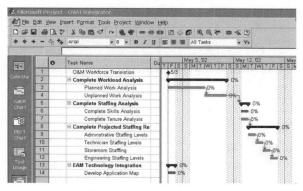

Figure 11.1 - O&M Integrator Project

The SMRO material team followed the steps of Strategic MRO supply chain management redesign (refer to Chapter 9) and began its team efforts. Sample activities included:

- Perform MRO parts commodity analysis.
- Design integrated supply activities with the O&M integrator.
- Conduct supplier analysis and selection activities.
- Develop performance-based pricing arrangements.
- Formalize supply contracts.
- Implement smart storeroom practices.
- Begin inventory consignment activities.
- Develop MRO order fulfillment workflows.
- Initiate e-commerce procurement strategies.

Figure 11.2 shows the use of project management technology to orchestrate Strategic MRO material project activities.

Both project teams were tasked with establishing value density metrics to drive performance and cost improvements. A number of these new metrics were designed into the company's ERP system as well as the O&M integrator's EAM system. Paul continued his emphasis on associating all metrics with a definable asset.

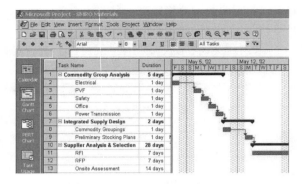

Figure 11.2 - Strategic MRO Materials Project

Quick Phase Observations

The quick phase was not taken lightly by leadership or the SMRO team. Paul wanted tangible results as soon as possible. He was confident his company's use of the DSC guiding principles was not sacrificing long-term success to achieve short-term gain.

The quick phase was costly in resources and time. He estimated that the SMRO teams alone were costing his company nearly $3,000 per day to operate. Denise was the only full-time member, as the other team members had no backup for their existing jobs. But the potential savings were real and significant. Paul's sense of urgency paid off. Because of his desire to apply industry best practices and a structured program management approach, Paul's company was on the right track.

Paul was keenly aware of the benefit of using external resources to guide his company's efforts. Even so, his staff insisted they could do it on their own. Reflecting on his initial leadership meetings when this topic first was discussed, he knew better. The DSC facilitators easily shaved six to nine months off the project duration. In some cases Paul's internal resources could not have accomplished certain tasks, much less done them right. Their DSC facilitator's knowledge and ability to work with his resources was instrumental to his company's success.

Phase 4—Agile Phase

Paul and Denise made sure improvement efforts did not stop with their first set of efforts. With both the O&M integrator and the redesigned MRO material supply chain in place, it was time to move on to asset condition assessments. These would be used to drive overhaul and repair decisions. With the help of engineering and procurement, and the support of their O&M integrator, they began work on early equipment management strategies sooner than planned.

Paul knew his Strategic MRO tasks would never end. The market began to turn positive; his internal efforts had been noticed by his customers. He began setting corporate sights on plant expansion and possible plant openings in two different countries.

Paul did not want to make the same asset mistakes he made previously. He insisted that DSC guiding principles and compression strategies be applied to all "green-field" sites.

The SMRO team recommended that a recognition process be established for Strategic MRO. Awards would be given for participation and results. Their affiliation with the DSC coaches created a communication source of new ideas and insights on industry best practices. The SMRO team recommended that the DSC coaching organization perform annual independent audits of their plans to benchmark progress and stay focused on achieving future perfect.

Denise was permanently assigned as the Director of Strategic MRO; she was a new member of Paul's leadership council. She continued to coordinate with all departments to ensure that systems were working, people were following the systems, and constant improvement was commonplace. With a never-ending set of tasks, Denise realized how important her role was to the continued success of her organization.

Chapter 12

Solution After Next

Executive Summary: This chapter synthesizes the journey of Paul, the CEO of a chemical company, who started on a quest at the beginning of this book. His company is on the right path—managing assets strategically to gain competitive advantage.

At the beginning of his Strategic MRO journey Paul knew his company faced significant challenges. The market was slowing, cash flow was tightening, new sales for future deliveries were much slower than usual, and uneasiness was settling in on his leadership team. His business experience had taught him the traditional business options of cutting production, reducing inventories, and extending payments. These options simply were not enough to keep his company competitive and maintain investor confidence. He also knew that the market experienced sales cycles and that he and his leadership could weather the storm... but at what costs?

What Paul discovered, almost by profound luck, rather than by business school teachings, was that tangible and less painful improvement options existed for asset management. He quickly discovered the benefits of viewing asset management as a business problem rather than an activity management challenge of keeping the maintenance resource busy and the MRO stores full.

The simple question of asking how many electricians were actually needed changed Paul's entire perspective on assets. He marveled at how his maintenance budget was simply taken for granted as necessary and perhaps unmanageable. He was amused that his company was in the MRO inventory management business and that a significant portion of his entire staff's time was spent hunting for the all-important gasket that would restore production capabilities. He had been alarmed that little, if any effort was spent preventing failure.

Paul became keenly aware that blindly slashing maintenance costs was just as foolish as blindly slashing production. The unintended consequences of "cut maintenance at all costs" were that the plant and customers would suffer considerably. Paul needed a defined logic to help improve his asset management decisions and work methods.

Over the past decade Paul's company had done well. In the past, they had resisted outside interventions that hinted at better ways to manage assets and the MRO supply chain. His company was a self-contained unit with all costs reasonably covered through product sales. The Strategic MRO experience had opened his eyes to the fact that the MRO service industry had evolved to where he could literally outsource everything having to do with the production. For example:

- Asset management.
- Engineering.
- Maintenance.
- Procurement.
- Storeroom and inventory management.
- Information technology.

These business options existed because they made sense. He needed to discover what made sense for his organization.

Paul began his journey with a simple sketch of future perfect. Later this sketch was supported by future perfect precepts. His company could no longer afford or tolerate decisions that impeded progress and increased costs of operations.

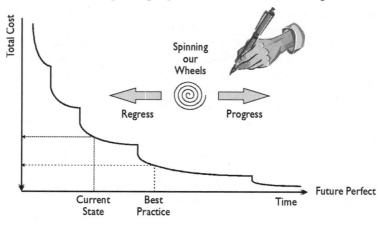

Figure 12.1 - Future Perfect Precepts

- Only produce exactly what is consumed in the market.
- Only invest in assets that produce exactly what is consumed in the market.
- Only invest in assets that never fail over their useful life.
- Achieve zero total cost of ownership (TCO) for all assets.
- Only invest in resources that enable the first four future perfect precepts.

Paul quickly realized that his leadership team did not have a collective vision that guided their decisions. Their decisions were based on narrowly focused future perfect objectives for their assigned business functions. Out of these narrow views of the world grew significant and plentiful islands of pain. *Operating as if all assets are exactly the same, all asset failures are the same, 80% of MRO costs are designed and redesigned in, the lowest acquisition costs wins out over the lowest TCO, our problems would be solved if we had more maintenance resources, internally supplied functions have no costs to us,* ... Paul had to refocus his organization and do it quickly. Without direction the company became a political morass where the boss became more important than the business objective. He would use the future perfect precepts to guide corporate decision-making and to regain control of business sanity.

Through his research Paul discovered a clear set of guiding principles that could restore business objectives as the boss. These guiding principles were part and parcel to Demand Supply Compression (DSC) methodology and could be used to overhaul poor thinking and doing. The five guiding principles were simple and their logic defied debate.

1. Define the value stream.
2. Connect the asset to the value stream.
3. Connect demand to the asset.
4. Connect supply to demand.
5. Compress demand supply connections.

Each guiding principle had a clear business objective driven by an associated future perfect precept. Supporting compression strategies were plentiful. Paul's executive forum experience opened his field of vision. Superior Water, EuroCar, MobileTel, MilBase Ops, and TL Freight each selected various compression strategies that made sense for their operations. However there was a common and logical message that prevailed throughout each application of the DSC guiding principles. These management strategies suggested that not all assets are equal in their importance to the value stream. Thus, there was the need for an agreed upon asset criticality classification that could be applied across the board.

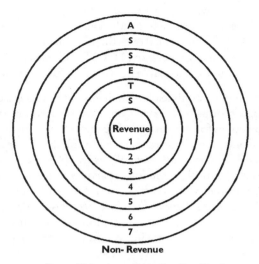

Figure 12.2 - Asset Criticality Classification

1. Assets required for conducting value stream functions that produce the unit of value. These might include mixers, lathes, distillation columns, milling machines assembly robots, and others.
2. Assets required to ensure that revenue producing assets are powered or controlled. These include power plants, generators, engines, compressors, distributed control systems, manufacturing information systems, and others.
3. Assets required for order fulfillment functions such as sales orders, production planning, shipping, and accounting. These include computers, software, telephone systems, fax machines, and others.
4. Assets required for other core production or service functions such as material handling or warehousing. These might include trucks, conveyors, fork trucks, pipelines, and others.
5. Non-revenue producing assets required for protecting revenue-producing assets from inoperable conditions. These include buildings, structures, HVAC systems, sewage systems, and others.
6. Non-revenue producing assets required for conducting supporting business functions. These include computers, software, telephone systems, desks, chairs, tables, and others.
7. Non-revenue producing assets that impact quality of life. These include cafeteria equipment, vending machines, access roads, parking lots, playgrounds, childcare facilities, and others.

The executive forum recognized that not all failures were equal as suggested by the demand criticality classification. The demand criticality is defined as the combination of failure effect type, availability impact, failure frequency, and cost impact.

Demand Criticality Classification
Failure effect types are:

1. Asset condition creates unsafe or hazardous work environment (highest priority).
2. Asset unavailable for use.
3. Asset does not produce a quality output.
4. Asset does not perform to design or operational efficiencies.
5. Asset use drives up cost of operations (lowest priority).

Availability impacts are:

1. Catastrophic—greater than 24 hours downtime.
2. Very significant is 8 to 24 hours (one production day) downtime.
3. Significant is between 4 to 8 hours (one production shift) downtime.
4. Insignificant—less than 4 hours downtime.
5. No effect—Asset availability is not impacted.

Failure frequencies are:

1. Chronic—Daily.
2. Chronic—Weekly.
3. Chronic—Monthly.
4. Sporadic—Quarterly.
5. Sporadic—Yearly or greater.

Cost impacts are:

1. Catastrophic—greater than 75% of the asset replacement value.
2. Very Significant—50% to 75% of the asset replacement value.
3. Significant—between 10% to 50% of the asset replacement value.
4. Insignificant—between 5% to 10% of the asset replacement value.
5. No effect—less than 5% of the asset replacement value.

Certainly if all assets are not equal and all failures are not equal, the executive forum correctly surmised that not all responses had to be the same either. Proactive and reactive demand responses had to be driven by the asset and demand criticality classification. Each asset portfolio needed a primary and pursuit strategy. For example, for Class 1 assets planned maintenance would be the primary strategy and autonomous maintenance would be the pursuit strategy. And for Class 7 assets autonomous maintenance would be the primary strategy and run to failure would be the pursuit strategy.

Demand Response Strategies

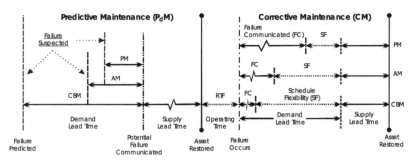

Figure 12.3 - Demand Response Strategies

Paul quickly found himself immersed in the technical details of asset lifecycle management as he attempted to connect the asset to the value stream and connect demand to the asset. This drove his decision to create an umbrella Strategic MRO program, entitled demand driven maintenance. He knew that strategically, his company needed to pursue the doctrines of early equipment management (EEM) and reliability centered maintenance (RCM). Tactically he needed to incorporate the tenets of total productive maintenance (TPM). Ultimately he needed to identify ways to extend asset life, improve asset condition assessment practices, and make better decisions regarding maintenance, overhaul, and disposal of assets.

Labor and Materials

In connecting supply to demand, Paul was now aware of his labor disconnects. The goal of matching skills to the task and the benefits of multi-skilling to increase flexibility made too much sense. He also knew that he needed to plan and schedule much smarter than he had in the past to improve resource utilization. Eventually he would have an answer to his straightforward question…how many electricians do we need?

By exploring compression strategies for MRO materials, Paul was struck by the tremendous cost of being in the MRO material ownership business. Each penny spent quickly added up to a dollar, then hundreds, then thousands, and then millions of dollars of excess inventory. All this time he was convinced that he was getting the best prices in the industry. His attempt to control material demand through procurement and inventory management was based on demand thinking and not consumption thinking. His company needed to understand and communicate consumption if progress was to be made.

Paul, as well as the executive forum, now got the message…loud and clear. Assets create the demand for labor, materials, and special equipment/tools. If asset management was to be operated like a business, then all demands must be associated with the originating asset. Only through a disciplined approach to asset management could Paul expect to forecast a reasonable budget and begin to develop cost control and improvement initiates.

Technology Connectivity

Paul knew he could not achieve organization discipline without technology. He now knew that technology served three principle roles: Enabling processes, ensuring organizational and MRO channel compliance, and capturing information to drive process improvements. Even though Paul's company outsourced maintenance activities to an O&M integrator it was of critical importance to him that the supplier's technology enabled the business objectives his company sought. It made business sense that the selected O&M integrator must have the best EAM technology. He knew that difficult decisions still remained regarding integration of multiple systems to improve information and workflow. He understood the complexities of Strategic MRO and favored the best in class technology specialist who focused on maximizing his return on assets.

Strategic MRO Program Management

Paul had discovered a hidden organization that needed oversight. This organization was comprised of assets. He had focused on products and using assets to produce products, but he had hardly focused on the asset itself. The appointment of the Strategic MRO program manager was essential to achieving near and long-term success. He was proud of the way the SMRO teams committed their time and energy to learning new skills and immediately applying them to the benefit of the company. He was also encouraged by his new relationship with an O&M integrator. Until the topic of Strategic MRO consumed his thoughts, he had never realized or sought to realize how many great service solutions existed in the market. Finally he had to thank his DSC coaches who shed new light on his organization. They provided strong, common sense guidance, based on practical experience and profound insight.

Solution After Next

As authors of this book we recognize that Paul's organization is clearly on a path to achieving asset agility. His organization, just like Superior Water, EuroCar, MobileTel, MilBase Ops, and TL Freight, has to leverage assets to accomplish its missions. This book was written to cause organizational leaders to pause and consider whether their assets are truly working for or against their strategic objectives. Is asset management being run like a business or is it simply a coordinated set of labor and material activities? The complex and varied topics introduced in this text were covered at a high level to show their interrelationship, dependencies and ultimately, where they fit in the challenge of Strategic MRO.

Early in our discussions we discussed complex channel dynamics that exist for asset owners, asset makers, and asset service providers. As new channels are formed and reformed, it is clear that business and technology solutions must address collaborative environments. Simple cost shifting maneuvers do not benefit the channel and almost always cause less than desirable practices known as islands of pain. All MRO channel participants must understand and work toward the future perfect precepts.

The premise that the asset creates the demand must be well understood by those who design, build, use, maintain, and dispose of assets. All MRO channel members must have a fundamental grasp of varying asset criticality and demand importance that creates the need for varying supply responses to eliminate waste in labor and material utilization.

Price breaks based on a false notion of demands continue to stockpile shelves throughout the channel. Transparency of consumption data is an absolute essential ingredient to achieving improvements in MRO materials production and acquisition. Fortunately the information system connectivity exists to make this happen. Unfortunately we have not seen the cross-organizational efforts that will make it happen.

The notion of Web-enabled technology solutions creating six and seven figure cost savings is nonsense if assets and the MRO channel are not designed and managed like a business. Clear business objectives, clear practices and clear technology integration strategies that result in practical solutions are the only way to achieve the hard cost savings that improve investor confidence, keep companies profitable, and employees focused on the collective success of the channel.

We suggest that the next set of best practices will now begin to occur as a result of looking at assets from the perspective of their value proposition. Managing assets from a business perspective is far more powerful than controlling maintenance and MRO supply chain activities. In breakthrough thinking, the first solution gets you equal to your competition, but it is the solution after next that puts you in the lead. Demand supply compression represents the solution after next for RCM, TPM, and other asset management strategies.

We look forward to this next generation of discovery. Where Strategic MRO powered by DSC is the recognized roadmap for transforming assets into strategic advantage.

Index

A

H

I

J

L

M

N

O

Time–based maintenance 161
TL Freight 82, 102, 139, 188, 249
total cost of ownership 4
Total Costs 156
Total productive maintenance (TPM) 117
Trade discounts 212

V

Value Density Metrics 78, 90, 114, 154, 198
Value engineering 79
Value generating asset value to total asset value 91
Value stream analysis 93
Variable pricing strategies 212
Velocity 14, 16, 17

W

Weibull analysis 110, 119
Work geographic density 157
Work Management Technology 266
Work type costs 157
Work Type Management 167
workflow 266
Wrench time 156

Z

Zero breakdown maintenance 117

About the Authors

Rich MacInnes is the President and CEO of Net Results Inc., an international consulting and training firm specializing in Market Driven System, powered by DSC™ and Strategic MRO, powered by DSC™ practices. Rich is the primary architect behind the Demand Supply Compression™ methodologies. A graduate of the United States Naval Academy and former marine company commander, Rich's extensive industry backgrounds include engineering and leadership experience in manufacturing, industrial distribution, engineering, and construction industries. Rich's work has taken him around the world, working in virtually all major industries, supporting strategic planning, business process redesign, lean manufacturing, supply chain management, and demand driven maintenance initiatives. Rich can be reached at RichMac@netresultsgroup.com or you can learn more at www.netresultsgroup.com.

Dr. Stephen Pearce is a consultant to the distribution and manufacturing industries and a leading authority on distribution and inventory management practices. He is a frequent speaker to companies and industry associations on the subjects of inventory management, the quality process in distribution, integrated supply, statistical process control, and the use of bar codes in distribution. Complementing his consulting endeavors, Stephen owns a software development firm dedicated to PC based solutions to specific problems facing the distribution channel. Most recently, he has been a consultant with Net Results working on projects involving lean manufacturing, supply chain optimization, and production planning and scheduling. Dr. Pearce served at Texas A&M University for over eleven years as Assistant Professor of Engineering Technology and Assistant Director for Research at the Thomas A. Read Center for Distribution Research. He earned his undergraduate degrees at Texas A&M and completed his Ph.D. in 1995.